D0290787

SETTING IT RIGHT

MICHAEL COREN

SETTING IT RIGHT

Published in 1996 by
Stoddart Publishing Co. Limited
34 Lesmill Road
Toronto, Canada
M3B 2T6
Tel. (416) 445-3333
Fax (416) 445-5967

Stoddart Books are available for bulk purchase for sales promotions, premiums, fundraising, and seminars. For details, contact the **Special Sales Department** at the above address.

Canadian Cataloguing in Publication Data

Coren, Michael
Setting it right

ISBN 0-7737-2940-2

I. Title.

PS8555.073S4 1996 081 C96-930058-1
PR9199.3.C67S4 1996

Cover design: the boy 100 & Tannice Goddard
Text design: Tannice Goddard
Typesetting: Image One Productions Ltd.

Printed and bound in the United States of America

Stoddart Publishing gratefully acknowledges the support of the Canada Council, the Ontario Ministry of Citizenship, Culture and Recreation, Ontario Arts Council, and Ontario Publishing Centre in the development of writing and publishing in Canada.

To Guy and to Susan

CONTENTS

PREFACE *ix*

POLITICS 1

MEN AND WOMEN 25

FATHERHOOD 59

THE ARTS 85

THE MEDIA 133

THE MILITARY 147

RELIGION 165

MORALITY 193

PERSONALITIES 211

Preface

There can be few more salutary tasks for a columnist than to look back over a collection of earlier work and see the evolution of his own style and approach. One conclusion is inevitable. There are some, though not many, things that I wrote in the past that I would not write now, and some that I would say in a slightly different way. But to change these would be to cheat, to defeat the object of this book. This is a collection of my writing from a specific period, reflecting my attitudes and reactions at a particular point in my life. Let me stress, however, that to a very large extent, I continue to hold the opinions expressed in these columns and essays, perhaps more firmly and confidently now than ever before.

As I say in one of these pieces, if newspaper and magazine columns were cassettes or CDs most would be tucked away in the Easy Listening section of the music store. I like to think that mine are often classical, sometimes heavy metal, occasionally folk and once or twice composed of just a little jazz. I am not one of the Perry Comos of the world.

Nor am I one of those columnists who embrace what might be described as "economic conservatism," or a modernized form of Victorian liberalism, and seem to have an obsession with the market and the supply of money. These are important issues, to be sure, but to believe that we can achieve lasting economic change in isolation from political, social and cultural reform is arrant and arrogant nonsense. When the social fabric of the country can be heard ripping down the middle, I wonder if heartfelt columns about subsidies to insurance companies are really the order of the day.

The responses to my newspaper and magazine writing are often morale-boosting, even inspiring, but sometimes intriguing and amusing. My opponents tend to react less with disagreement than with efforts at censorship. "I will not read the newspaper again," "You must get rid of him," "How dare you publish this man" and so on. When I wrote a men's column for *The Globe and Mail* I was told in no uncertain terms by critics at the newspaper that I should be filing Laodicean accounts of taking junior to his baseball game or of my first experiences of a dirty diaper — don't rock the boat or, more accurately, say nothing when the boat comes under attack. Not my style at all.

There have always been a large amount of letters written to me or to the editors of various publications about me, usually of a ratio of ten to one in my favour. It is genuinely moving to receive dozens of letters a week from people who tell me that they rely on my writing for, what one described as, "a voice of sanity, clarity, morality and wisdom." I quote these words because they are hers and not mine. And because they mean a great deal.

This even occurred when I wrote an arts column for *The Globe and Mail* — surprising, since the column was seldom put into the national edition of the newspaper and was usually tucked away on an inside page of a very thin Monday paper, sometimes almost hidden on the penultimate page. Apparently when the editor of the section was informed that I was writing a column for her she "became ashen-faced."

Indeed, life at *The Globe and Mail* was sometimes worthy of a comic novel. There were several columns written by staff writers criticizing me and even a petition that managed to prevent one of my pieces from appearing. The editor of the newspaper and my page editor were absent at the time. One of the signatories has since apologized for her actions; her four colleagues have yet to do so. Those poor souls really should have learned by now that good journalism has nothing to do with a bland little comfort zone. But they probably never will.

The work assembled here was originally printed in *The Globe and Mail, The Financial Post, The Toronto Star, Books in Canada, Saturday Night, Toronto Life* and *The Idler.* I wrote two columns for the *Globe* — an arts column and a men's column — for almost two years. I decided to resign from the men's column because I wanted to discuss other issues and, frankly, because it is always advisable to quit when ahead. Diane Francis at *The Financial Post* made me a generous and tempting offer and the timing was perfect. When I told *Globe and Mail* editor William Thorsell of my decision he was understanding and gracious. This came as no surprise as he had been thus throughout my time at the newspaper. I thank him.

I have never for one moment regretted moving to *The Financial Post* and I must in particular thank Diane Francis, Natasha Hassan, Bob Catherwood and Tracy LeMay for making my life at this newspaper so very happy and rewarding. My weekly column, "All Things Considered," began in early 1995 and is now syndicated through the *Sun* group. For the latter I am indebted to Paul Godfrey, Peter Stockland and everybody concerned with the Toronto, Calgary and Ottawa *Sun.* It is a privilege.

Paul Stuewe edited me at *Books in Canada* for two years and I know that he had to defend me against those in the literary community who are not partial to contrary points of view. When Paul left the magazine the new regime fired me. This new regime, however, lasted only a few weeks. They were replaced by Norman Doidge and Gerald Owen, who immediately reinstated me. What a funny thing is life.

The articles from *Saturday Night* in this collection were published by Kenneth Whyte, who also made me a Contributing Editor of that ever-improving magazine. Thank you. Gratitude also to John McFarland at *Toronto Life* for friendship and guidance and to those at *The Toronto Star* and the sadly missed *Idler*, for all of their help.

To my agent Bruce Westwood, and to my publisher Nelson Doucet and to my editor Lynne Missen I say a loud and heartfelt "thank God you were there" and to my many friends and advisers who will not find their names listed here, please forgive me. And to my life's meaning —

Bernadette, Daniel, Lucy and Oliver — well, you know what I think, and that is what matters.

Finally, two men long gone but never forgotten; two sides of inspiration and influence; two sides of spirit and soul. Jack and Hilary. C. S. Lewis and Hilaire Belloc. Blessings.

SETTING IT RIGHT

POLITICS

Man is by nature a
political animal.

ARISTOTLE
POLITICS, BK. I CH. 2

Contempt for Democratic System Is a Dangerous Thing

Nobody said that democracy would be easy. It hurts. It is meant to. It involves winners and losers, and if both sides sincerely believe in their ideas they will, naturally, resent their opponents' victory. But resentment and opposition are one thing, hatred and contempt quite another.

I refer to that legion of journalists, activists and zealots who have spent this past month arguing that the Ontario Legislature should be recalled, that Premier Mike Harris should be ashamed of himself, that Ontarians are breaking "The Canadian Way," that our method of election is all wrong, that it is now time for civil disobedience and that those who support the government are either fools or fascists.

Less a Greek chorus than a Gecko choir, these people are abhorrent not because they are critics of current policies — that, of course, is a valid role for an estate of media or opposition in a democratic system — but because they exhibit contempt for the decision to elect the Progressive Conservatives in the first place. And by being contemptuous of the decision they are also being contemptuous of the people who made it and, worst of all, the process and system by and through which it was made. Contempt for democracy. A dangerous thing. As G. K. Chesterton said of such types: "They love ordinary people from afar and talk about them often. But proximity to the people and their beliefs frightens them and confuses them."

Let us put all this in proportion. A democratically elected government, now even more popular than when it came to office, has decided to stop spending so much of the public's money and to give some of that money back to the people from whom it was taken in the first place.

The same administration is determined to reduce the deficit, liberate individual initiative, rejuvenate the economy and put into reverse the steam-roller of interventionist government. Hardly extreme. Especially, one could reasonably argue, when compared with the ideas of the former socialist regime in Ontario. Yet it must not be forgotten that that socialist regime, whatever I or anybody else thought of it, had the same right to implement its policies as does the current conservative one. Again, it is called democracy.

Rival ideologies and personalities throw down the party gauntlet and after an equitable campaign governed by the rule of law, by time-honoured codes of ethical behaviour and by electoral legislation, the enfranchised people vote and a leader is chosen. In Canada, as in many democracies, the British-style first-past-the-post system of voting is used. Some experts prefer a form of proportional representation but all genuine democrats agree that the results from any existing system have to be accepted unless and until that system is changed.

The squeals from the left, from the tired terriers of the establishment, are as sad as they are silly. "It is my ball, I've lost the game and I want to change the rules," says the spoiled brat in the park, too used to having his own way.

At heart and by origin democracy is a revolutionary system. The politics of shock. Winston Churchill, for example, heard the news of the Labour Party's election triumph while he was in his bath. The lion whose roar had saved Europe now gently purred that the chance of defeat was the essence of democracy, and democracy and all of its blessings were the very things for which the western allies had been fighting.

The voice of the people is articulated through an election, listened to and acted upon, in this case by Mike Harris. He has not only the right but a duty and an obligation to cut back on spending, precisely because he said he would do so in his election manifesto.

To submit to the pressure of radical interest groups, to dilute his policies, would be not only cowardly but, yes, undemocratic. Mike Harris, Ontario's honest politician. Not the sort of thing that the journalists of Canada and their friends are used to at all. Again, the politics of shock. Now if only Harris had promised to abolish the GST, but once in office had instead . . .

Canadian Socialists Still Manning the Barricades of the Past

I think I have seen a ghost, one that is more curious than frightening. It rattles its chains when it is challenged and threatens all sorts of horrible consequences if it is not taken seriously. But it is by its very nature linked only tenuously to the world of reality.

I speak of the New Democratic Party and of its anachronistic obsession with socialism and class warfare. It is fascinating to watch the party thrash about in confusion and to observe its quixotic charges at windmills that have not existed for a very long time. Indeed the "new" in the party name is singularly inappropriate. All this talk about welfare, class and the state is merely an inheritance from the old political grouping that was an aged parent of Canadian social democracy — the trade unions and the Labour Party in Britain.

Two generations of British trade unionists and Labour Party stalwarts made their way to Canada after the Second World War. Even now a disproportionate number of the NDP caucus in the Ontario Legislature, for example, were born in Britain. Throw in Northern Ireland's Bob White and the layer of other class-warriors from Britain in the other unions and we have an absurdly archaic labour leadership.

The irony of all this is that in Britain itself Tony Blair during his entire time as Labour Party leader has tried to expunge any residual trace of socialism from his organization. He knows, as do the electorate, that socialism is discredited and unworkable. In the British context it is also based largely upon a lie.

In 1945, the British people were told that the loyal trade unions had through their sacrifices made an overwhelming contribution to the defeat of Nazism. These unions were owed, voters were told by the media and the chattering classes, a nation better than the one that had existed in 1939. Yet as British historian Andrew Roberts has shown, large elements of the British trade union movement had acted in a repugnant manner. In 1940, communist-led Glasgow miners went on strike because of demarcation protocol. Shipbuilders throughout Britain also stopped working on three separate occasions in the same year. One strike at the De Havilland factory cost 4,426 working days over a three-week period. The reason was the "transfer of four capstan fitters from the firm to other work of national importance." All these men were already privileged, in that they had been excused military duty.

But the legend that the working class had been oppressed and the bosses didn't give a damn had been created. In fact, the bourgeoisie was growing at an extraordinary pace, the economy was doing very nicely under capitalism and the class divisions of the past were fading into the stuff of May Day mythology. By 1951 Britain had brought back the Conservatives and that party would dominate postwar politics.

More than this, the innovations of the Labour Party had obviously failed. By the end of the 1960s the National Health Service was in chaos, state education was melting into a nasty goo, welfare parasites wore their shame like badges of honour and increasingly zealous trade unions were prepared to "hold the country to ransom" on the most flimsy of pretexts.

The Tories' long run was highlighted by Margaret Thatcher's tenure, but she eventually left office and the revitalized, highly moderate and conciliatory Labour Party will probably win the next election. But the Thatcherite triumph was about more than a mere electoral victory. She moved the centre ground, the common ground, to the right and restored a sense of priority and balance. Parties of the left now embrace traditional ideas of economic and social responsibility. Scandinavian socialism failed; Germany and France jettisoned their radical fringe; and the newly liberated Eastern Europe looks to Monetarism rather than Marx. They understood that the notion of class warfare was nothing more than a chimera embraced by politicians anxious to maintain their power.

Charming little souvenirs of the past still exist, however, and Canada is home to one of them. The mother countries have been rejuvenated yet the child stubbornly refuses to grow up. And to think that these people like to refer to conservatives as dinosaurs. Bring on the Academy Award winner of 1995, Socialistic Park. With a cast steeped in British trade union folklore and tales of life on the state-subsidized barricades.

Recent Mail-Bombs from Left-Wing Terrorists Nothing New

Last week a series of potentially deadly mail-bombs were sent by something called the Anti-Fascist Alliance to various people disliked by Canada's hard left. Two Nazis, a genetics laboratory and a research body devoted to the study of security and terrorism, received these missiles as missives. At the latter recipient, the MacKenzie Institute, the package was opened by a secretary, who would have been killed if the battery of the bomb had not come loose in transit. Several prominent conservatives were told to take special precautions but few of them were particularly surprised.

Left-wing terrorism is nothing new. The anarchists of the late nineteenth and early twentieth century were not harmless caricatures with waxed moustaches and top hats, carrying fizzling grenades emblazoned with the word "bomb." These bloodthirsty men and women, in fact, mutilated and murdered anyone they considered politically objectionable, invariably killing innocent by-standers in the process and usually provoking strong reaction from the police. It was just such a climate of violence and fear, of course, that these monsters desired to create.

Such terrorism was also successfully used by the Bolsheviks and their allies, within and without Russia. When Lenin and Trotsky came to power, one of the first things they did was to create death-camps for the people who had opposed them. Their successor, Stalin, murdered his former friends and current enemies and during the Spanish Civil War the communists "dealt with" non-Stalinists who were fighting on the same side — several American and Canadian volunteers "disappeared" during the war in Spain and new evidence from the Kremlin's security files will probably provide shocking details.

Within Canada itself examples of leftist terrorism are numerous. In 1992 during an acrimonious strike at Yellowknife's Giant gold mine, Roger Warren planted a bomb that killed nine people. Three union activists are now publishing a newsletter intended to raise money for their mass-murderer buddy.

Then we have the environmental demonstrators. Amongst these zealots are terrorists who put spikes in trees likely to be cut down so that when the tree is put through a saw the spike will shatter and kill the saw's operator. In an effort to protect their employees the logging companies introduced metal detectors. The friends of the environment reacted by replacing their deadly weapons with equally dangerous but undetectable non-metal spikes.

In the early 1980s a representative from the Construction Labor Association acted as an arbitrator in various union disputes. One day he was accosted in the street, had a jacket thrown over his head and a baseball bat was taken to him. He received multiple and profound bone-breaks, to his face and body. There have been myriad examples of anti-union workers and conservatives being attacked and having their tires slashed and antenna wires bent, of death threats, of mailed excrement and of organized intimidation. Conservative organizations have received smoke-bombs, pro-life activists have been beaten and threatened, Reform Party members have been punched and kicked.

Then we have Indian chief Ovide Mercredi recently telling his people to be "more aggressive, more militant" and to occupy government offices. This after the death of a Quebec police officer and stand-offs with automatic weapons. If Canada's leaders were not so tied by misplaced guilt and cowardice their reaction to Mercredi would be something other than benign indifference.

The thuggery of the IRA, the blood-lust of animal rights protesters prepared to kill men, women and children so that rabbits and rats might not be used to advance medical science, the throwing of condoms filled with broken glass by radical homosexuals at Roman Catholic priests: the list goes on. But if we believed most newspapers and television stations we would assume that all terrorists are either militia members in Idaho or gun-owners in Alberta. How terribly odd.

In conclusion, I was one of the conservatives advised to take special security measures. I, my wife and three children no longer regard the receiving of mail as one of the small, charming aspects of daily life. That letter might be from grandma in Britain to wish tiny Lucy a happy birthday. But then again, it might not. Welcome to democracy, Marxist style.

Rising Above "The Troubles"

People in oppressed, troubled or divided countries are often described by trite television reporters as being particularly attractive. You know the sort of thing: "Between the craters and in spite of the unemployment, these are a vivacious and inventive people who . . ." As a superficial observation, it stinks of voyeurism and sound-bite naïveté.

The problem with Northern Ireland as a whole, and Belfast in particular, is that here the conclusion is true.

Tragically, however, what are known as The Troubles have ravaged this beautiful and beguiling little country for a generation now. Thousands of people have been stained by death or its propinquity, and the two communities here are probably more distinct and mutually antagonistic than ever before, in spite of — or perhaps because of — the peace initiative by far-away Dublin and farther-away London.

The irony is that for all of the hostility between Protestant and Roman Catholic, Loyalist and Nationalist, Unionist and Republican, these people are as much sustained by symbiosis as they are destroyed by internecine hatred.

The current habit is to make conversation about Bosnia and to shake your head and say that next to the former Yugoslavia, Northern Ireland is a tea party. To a very large extent, this is correct. There are self-imposed no-go areas in this country, people and places that are considered to be off-limits. Children are not harmed on purpose, women are usually considered non-combatants and clergymen of all varieties are seldom targeted. But this did not prevent the Irish Republican Army from murdering a Roman Catholic policeman (he had committed the crime of giving out parking tickets and making sure that store doors were locked at night, hence aiding the British war machine) in front of his five children as they came out of mass, the family saved from the bullets by sheer chance. Nor did it stop the Ulster Volunteer Force from firing indiscriminately into a bar crowded with merrymaking Catholic men and women.

As for the coming few years, politicians may claim to be sanguine, but those who know Northern Ireland are pessimistic. If the IRA perceives weakness in Britain's peace efforts, it will push all the harder for victory. If the UVF genuinely fears British abandonment, it will escalate its violence.

Indeed, militant Protestants are increasingly advocating a policy of Ulsterization; they reluctantly realize that they are being abandoned by Britain and hence propose a new Northern Ireland ruled *from* Northern Ireland by the Northern Irish — that is, a Protestant province unhindered by the restraints of agnostic, moderate England. The policy is workable but terrifying. Lest we forget, the British Army was sent there in the 1960s to protect the Roman Catholics from their Protestant neighbours; if the Loyalist paramilitaries and their Scottish allies were to be given free rein, the IRA and its supporters would be nothing more than a tattered tricolour in a matter of weeks.

Of course, in between these polarized, ghettoized extremes, there are tens of thousands of sensible, relatively apolitical people who are more concerned with lower income taxes than with the denomination of their representatives. But they are in the centre of an enormous net, the ends of which are held aloft by hardened and relentless people. When the terrorists rise, the net closes and everybody gasps for air.

As that gentle genius William Trevor commented, "The only real hope is time. At its present rate of increase, the Catholic population will overtake the Protestant population within 20 or 30 years. A referendum, and Irish union. It's inevitable. And I'm sure it'll be accepted by everybody when the time comes."

Mr. Trevor, of course, is a short-story writer of world renown, and the product of a north-south, Catholic-Protestant union.

Why the Leopard Changed Its Spots

Surely nobody can love a peace treaty or a cease-fire more than a Canadian. Warms the heart during a long, cruel winter. And surely nobody can know so little of what is really going on in Northern Ireland as a North American.

The Irish Republican Army has declared a cease-fire. After a quarter-century of murder, it has decided to stop its campaign of killing, not only soldiers and policemen but labourers working on projects with any connection with the government, innocent civilians walking past a car bomb or ordinary people who just happen to be English or Protestant. (Witness those wretched men and women during their Christmas shopping in London's Harrods, or drinking at a pub in Surrey. There was not even a warning given on the latter occasion.)

The mystery

So, what has really happened here? A cease-fire assumes a two-sided conflict, a war. Only the IRA describes the terror campaign in Northern Ireland as a war. The British disagree — well, they would — but so does every neutral international organization in the world.

The British Army was called to Northern Ireland three decades ago by the Roman Catholic (or republican) population, to protect it from an increasingly bellicose Protestant majority, who call themselves Loyalists. Soldiers were given cups of tea in Catholic West Belfast. It didn't last long. Old tensions soon awoke and the largely moribund IRA muscled into life, particularly after the Bloody Sunday killing of thirteen Catholic demonstrators by British soldiers in 1972.

Northern Ireland has 1.6 million people, 57 per cent of whom are Protestant. While only the tiniest number of Protestants wants to unite the six counties of their country with the republic to the south, they are no longer convinced that union with Britain is possible or even desirable. Ulsterization, or the rule of Northern Ireland from Belfast, is increasingly the policy of Ian Paisley's Democratic Unionist Party, and of the outlawed paramilitary groups — the Ulster Defence Association, Ulster Volunteer Force, Ulster Freedom Fighters and Red Hand Commandoes. You no longer have the will or the stomach to do it, they tell London, so let us take charge from here.

If this prospect sounds inviting, like some dismantling of colonialism, be aware that unleashed Protestant extremists would not observe the niceties and restraint of British regulars.

The main factions

The Ulster and Official Unionist Party: Moderate, it still represents the majority of Protestant opinion — as well as more than 10 per cent of Roman Catholic voters. Many middle-class Catholics would rather be tied to secular, modern Britain than to their co-religionists in good old, green old Ireland. Romanticism aside, there are few advantages to a united Ireland. The British government is pumping millions of pounds into Ulster, and much of it, as bitter loyalists will readily explain, is being injected into republican areas. Compensation for past wrongs.

The Social Democratic Labour Party: Also non-violent, it speaks for the overwhelming majority of republicans, and has condemned terrorism since its beginnings. Some of its leaders have even been targeted by IRA gunmen.

Sinn Fein: The political manifestation of the IRA (to a very large extent, the two are interchangeable), Sinn Fein receives the support of less than one-third of Catholic voters in Northern Ireland, and the number is declining.

The strategy

The IRA has long been intolerant of internecine disagreement. Its full name is the Provisional IRA, and it successfully and brutally destroyed its rival, the less nationalistic and less military Official IRA, in a brutal war. Subsequently, it dealt a near fatal blow to the Marxist and wildly violent Irish National Liberation Army. Now, it will have to be similarly thorough with dissidents in its ranks who disagree with the cease-fire.

The cease-fire is less an act of compassion and moderation than one of desperation, brought on by declining support, a lack of progress in the terror campaign and also spiralling losses to British units such as the Special Air Service.

Yet if the cease-fire is less than noble, it is more than cunning. This could very well be a game of diplomatic double-bluff by the leaders of the IRA. They know that loyalist groups will not assume, from all the good ink the IRA has received from the more naïve media, that blackmail works. That launching a campaign of violence and then halting it brings results.

There are myriad rumours within the Protestant community that even now London is negotiating a deal. Because of this, Loyalist paramilitaries will try to smash the cease-fire by attacking the Catholic population. This will oblige the British Army and the Northern Irish police to concentrate on them rather than the IRA.

As a result, the IRA will face an enemy divided — Brit against Protestant, extreme loyalist against moderate loyalist — and, in foreign and even British civilian eyes, its violent past will be forgotten as another drive-by shooting in the Falls Road is reported in the media.

The future

When Irish Republican Army eyes are smiling, everybody else suffers and bleeds.

The Loyalist paramilitaries are no longer the heavy-drinking hard men they used to be, when their own community would joke that "the trouble with our boys is that they can't shoot straight."

Already, there have been murders and bomb attacks on Sinn Fein offices, and reports from sources on the ground predict many more.

The violence may well extend to the Irish Republic and probably to Dublin, where a weak and inexperienced Irish security service will be hard-pressed to cope.

As for the IRA, less than one-third of the 1,000 people interviewed in a *Belfast Telegraph* survey said that they believe that its campaign of violence has ended for good.

Are they right? London and Dublin would love to be rid of this expensive and embarrassing problem, and U.S. politicians who boast of Irish ancestors are easily hoodwinked.

However, wise Catholic politicians in Belfast and Londonderry, Protestants who still sing "No Surrender" every July 12 and all those who know the truth about beautiful, troubled Ulster realize that yesterday's bomber does not become tomorrow's pacifist.

Political Lives

There are currently two biographies of General Franco being written and another, by Paul Preston, has just been published. All are inadequate and misleading. My Uncle Lou was an English member of the International Brigade and was a prisoner of the Nationalists in Spain for over a year. I myself am half-Jewish and have every reason to hate fascism and all its works. But I do not believe that Franco was a fascist. Are these new books objective? Or, can political biography be objective?

The established wisdom states that the Spanish Civil War was a battle of good against evil. So influential is this view that almost sixty years later, some Canadian writers campaign for a monument to the men who fought on the Loyalist side with the Mackenzie-Papineau Battalion.

Franco's Nationalists were supported by Nazi Germany, that national manifestation of a new dark age. There was also a powerful fascist element within the forces General Franco eventually led. But what about the support for the other side? This came from a Moscow regime that began its massacres earlier than the Nazis. We ought also to consider the new evidence from KGB files suggesting that members of the International Brigade, including Canadians, who went missing during the civil war were actually executed by Soviet commissars. This occurred because they questioned the Stalinism that was becoming increasingly dominant within the Spanish left and was intent on emasculating its Anarchist and Trotskyist allies.

I acknowledge the bravery of those men who fought for the Loyalists in Spain, but I cannot condone their logic or their politics. We need to look at the conflict with a clear eye. The Nationalists won the war and Franco established a dictatorship, a government that, according to Holocaust and Second World War historian Martin Gilbert, "really should not be compared to Hitler, Mussolini or Stalin. More like Catholic monarchism than Nazism." Whatever the repugnance of Franco's regime, he steadfastly refused to side with Hitler, maintaining a more honest neutrality than, for example, the Irish Republic. He refused the Germans marching rights through Spain and took in many Jewish refugees, to the horror of the little man Franco described as "the Austrian fool in a bad suit." As the Anglo-Israeli author Paul Rose has it, "Jews probably ought to thank rather than condemn Franco."

Try a leap of imagination. Say the Loyalists won the civil war. Not all of those who fought on this side were Communist, but the Communists always out-manoeuvred their alleged friends and dominated any leftist government. This happened in Russia in 1917, in Greece at the end of the Second World War, in Eastern Europe in the late 1940s. Indeed, members of the Communist Party often seemed to take a greater delight in murdering their non-Communist allies than in fighting fascism. If you doubt me, read George Orwell.

So a Loyalist victory would almost certainly have meant a Communist victory and, as with all the other Communist parties, this Madrid regime would have played poodle to their master Stalin in Moscow. When Hitler and Stalin signed their infamous non-aggression pact the Soviets handed back German Jewish refugees, and trusted their Nazi friend so much that in its initial stages the German invasion of their country was disbelieved by the Kremlin.

If the Germans had asked for marching rights through Spain, the Spanish Communists would probably have granted the request. This would have enabled the Germans to attack Gibraltar from both land and sea and would almost certainly have led to a British defeat. The war in the Mediterranean would have been over. The British, and Canadians, would have been forced to surrender and the entire Second World War would have come to an unimaginable conclusion. Mere speculation? "Not really," says Paul Rose, "and quite terrifying. Better a Franco at that time than a Soviet tool in vital Spain."

Once in office Franco isolated and suffocated Spain. He kept it firmly within the authority of a reactionary Church and an authoritarian police force. His rule was anachronistic, rigid and, ultimately, futile. But Franco was no fascist. He hated and abandoned the straight-arm salute as soon as he could, tried to establish diplomatic relations with Israel and maintained open borders. Before he died he groomed his successor and made certain that the young monarch would assume power. Because of this Spain slipped easily into becoming a key state in the world of parliamentary democracy. On the other hand, when the Communist leaders were forced from power they left only ruin and war.

We are still, by the way, waiting for a sound biography of the monster Lenin, and Stalin and Mao were lauded by biographers while they lived. Biography, just like politics, seems to have a little growing up to do.

The Paradox at the Heart of an Arts Debate

The year is 1982. Warren Beatty has made and starred in *Reds,* a risibly hagiographical film about the U.S. Marxist John Reed, who witnessed and chronicled the Bolshevik Revolution. Beatty is proud, euphoric. He grins as he climbs the stairs of a California stage to receive an Academy Award for his work. As he does so, the Hollywood orchestra plays a brassy, jazzed-up version of "The Internationale" — the socialist anthem performed in the heart of the capitalist empire. Hilarious, but meaningful. One evening that shook the world.

This apparent paradox has become an issue at the centre of the arts debate within the conservative movement and, for that matter, within the more thoughtful areas of the arts community in general. How is it that capitalism is constantly attacked by radicals for its cultural failings when this is evidently a vehement untruth? The creeping irony is almost palpable. Those on the left of the cultural and artistic spectrum criticize capitalism and liberal democracy, while at the same time they are sustained by it and often directly financed by it.

In a recent edition of *Commentary* magazine, politician and philosopher William Kristol wrote that "Liberals continue to dominate. They shape most of the products of the mass media, journalism, book publishing and Hollywood." Kristol is Chairman of the Project for the Republican Future and is considered to be one of the finest minds in U.S. politics. He was also Chief of Staff to Vice-President Dan Quayle, and is a man who can spell not only potato but many very long words as well. Kristol was in Toronto recently, where he continued the arts debate, protesting that "the best argument for capitalism has always been the awful nature of alternative systems, and this is particularly the case with the arts. We in the West seem almost apologetic for our achievements in this area, when in fact we should be boasting of them. They are unprecedented."

The indisputable fact is that capitalism has been and is culturally triumphant and will be so in the future. Those rival systems that have been tried since the advent of capitalism — Marxian socialism by the Russians, Chinese and their puppets in red shirts; National Socialism by the Germans, Italians and their allies in black shirts — have produced little other than banality and formulaic dross. The Nazis in particular injected enormous amounts of money into their arts industry but produced little outside of some anachronistically interesting movies. The proto-Nazi composer Richard Wagner, we must not forget, advocated an end to liberal capitalism and the introduction of a fascistic society while working in just such an emergingly powerful liberal capitalist Europe. In their several generations of rule, the Soviets produced one or two fine composers and authors of Russian birth, but none as spectacular as those who preceded them in the Tsarist state. The vast majority of Slavonic artists who achieved brilliance during the dictatorship of communism did so outside of that oppressive and stifling system.

One of the most discernible artistic legacies of far right and far left non-capitalist regimes has been the numbing regularity of Socialist Realism, in its musical and theatrical as well as fine art versions. Central direction, politicized funding and iron control do not produce a meaningful culture. This really should come as no surprise, particularly in Canada. Subsidized art is frequently bad, socialized art invariably bad and state art always bad.

In those social and economic systems that existed before capitalism, the arts were sometimes startlingly good, but they were always preserved for religious, economic and political elites. Capitalism, we must not forget, liberated the arts and made them far more egalitarian. That apotheosis of early capitalism, the printing press, changed everything, and everyone. And the fecundity of the Renaissance travelled its splendid road hand-in-hand with the ambitions of the merchant princes of late fifteenth- and early sixteenth-century capitalism.

So on a second glance the entire equation looks a little different. Under socialism, the zealots of the new left tell us, a new cultural dawn will emerge. The old left and the old right said the same thing. Trotsky wrote speeches about it, Goebbels broadcast radio talks about it. Their heirs will deliver the same arguments. It is right and fitting that a capitalism-financed orchestra played "The Internationale" at a capitalism-created ceremony, because it proves the tolerance and maturity of the system that begot such a situation. It is only raw, fragile and childish systems that oppress their dissident or challenging cultures. Similarly, it is a thing of political beauty that a tired, capitalist, parliamentary democracy like Canada tolerates myriad leftist cultural projects and magazines whose ostensible intention is to undermine the very system that allows them or even encourages them to exist. Whether that state should go a step further and establish cultural agencies to actually fund such entities is another issue. And, I think, another column.

The Radical Chic of Thespian Politics

I wonder what it is about the arts community in general, and actors in particular, that makes so many of them lose all sense of humility, self-perception and intellectual integrity whenever a glamorous political issue comes to the surface. British musician and actor Sting became an authority on the decay and exploitation of the Latin American rain forest for a brief period of time; for a week or two, he was seldom seen without a wretched, bewildered Brazilian native on his arm. Of course Sting understood the intricacies of environmental politics; after all, he wrote nice pop songs.

Jane Fonda thought that liberalism, feminism and the Democrats were most desirable. Vanessa Redgrave went further, embraced Trotskyism, the IRA and the PLO and stood for Parliament in Britain. She received fewer votes than the Monster Raving Loonie Party, led by someone called Screaming Lord Sutch. Actress Glenda Jackson also tried to become an MP, for Britain's Labour Party. She succeeded.

One would have hoped that this muddy and fatuous spectacle of thespians throwing their meagre weight around on the political stage was a tendency that Canadian actors had not inherited from their British and American cousins. But no. Recently a group of performers banded together to express their approval, if not adoration, of Bill 167, the flawed legislation that would have given spousal recognition to homosexual couples and was democratically defeated at Queen's Park a week and a half ago.

Al Waxman, Helen Shaver, Sheila McCarthy, Ralph Benmergui and most of the cast of the cancelled CBC drama *Street Legal* portentously recited their beliefs, as though their views were somehow ex cathedra. The lachrymose Sonja Smits was most emotional when interviewed, her presumably trained voice breaking and cracking as she told us just how important this bill was and how we had an obligation to support it.

Of course, performers have the same rights as anyone else. Not more, not less. Yet they abandon that precious jewel in the democratic crown, the right and even the duty of an individual to act as, and be represented as, a single voice. Instead, we are forced to endure Act 1, Scene 1: enter several actors in search of a cause.

Should we revere public comments just because they are made by people who are in the entertainment industry? That certainly appears to be the implicit nature of any political campaign or statement made by a performer. There is an inherent danger in this as well as a leap of sheer rodomontade. Actors are not known for their true, authentic selves, but for the roles they play on stage and on the screen. When Sonja Smits tells us about the importance of a bill granting benefits for same-sex couples, we do not perceive a woman whom we have never met, whose character and intelligence we are not familiar with and whose name we hardly know; we perceive a campaigning lawyer who came into our homes through our television screens for several CBC seasons. This is an exploitation of an insidious influence; we are led vicariously by characters we have grown to know or even love in an artificial form.

That the causes pursued are invariably leftist should come as no surprise. The American conservative magazine *National Review* tries constantly to produce more stars to support its position, and always has to make do with poor old Charlton Heston and his friend Tom Selleck. Change is thought to be romantic, the sort of thing that should attract actors and rock musicians. Tradition and orthodoxy, on the other hand, are less instantly attractive, certainly less so than ostensibly chic political struggle.

In Canada, this show-business pressure was applied at the same time as Bill 167's partisans complained that members of the clergy, notably the Catholic Archbishop of Toronto, had no right to interfere in politics from their pulpits, because external opinions on this controversial debate were unfair. Interesting. I for one would rather have someone concerned with the soul than someone concerned with a script give me advice about matters of significance.

It is not that there should be a complete abnegation of politics among members of the show-business community, but that we must know, and they must realize, that their words are not oracular — in fact, perhaps even less so than the opinions of others, because they have spent most of their working lives reciting the words and thoughts of other people. All the world's a stage, and all the men and women merely would-be candidates for the NDP. To borrow from those who demonstrated so loudly against the outcome of the vote: Shame, shame, shame.

Writers and Politics

I have an enormous problem with writers who become overtly political and ally themselves to a particular political party. It is for this reason that I am not a member of The Writers' Union of Canada. Although I admire and respect some of the union's work, I question the political infighting and strutting that occurs, which is often initiated and carried out by people who have in common the single fact that they do very little writing. There is a clear "line" on display here and it is not for me. Fair enough. Nobody is obliged to join and I would hope that those who are members of the union would respect such a decision. I would also hope that they would respect the decision of those who, in the light of recent events, have decided to resign.

But at least Canadian writers do not identify with actual parties in the manner or to the extent of their more fatuous American and European comrades. A writer entering the political arena in such a way is, to tamper with the former British prime minister Stanley Baldwin's remark about those he called the prostitutes in the press, a case of no power and no responsibility— the prerogative of the fool down the ages.

In Britain during the last election, all the major political parties pillaged reference works such as *The Oxford Companion to English Literature* in an effort to grab a few names for their propaganda. Travelling back through the centuries: Christopher Marlowe wrote anti-immigration pamphlets for the government, Grub Street bulged with hacks who would promote Whig or Tory in return for a good beef-and-ale dinner, and, of course, Benjamin Disraeli made his reputation as a rather fine novelist.

If we look a little deeper there is Henry Williamson, author of *Tarka the Otter*, amongst others, spreading the bloody and bloodstained cause of fascism, and dozens of useful idiots fellow-travelling along the road of dialectical materialism from Wigan Pier to Siberian Gulag. Ezra Pound supported Mussolini, Hemingway threw in his lot with the Spanish republicans, Bernard Shaw thought he had seen the future in the new Soviet Union; even more oddly, he thought that it worked. In Canada we have the likes of the Quebec poet Gérald Godin, who is also a well-known politician.

But there have always been the others, the more sensible, the less arrogant, the laudable Laodiceans. In Canada, with the rare exceptions of people such as Godin, they have dominated, and blessings on them for that. The point to be made is that as soon as writers join or offer full commitment to a political party they are, at best, lending or, at worst, giving part of their souls to an organization that stands for all sorts of policies and platforms. This is precisely what happened to so many well-meaning men and women in the 1920s and 1930s when they saw the rise of fascism in Europe. In reaction to this they submerged their capacities for original and mature thought in a sea of facile emotionalism. The Communist Party, they cried, was the only body standing up to the dictators in black — so they embraced the dictators in red.

When the Montreal intellectuals and the Toronto activists thought that Bolshevism might be nice, they signed a document metaphorically in favour of mass murder, social engineering, death-camps and crass imperialism. They should, they really should, have known better. Yet the century of the political party, of the National Socialists, the Bolsheviks, the Khmer Rouge, appears to have taught some authors hardly anything at all. We still see the bright young novelists, the aged writers of historical tomes, the pillars of conventional liberal wisdom, leaving their expensive houses and their book-lined studies and arriving at the conference and the convention centres, announcing to sound-bite-addicted hacks that the party knows best, waving the flag and wearing the rosette.

The good news is that the party never knows best. Nor does the community or the commune, the collective or the club, the union or the association. Truth lies with the individual. As long as that is engraved on the thought patterns of every author we will be safe from party harm. Once we give up personal, individual thought we are standing at the top of an intellectual and moral slide that has its end placed firmly in hellish oblivion.

I have no respect for writers who boast that they have just come from a party meeting. I would have far more regard for them if they told me that they had spent the weekend behind a dusty desk, reading dusty books in a dusty library. There are no political dictates in libraries — not yet, at least, nor will there be while the supremacy of unique and individual thought is championed by all those who describe themselves as writers.

Men and Women

To gain the supreme victory, it is necessary, for one thing, that by and through their natural differentiation men and women unequivocally affirm their brotherhood.

Simone de Beauvoir
The Second Sex, pt. VII, Conclusion

No Matter How Much They Like Women, Men Will Always Get Together

I have often thought that the relationship between men and women resembled an enormous mediaeval tapestry depicting a lord and lady, king and queen, serf and wife. From the front, the picture is pristine in its clarity — distinct, formed, sometimes staggeringly beautiful and placid, often quite grotesque and painful. Yet if we look behind the cloth we see a mess of stitches, a mass of hanging threads, a labyrinthine map of surprising connections and interwoven characters. Though the two figures appear to be apart, they are, in fact, joined at every point.

The image of the tapestry applies to a private dining club to which I belong. It is composed of about fifteen men in their thirties from the fields of journalism, publishing and politics. The ingredients are most appealing: a candle-lit table, fine food, plentiful and often fortified wines, good conversation and better cigars. To some, this rarefied scene would indicate that we have the blood of millions on our hands. But in the twilight period before my moribund gender shuffles off the masculine coil I prefer to believe that it merely indicates a penchant for civilized and urbane behaviour.

There is also one last spice thrown into this rich stew that I should mention: the sin of gender exclusivity. No women. Not invited, not required, not allowed.

How dare he? How dare they? One of the sacred cows — bovine and moralistic — of the egalitarian movement is the assumption that men and women not only *should* be granted equal access to clubs, associations and organizations, but *want* equal access to clubs, associations and organizations. In the public field, of course — in education, politics, employment — this is definitely the case and affirmative action is sometimes required to rectify past wrongs. But in the context of private gatherings it simply does not apply.

In a recent magazine interview, the actor Sean Connery expressed this with a rough and unpolished candour bordering on earthy wisdom: "At the club where I play, there's a men's bar and then there's a mixed bar . . . Women don't go into the men's bar. I think that's perfectly normal . . . It's harmless, really. It's just camaraderie." Mr. Connery is right. If there is such a thing as male bonding it may take place in a golfing watering hole or a Toronto club just as well as at a contrived men's-group meeting in a suburban basement.

Most of the better philosophies consist of the intellectualizing of the instinctive, a cerebral extension of a natural inclination. There is an inevitable bifurcation of the genders in some areas and this is by no means a bad thing. Because propinquity does not necessarily lead to familiarity or to mutual understanding and sympathy. Or, to put it in a more constructive manner, it is only by genuinely understanding ourselves can we even hope to understand others.

Of course, one of the valid fears and apprehensions of women about all-male clubs is the suspicion that such places will serve as nothing more, and nothing less, than surreptitious venues where men bolster their power and women are pushed even further from positions of influence. In fact, this scenario occurs far less often than some would have us believe. If it did become the purpose of an all-male group, however, and if it became the purpose of my club, I would leave it.

Women have used all-female meetings and groups to express their feelings and rationalize their situations for years, often out of necessity. As a close female friend, a columnist for *The Globe and Mail*, explained, "I have fallen down laughing when joking with some of my girlfriends. It's a different type of humour when I'm with men. Not worse or better. Different. I feel freer." But men are only thought sensitive in the 1990s if they gather not to laugh and enjoy but to offer contrition and share guilt. How sad, and how fatuous. We should not, must not, confuse neurosis with empathy, masochism with responsibility.

Men who like, love, regard and respect women will always gather with other men to the exclusion of women, and no amount of self-righteous indignation will change anything at all. And that mediaeval tapestry still hangs. And lord and lady, king and queen, serf and wife, still seem to be yards apart — until we take another, less direct but much closer look. The trick is to want to.

"Misogynist" an Overused Epithet

A curious but perhaps predictable phenomenon has developed within the sexual debate, that concerning the political and social relationship between men and women. It is best described as a form of Stalinism, a condemnation of individuals and ideas that does not rely on thought, consideration and argument but on abuse, stereotyping and name-calling. The name called is extremely specific. Misogynist. "One who hates women." A venomous, dreadful word and a venomous, dreadful thing. And not to be used lightly.

The word was hardly used at all in the past but has become part of the nomenclature of radical feminism. If a man disagrees with your opinion, he is a misogynist; if a man expresses a contrary point of view, gained through objective observation or subjective experience, he is a misogynist. In fact, men who express a view about a particular kind of feminism that is in any way negative or critical will certainly be labelled with the epithet at some time in their lives. It does not matter that those shouting the word are not very intelligent or sophisticated, they still do a great deal of damage and try, sometimes successfully, to stifle opposition by linguistic mugging. The last resort of the defeated and the debunked.

When I speak of a man who has reservations about feminism I am not talking of the wider, representative feminism that advocates equal rights under the law, pay equity, shared parenting of children and housework, and full opportunities for women in any profession they choose, or the balanced and astute feminism that condemns outrageous sexist behaviour and workplace harassment. Those beliefs, one would think, constitute a self-evident truth. Any man who had difficulties with them would be, if not misogynistic, certainly rather foolish.

No, I speak of the radical feminist agenda that is based on extremist notions and is articulated by a tiny, elitist group that claims to speak for the mass of women but, in fact, represents a zealous few. That this name-calling might destroy all debate on one of the most interesting and important issues facing the contemporary world seems not to concern this tiny band. But then, it is perhaps what the culprits actually want. Who could forget the repugnant scenes of extremists screaming and whistling into silence the professor of psychiatry trying to deliver a lecture at a Canadian university about the possible errors of suppressed memory syndrome? Echoes of the nastiest of authoritarian regimes of the century. This man was apparently a misogynist. He hated all women, all of the time, forever. I see.

The nearest comparison I could imagine would be someone who condemned, for example, the Jewish Defence League, Kach, in Israel and the United States, and was then labelled an anti-Semite. This group is supported by only a fraction of Jews, and is openly rejected and even banned by the overwhelming majority of Jewish people and, indeed, by the Israeli government. So what we have is political and intellectual terror by mythology and innuendo.

The truth of the situation is that to oppose one fringe political expression of a race, religion or gender is not to oppose that race, that religion or that gender in general. On the contrary, to oppose damaging extremism is to support the group being thus ill-represented. I condemn real misogyny not because I hate all men but because I care about men. I condemn fundamentalist and hysterical feminism because I care about women and about genuine feminism.

Of course, those to whom I am referring would say that the reason I have written all of this, the reason that I think all of this, is that I am "threatened." This is the meeker but related secondary attack after cries of misogyny have been dismissed. And you know, the substandard sophism of this tawdry attack aside, in a way I am threatened. Just as I would be by real misogyny, by wrong thinking, by real racism, by real sexism, by badness and by hatred. Because they are wrong. Because all decent people should be threatened by them. Not frightened, but threatened. I wonder if there is a word for that, and whether it will be perverted and exploited by those who refuse to listen, and those who refuse to learn.

Sexual Harassment — Two Very Different Outcomes

A story about two very different men that illustrates the paradoxes, the amorphous rules and guidelines, the innate hypocrisies and the inherent dangers that exist within the issue of sexual harassment:

The first man is black. He is a respected lawyer, a conservative figure renowned for championing traditional causes. He is also a little stuffy, lacking glamour and instant panache. Ironically, there is no real sex appeal here, either in a physical or metaphorical sense.

At the very point that this man was offered a job of enormous prestige and influence, a woman alleged that ten years earlier the man had sexually harassed her, made obscene jokes and commented on his and her genitalia. She may have been telling the truth, she may not. The man was questioned in a televised pseudo-trial in front of millions.

Many women who had worked for and with him said that the accusations were unbelievable. The man said there was racism at play.

The chattering classes, the mainstream media, the opinion formers of North America tended either to mock or condemn him. His accuser, on the other hand, could do no wrong in their eyes.

One CBC reporter interviewed the woman's aged father, who said that he had raised his girl as a church-goer and hence she would never lie. The credulous, unctuous reporter nodded enthusiastically. The journalist did not interview any of the accused man's relatives. Presumably, they did not raise him as a church-goer.

There were questions about the accuser's credibility, and after a thorough and strenuous period of interrogation the charges were dismissed. Yet the woman is now treated as a feminist hero and is a highly paid speaker — she will not, by the way, answer any questions about this case.

The man was, of course, Clarence Thomas. The woman was Anita Hill.

The second man is white. He is a politician who has been accused of being unfaithful to his wife, and around whom there is a stench of financial and personal scandal. But he is a press favourite for initiating or supporting liberal campaigns. He is modern and has a certain popular appeal. He is media savvy, personable, likable.

The man was very successful. He became, in fact, the most powerful individual on the face of the Earth. And he was accused by a former employee of sexual harassment, of removing his trousers and asking her to perform sex acts with him.

This was not the first time that the man's sexual propriety had been questioned. Nor had this woman, unlike the first, waited almost a decade to bring forth her charges. She claims that her ordeal took place less than three years ago and that she was too frightened to do anything until now. There are witnesses who say the woman told them what had happened on the day the incident occurred and was badly shaken.

The media are less than sympathetic, even openly hostile, to this woman. They have referred to her as being white trash, as having "big hair," of being promiscuous, the product of a trailer-park culture.

Whether any of this is true or not is irrelevant. Sexual harassment is the issue, not the character or class of the plaintiff. Feminism has taught men this reality and most of us have learned it well. Surely in this case there is a repugnant double standard on display.

The man, of course, is President Bill Clinton. The woman is Paula Jones.

So what should be construed from all this? Perhaps that if a man is black he is more easily attacked and less readily believed? Or that if a man symbolizes and represents beliefs that are contrary to the prevailing ethical and social fashions of the day he is a more likely target?

A spokesperson for the National Organization of Women has said she is concerned that some of the people supporting Ms. Jones "don't have the best interests of women at heart." Interesting. It is not only sex, sexuality and race that qualify us for victim status, it appears, but also our political ideology.

Either way, and whatever other permutations we employ, this is a gender issue that is evidently as political as it is moral, and we have a very long way to go and a great many answers to provide to enigmatic questions before justice can be done, and be seen to be done. For men as well as for women, let us hope that progress is rapid.

Sexual Harassment of Men Barely Out of the Closet

The casting is terribly wrong. In the movie *Disclosure*, adapted from Michael Crichton's novel of the same name, we see Michael Douglas sexually harassed and finally seduced by sultry American actress Demi Moore. Men in the audience are, presumably, obliged to try to sympathize with poor Mr. Douglas's plight. Difficult indeed. A nightmare or a dream? Actually, it is neither, but just another example of Hollywood trivializing and commercializing a subject that deserves better treatment.

That is a shame. Because if we dismiss the sheen of glamour, the whole issue of the sexual harassment of men takes on a very different focus. That was certainly the case recently just a few miles away from Hollywood in central Los Angeles. There, Sabino Gutierrez, a thirty-three-year-old male factory worker and Mexican immigrant with a fourth-grade education, accused Maria Martinez of sexually harassing and assaulting him over a six-year period, culminating in his forced resignation. The jury, composed of two men and ten women, was so outraged at Mr. Gutierrez's treatment that it awarded him more than $1 million (U.S.) in damages.

Anyone familiar with the extremely liberal mindset of the contemporary American judiciary will comprehend the importance of this decision and understand how obvious the crime must have been. To confirm the fact, the plaintiff was represented by Gloria Allred, the most renowned feminist lawyer in California.

Elsewhere in the United States, staff at the Jenny Craig diet company have been accused by two male employees of sexual harassment, of repeatedly making sexist remarks and of passing the pair over for promotion for gender-related reasons. Tip of the iceberg or tip of the ice cube? Most objective political commentators and legal observers believe that it all goes deeper than a gin and tonic.

Harry certainly does. He knows all about sexual harassment from his days in a Montreal computer company. He resigned from his job, without references, rather than go to court to fight his case. He was afraid of revealing to his friends and to his wife something he then thought of as being a sign of weakness and humiliation.

"What I find most disturbing is that when the subject comes up in conversation, people think a man has to enjoy harassment, has to be turned on by it," he says. "Well, maybe some men are, but not this one. Frankly, my boss in Montreal was ugly. Nothing sexy about this woman old enough to be my mother holding my crotch and rubbing up against me. It happened first at a Christmas party, so I put it down to high spirits and too much wine. But my boss saw my failure to complain as a sign on my part that it was okay. It didn't stop after that."

The notion that men have to be erect and hence aroused to participate in a sex act is patently false. Sexual harassment seldom involves penetration, and even when this does occur the necessary tumescence is forced and involuntary and thus constitutes harassment. And the idea that men cannot be sexually assaulted because all men want sex all of the time is eerily similar to that pestilent caricature that was formerly applied to women.

"When I told my brother about what was going on, he looked at me as if I was crazy, as though I was the lucky one," Harry says. "I told him that even after I came back to work with photos of my baby son, just born, this woman still fondled me, still rubbed up against me. When I told her that if she did it again, I would make a complaint, she just laughed. Nobody will believe you, she said. Then she got angry, told me that my career was finished. It was a couple of months after that remark that I left. Her last threat broke the circle. It made me realize that I had to be stronger."

Will he ever seek legal or financial compensation? "No, no, it's too high a price," he says. "My wife trusts me implicitly, but imagine the response of her friends, her family. The question will be, 'Did Harry encourage the woman?' The answer will have already been decided. No, I'll just move on."

As will society, with all of its pert preconceptions and its refusal, even inability, to peel back the thermal-thick layers of traditional and conventional wisdom. Yet the issue is more than Demi Moore and more than demi-serious. It is important, damaging and sufficiently common to require a consistent and intelligent response. Just like, in fact, the sexual harassment of women by men.

Humour's Double Standard

What is good for the feminist, liberated goose is surely good for the poor old gander. Or in other words, we should not observe a double standard when it comes to the depiction of politically and socially sensitive issues such as power, sex and abuse.

Last year, Dr. Frederick Mathews, director of research at Central Toronto Youth Services, published a report entitled "What's So Funny About the Abuse of Boys and Young Men?"

In the paper he argued that while we no longer accept the portrayal in the movies of racism or sexism towards women as being amusing, "If you have rented a comedy video for your children in the last ten years, chances are you and they have witnessed scenes about the sexual abuse of boys and young men — and laughed."

Dr. Mathews' examples are intriguing. In *Police Academy II*, for example, a "bad guy" is anally penetrated with a gloved finger by an ugly, aggressive nurse. When the victim protests and tries to escape he is held down by two of the nurse's assistants and his mouth is taped over.

The slapstick comedy *Airplane II* features one scene in which a priest is reading a magazine called *Altar Boy*, the cover of which shows an innocent young boy with his hands clasped in prayer. After a few moments the priest turns the magazine on its side, however, and is supposed to be looking at a centrefold of a nude altar boy.

In *Ladybugs*, a young boy is obliged to dress as a girl so as to play for a female soccer team. One scene, played for laughs of course, shows the star of the movie, a grown man, driving his car alongside the cross-dressing boy and bothering him, as in an attempted pickup and molestation. A passerby tries to intervene and stop what is happening, only increasing the level of laughter.

In *Wayne's World*, another of those bad guys who almost seem to ask to be violated or raped is stopped by a policeman and anally penetrated by the man with his finger, ostensibly in search of hidden drugs. Later the actor, Rob Lowe, is seen walking bow-legged and in extreme pain.

In the more serious *Rambling Rose*, a young woman climbs into bed with a thirteen-year-old boy. The boy is extremely naïve but naturally curious and asks if he can touch the woman's genitals. She says yes. As the boy touches the woman she reaches an orgasm. The boy is so callow that he even asks her if her heavy breathing is a sign of ill health. Although the woman cries and pleads with the teenager not to tell on her after the act, the film still depicts the skinny little boy as the seducer.

Private Lessons is about a fifteen-year-old boy who is gradually seduced by an older woman and is shown growing to manhood and maturity as his sexual experiences multiply. In one scene, the boy's penis is touched by the woman without his permission, causing him to run out of the room and away from his abuser. The woman follows him and tries to convince him to get into bed with her to talk things over.

Dr. Mathews argues: "At a time when female victims are finally finding a voice to express their fears and talk about their experiences, abused males are being laughed at. Not only is violence and sexual abuse directed towards males not taken seriously in North America, it is seen as material for comedy and entertainment!"

It is true that we cannot even imagine an audience laughing, and the writers expecting the audience to laugh at, the sight of a young woman limping away from a physically invasive examination by a police officer; or approving of sexual pressure being applied to a teenaged girl by a middle-aged man.

Yet I must confess that none of this particularly bothers me, and I believe that an increased capacity for laughter from all Canadians would make this country a much saner, more tolerant place in which to live, particularly in the context of gender issues. Nor can I think of many experiences more pleasing than a sexual rite of passage involving a boy in his teens and a mature, attractive woman.

But this is not the point. Once again we are obliged to live under the rule of hypocrisy and an ugly dichotomy of morality and a division of standards between peoples. It is not a very good idea. It never has been.

Statistics, Damned Statistics and Lies

Some people found the recent report on the subject of violence against women issued by a group of zealous pollsters in Ottawa to be frightening and offensive. They could not believe the extraordinarily high figures included in the paper of alleged abuse, rape and incest, and rejected the almost blanket condemnation of Canadian manhood. I remain unmoved. There is an aphorism that says that there are lies, damned lies and statistics. I prefer the explanation that there are statistics, damned statistics and lies.

If it is really true, as the report by the Canadian Panel on Violence Against Women exclaims, that half of the women in Canada have been victims of attempted or fulfilled rape, and if, like me, you know many women who have not been thus treated, to balance out the average there must in this country be entire cities whose populations are composed entirely of raped females. The report is evidently an example of the workings of a group of people who have screamed before they have learned to listen.

The only remotely interesting aspect of the task force's conclusions and recommendations was its demand that men and women "not laugh at sexist and racist jokes." Now, this does move me. God forgive me, it moves me to tears of laughter. Oh dear, I do hope that the task force's action squad does not come to my front door at dawn to arrest me, send me to a re-education camp and torture me for being an enemy of the nanny, or sister, state.

Of course, it had to come. We will tell you when to smoke, when to drink, when to wear a seat belt and a bicycle helmet, and now what to laugh at. The hubris of the liberal authoritarian is quite overwhelming. Such invincible ignorance, such invincible arrogance, such invisible common sense. People will laugh at what they have always laughed at and no directorate or committee or cabal will change matters. More than this, just because a man laughs at a joke that has as part of its equation a woman does not mean that he is hence a purveyor of galloping misogyny.

Only the genuinely perverse or insane could laugh at a joke that glorified or minimized rape or authentic violence against women, but most jokes that feature women in any way at all are of the mother-in-law variety and are more innocuous than they are execrable. An antediluvian buffoon such as the U.S. comedian Andrew Dice Clay is not funny because he is not funny — he is a vapid and priapic bore. Those fatuous activists who formed Feminists for Healthy Humour in Vancouver in an attempt to ban Mr. Clay achieved two things: they increased his sales and profit, and they made a lot of people laugh because of their caricatured antics.

We would do well to recall George Orwell's observations when he compared the British and German attitudes towards goose-stepping soldiers. The SS march through Berlin and the crowds weep with pride, said Orwell. If English Tommies did the same in London the spectators would fall about laughing. One cannot throw a punch when one is giggling, lunge with a blade when one is guffawing. Humour is the great leveller and the great disarmer. And anyway, contemporary man is probably more joked against than joking — this is only right, and I would equally condemn an intolerant man if he objected to and tried to silence a feminist stand-up comic.

There is more to all of this than the mere censure of politically incorrect jokes. The strident are by their very nature emotionally arthritic individuals. They demand to be taken seriously and hate to be mocked. They also lust to control others, because they are so fundamentally convinced that they are the only ones to whom the truth has been revealed. People who laugh, however, cannot be controlled, and this is terrifying for those who would control us.

Samuel Taylor Coleridge wrote that "no mind is thoroughly well organized that is deficient in a sense of humour." Amen to that. But perhaps of even greater pertinence was playwright Edward Albee's line in *Who's Afraid of Virginia Woolf?* when he had one of his characters proclaim: "I have a fine sense of the ridiculous, but no sense of humour." Don't laugh at certain jokes. This is indeed ridiculous, and exhibits absolutely no sense of humour. By the way, I for one am in no way afraid of Ms. Woolf, though I do on occasion find her to be extremely amusing.

Why Are You Wearing That White Ribbon?

The results are now in and I am eager to reveal them. In the grand tradition of Statscan and the sociology and women's-studies departments of almost every university in the country, I undertook a survey. It was of men wearing white ribbons on the much-chronicled anniversary of the Montreal massacre. The responses were fascinating, and the conclusions drawn bring to mind Immanuel Kant's concept of an island of insight surrounded by the icy, foggy ocean of illusion.

My helpers and I asked one hundred men this question: "What is that ribbon you are wearing and why are you wearing it?" (The poll did not cost the taxpayer any money and was not tendentious.)

First, a few typical answers. Simon from Oakville: "It's about AIDS awareness. A guy at work died last year from it. It's terrible. A man came in to give the ribbons out yesterday. I gave two bucks. It's a good thing, I think. I'm not gay, but we have to do something to stop the disease."

Jack from North York: "You've got me there." An embarrassed laugh. "The boss was wearing one and some of the other guys began to, so I got one. I think it's got something to do with drunk driving and zero tolerance. The R.I.D.E. campaign. Christmas drinking. There are so many ribbons today that I get a bit mixed up. It might actually have something to do with AIDS. No, wait. No, that's the red one. There's a green one, too, isn't there? I'm late, actually."

Lee from Scarborough: "It's against violence. Everyone should be wearing one. You turn on the television — Serbia, Israel, Russia, killing everywhere. It's my stand against violence. It's easy to mock, but if we all stood together, some of these wars might stop. It's easy to be apathetic."

Roughly 35 per cent of the men interviewed had no idea what their white ribbons were meant to signify, 35 per cent had a vague notion and 30 per cent knew to a very large extent what the ribbons were about. Some were so wrong as to be hilarious, or horrendous. Yet they still wore them.

The organizers of the white-ribbon campaign claim that every man wearing the ribbon is making an unreserved statement concerning male violence against women. Not only do they appear to be wrong, but the package offered by the campaign includes more than this ostensibly innocuous and moderate comment. It involves any number of half-baked ideas about patriarchy, manhood, the inevitability of violence and the belief that only they have seen the light of truth about the relationship between the sexes and that for millennia every man has misunderstood the situation.

There is one particularly false and undeniably insidious tentacle emanating from the body of the white-ribbon phenomenon. This is the implicit, sometimes explicit, belief that any man who does not wear a ribbon is either in favour of violence against women or somehow insufficiently active against it. An example of one of the consequences of this is that various prominent television anchors have been pressured to wear the things.

More responses from the survey. Rick from Whitby: "I always buy poppies and stuff from people on street corners. Charity needs our support. I'm not really that concerned about the cause. I was a bit angry that the last mayor refused to let the Salvation Army on city property." George from Peterborough: "I don't bloody know, it's not my coat. Is that it? I thought you were going to ask me about the hockey strike." Finally, Dick from Toronto: "It's to show my sympathy with the women of the world who are abused and murdered, especially minorities but everybody, really. I'm ashamed to be a man sometimes. Hold on a minute, I know you. You're Michael Coren. I hate you, I'd stop you from ever being in print if I could."

If any of you believe my sample to be too small or my motives to be less than objective, you might have a point. My results are documented and genuine, however. Just like, I am sure, all of these gender-related surveys that have been conducted during the last decade and have had an untold influence upon Canadian society. What should we construe from such matter? Hard to tell. Perhaps it is time for a ribbon campaign for ambivalent pollsters. Or perhaps not.

Domestic Violence Against Men Should Not Be Dismissed

Although I have received myriad letters about individual cases of husband abuse, I have remained unconvinced that a woman could inflict genuine violence on her husband, and believe that a man's economic independence and physical strength would have enabled him to leave an abusive relationship.

It was a woman — it had to be — who convinced me that some of my preconceptions were wrong and, frankly, the product of prejudice. Holly-Anne Franchi, the twenty-seven-year-old director of a counselling service called The Easton Alliance, telephoned me and asked if I would write about the opening of her organization's new centre. She explained that she was an unpaid volunteer, was not political and only became concerned with this cause through meeting victims. I asked if we really needed another therapy or aid organization in a country that seemed to be drowning in them. Thus began a tale.

"I've spoken with thousands, met with hundreds, of men who are victims of domestic violence. Knifed, hit over the head with heavy ashtrays, with telephones, pushed through dining-room windows, run over, burned, noses broken, beaten, kicked," she says. "Do we need such a centre? Of course we do. The very fact that you would ask such a question shows why we need it, because so few people take domestic violence against men seriously."

The situation is evidently more complex than it initially appears. Men are not the violent time bombs that propaganda has led us to expect; this false image is the result of politicized hysteria and biased surveys.

Ms. Franchi lists a variety of reasons for the phenomenon of men remaining in violent marriages. "Most have been raised to believe that a man should never hit a woman and therefore [they] often accept spousal violence without retaliation. If there are children in the family, men are frightened of the marriage ending and their losing custody in an unbalanced legal system, even if they are the innocent party."

She looks to the ground, a little upset. "If they do call the police, the cops are extremely reluctant, if not effectively forbidden, to remove a woman from the home and the first thing they will ask is whether the man used any force, even in self-defence.

"And then there's the non-physical stuff, emotional humiliation, and that does not require physical strength. And the fear of being laughed at if you say that your partner is beating you. No laughing matter though, really not."

Ms. Franchi and her comrades also deal with other forms of abuse suffered by men. These include constant threats of divorce, threats to call the police or to deny access to the children. There is also the destruction of personal property and using the children or another family member to relay spiteful messages. The Easton Alliance is very busy indeed.

An extensive study carried out by the University of Calgary revealed that while 18 per cent of men admit to having physically abused their partners, 23 per cent of women say that they have assaulted their spouses or boyfriends. While we have to break the throttle-grip that professional statisticians have on government, the report is supported by an increasingly bold wave of anecdotal evidence. New feminists, usually younger women, are confirming that the ill-lit and potholed street of domestic violence is certainly not one way. Ms. Franchi is an appropriate witness.

"I'm not ashamed as a woman, but I am confused. The issue is about fairness, justice. I'd like to introduce some of these radical feminists who blame men for every act of violence to some of the broken, bashed men I talk to. It's comforting for some people to think that domestic violence against men is a rarity, an irrelevance in the grander scale of things." Her face reddens, her voice is raised. "I'm sorry, I'm really sorry, but that is absolute nonsense!"

Some readers might think that the discussion of this issue is meant in some way to diminish our abhorrence of male violence towards women. That would be sad. Our conclusion, on the contrary, should be that violence, just like hatred, racism and every other negative aspect of the human character, can emanate from any source, irrespective of gender or ethnicity, and that its victims are similarly universal. When that is understood, progress might just be possible.

The Abortion Debate Not Over

What is a man's issue? What is a column? The former is surely anything that concerns or involves men, and need not be exclusive to them in any way. The latter is a little more difficult to define. This I know — if newspaper and magazine columns were CDs or cassettes, most would be tucked away under the Easy Listening section of the music store. I'd prefer not. Better a bit of heavy metal, plenty of classical, some folk and perhaps a little jazz. But never let any musical form dominate or claim to be supreme, righteous and orthodox.

This column is about abortion, partly because half of all of the parents of unborn children are, of course, men and partly because almost half of aborted unborn children are men; cultural chauvinism in the Third World makes sure that more females are aborted than males. But most of all, it is about abortion because somebody wrote a letter to this newspaper recently, claiming that the abortion debate was over. If any debate around such a fundamental issue is over, we might as well raise the white flag and thrash about in a hedonistic and insouciant quagmire while we wait for a deserved armageddon. I say again, let no musical form drown out others with its cacophonous volume. I write this column as a man, and as a father.

The balance between the rights of women and the rights of men, and between the freedom of women and the freedom of the unborn child, is razor-like in its delicacy and in its sharpness. It can break so easily, and it can cut so readily. The truth can also cut and be acutely painful, but that does not diminish its truthfulness.

As a man, I find it fascinating that when MP Roseanna Skoke made her remarks recently about homosexuals, she was attacked for provoking violence towards gays. Possibly. Yet when various MPs call for abortion on demand, they are calling for extreme violence towards the unborn. Definitely. The former statement provokes hysterical condemnations and satirical attacks, the latter only an apparent indifference or a media approval. Perhaps we should extend the Human Rights Code to include unborn children. After all, the handicapped are already there — well, those fortunate enough to have made it past the compassionate doctors, the ones who appreciate how difficult it is raising a child who does not measure up to the physical and mental standards of the late twentieth century and offer a quick, convenient solution.

I have been told by objective medical reports that an unborn child feels pain. This has been proven during blood transfusions when needles are inserted into babies. They were hurt. We have also seen gruesome footage from abortions showing the baby moving away from the device that is ending its life, showing it squirm and struggle. So the rationale of this, and one that is accepted even by doctors who perform abortions, is that it may be necessary in the future to anaesthetize the baby before it is removed. Forget politics, forget religion, forget feminism, forget men, forget everything — this alone sickens this man to his stomach and screams out for justice.

I could say that 40 per cent of abortions are performed on women who have already had one or more abortions; I could say that a third of all abortions are performed on teenagers, usually without the knowledge of their parents; and I could say that almost three million couples in North America are on adoption-agency waiting lists. But surely the argument is more fundamental than this. We claim that we want a society that is less violent, less exploitative and less cruel. Yet we harm and exploit the most vulnerable in that very society. How dare it surprise us that others are also treated callously? As our elected rulers consider more gun control to reduce the number of people who are injured, they also give their blessing to abortion. Thomas Jefferson's remark that "the care of human life and happiness, and not their destruction, is the first and only object of good government" should still hold true.

As a man, I am thankful that I was allowed to be born. And as a man I say that if the debate is over, on this or on any other basic issue of life and liberty, then so is history. For the sake of us all, let the band play on, and on.

Do Canadian Men Really Want Golf Trophies, Joke Toilet Paper and Executive Desk Games?

The feared and respected male hunter-gatherer has filled his belly and earned his crust. His day is done. His terrifying roar is over. Now back to his den, a sacrosanct haven shining with playthings, intricate comforts and the eclectic personal possessions that give meaning and validity to life. This fellow with an atavistic memory of wrestling with wild beasts and fighting for sheer survival comes here to revel in his masculinity and to explore the deeper significance of his existence as a man.

In the corner, a set of highly attractive barbecue tools and gloves. Next to them, a group of extremely useful anchor-shaped key rings, a book of pithy golf quotations, some one-armed-bandit machines, a few pewter hip flasks, a pile of T-shirts emblazoned with examples of hockey humour, some dart boards and darts illustrated with shamrocks and snakes, a pot of moustache wax, a squadron of toy cardboard planes and a regiment of Swiss army knives — knives for the Swiss army, or knives made by the Swiss for other people's armies? Surely the latter, from a people who love neutrality even more than they adore chocolate and banking.

A flower bed of banality. But there on the wall, obscuring the Gary Player range of golfing accessories "including score watches, tee dispensers and gold ball monograms, $9.99–$34.99" is, perhaps, relief. But no. It is a board game called How To Host a Romantic Evening, and promises that players will "experience the rapture of romance without leaving home."

Where am I? In a branch of Den For Men, one of thirty-five such stores that began life in the 1970s and cater to the apparent needs of Canadian males all the way from the west coast to Quebec.

It is a unique case of the reversal of gender-pertinent commercialism and advertising. For once, it is not women who are being targeted with crass promotions for odourless toilet cleaners and softer tissues for blowing the sensitive female nose. This time it is an appeal to what men are supposed to find in their den, their inner sanctum, their special place where they go to be themselves, to reflect and consider the world. And, it seems, to play with golf trophies.

"We found a pretty uniform demand from Canadian men," explains Den For Men divisional vice-president Derrick Barnett. "The same sort of sales from city to city. We're trying to have everything that men would possibly want under one single roof." A pause. "Although I must admit that out west there was more of a call for imitation antique guns."

If the invisible hand of the market is as reliable as some would have us believe, maybe Canadian men really do want to wipe their bottoms with joke toilet paper while playing with executive desk games made popular in the 1960s. But can it be so? Can they be attracted by this stupefying and stultifying juxtaposition of the crass with the crasser?

There are also some dreadful and, one hopes, not too indicative omissions from the shelves. There are hardly any products about families, about men as husbands or fathers, about men relating to others. There is an enormous amount of material for people who are simply bored, possibly with themselves. It is difficult to imagine the attraction of owning a preassembled miniature model of the Santa Maria or H.M.S. Bounty when the entire point of such kits is that the owner is supposed to lovingly put the things together himself.

The positive result of all of it is that men might begin to wonder if this is what they are actually like, or whether they have been manipulated by the media or by the relentless force of sales pressure. It is, of course, a question that women have been obliged to ask themselves for generations. Self-analysis can only be good for men, in that it should strengthen their self-perception in the midst of a dramatically ambiguous age. If only it could be done without wearing that new range of "oversize BBQ aprons and chef hats." We can but hope.

Sammy the Way Out Seal

The first conscious memory I have of my tears dates back to the Christmas of 1966. I was approaching my fifth birthday and had been taken as a seasonal treat by my mother to the Rialto Cinema in Leytonstone to see *Sammy the Way Out Seal.* I think Haley Mills was in the movie, but I could be wrong. I know I had a crush on her. Certainly Sammy was present, and I definitely had a crush on him. So much so that the film's denouement was, for me, unsatisfying and ambiguous. Simply, I bawled my eyes out.

The irony of the thing is that the movie was meant to have a happy ending. Lucky old Sam is abandoned by his human friends so as to spend his life with an obliging lady-seal companion.

Yet the actions of these premature animal-rights zealots were difficult for a wailing prepubescent to comprehend. Poor Sammy, without Hayley and her friends to play with him. My mother urged me to consider the paradox of the situation and then took me into the ladies washroom to deliver my first lesson about the birds and the bees . . . and the seals. She also promised to buy me an ice cream if I shut the hell up.

Strangely enough, I have not been left with any profound neurosis about women's toilets or about bribes of confectionary. I suppose I am probably yet another victim of suppressed memory syndrome.

Nor since The Great Leytonstone Washroom Incident have I been at all shy, reserved or even particularly concerned about crying, in private or, to a very large extent, in public. I like to think that this is because I am abundantly secure in my sex, my sexuality and my self-perception, and I also believe that the reason that so few men are prepared to cry is that they consociate tears with weakness, and weeping with vulnerability or effeminacy.

They would do well to read up on their history, especially the period of the Elizabethan Renaissance in England. In the sixteenth century, the Anglo-Saxons were the piratical wild men of Europe. Sir Richard Grenville was one of the doyens of the breed, a choleric and terrifying man who, when he was finally defeated, chewed broken glass in front of his captors to evince his courage and contempt.

This was an individual more leonine than lachrymose. Yet on one occasion, he listened to his favourite lute player before battle and wept profusely in front of his men at a poignant chord; he then strapped on his breastplate and promptly transformed five Spaniards into paella.

He was a raw buccaneer, but one who realized that it is only a foolish man who will refuse to physically show his appreciation of the inherent beauty of a sonnet.

I recall standing with 60,000 other Welsh rugby fans and seeing hardened, coal-stained men with tiny pearls of saltwater dissecting their sinewy cheeks as they listened to their national anthem with its atavistic clamour and unabashed Celtic pride. Effeminate? Go and argue the point with those boys from the valleys.

I cry at great literature, at great music, at the untamed greatness of my children, at the innate beauty of a traditional mass. Yet it is essential that we are aware of the difference between falsified emotion and the genuine, abundantly natural and healthy phenomenon of crying. The group dynamic neurosis of pustulous teenagers and the rehearsed leaking sessions of ostensibly liberated and reconstructed men are irrelevant.

Similarly the tears of ostentatious talk-show circus fleas who submit so readily to the sedulous pornographers who masquerade as journalists are contrived, artificial and invariably pointless. Some people weep habitually and the act becomes as redundant and gratuitous as it is tiresome.

But Canadian men could do well to consider crying as not merely a means of emotional catharsis, but also a statement of quintessentially masculine strength and a means of communication, expression and feeling, especially in their relationships with women. This is not a discovery of the new, but a recapturing of the old.

Zeno and his Stoics were wrong on many issues, and you can be sure that those dull philosophers never went to see *Sammy the Way Out Seal* at the Rialto Leytonstone.

The British Gent Easier About Gender-Bending

Two nationalities divided by a common gender. Men in Canada and men in Britain. I think I am qualified to judge. Seven years in the former country, twenty-five years in the latter. Both periods, I hasten to add, as a man. And the differences are vast, from the cosmetic and the superficial to the meaningful and the profound.

One of the most obvious and indicative aspects of the dichotomy is the attitude towards homosexuality held by heterosexual males. Much as Canadians like to consider themselves to be extraordinarily tolerant, and even though gay rights are more institutionalized this side of the Atlantic, there is a far greater and wider acceptance of homosexuality in Britain. It is part of the English laissez-faire attitude towards individual lifestyle, but also reflects the intriguing Anglo-Saxon ambivalence towards sexuality that sweeps across all classes, from Brideshead posing and patrician rights of passage to proletarian guardsmen "obliging a gent" in St. James Park.

The English now have openly homosexual men playing professional soccer, and even the gruesome tabloid press in London does not "out" known gay politicians. This acceptance or indifference might offend those radical gays who stress the "differentness" of homosexuality and are obsessed with public declarations of sexual preference, but then the Brits have never been able to tolerate a bore, however he makes love. So while the government and the CBC tell us, interminably and expensively, which social attitudes are righteous and which are not, and while equality is increasingly legalized, British homosexual men are in a far superior position compared to their Canadian comrades.

Which leads to other manifestations of sexual identity. British men appear to be more comfortable than Canadians with gender-bending, the wearing of makeup, the New Romantic generation and unorthodox self-expression. Surprising. But the popular image of the tight-lipped Englishman in a suit is largely nonsense. Such sartorial and social stoicism might apply to the upper classes — "By God, I think I've lost my leg," said the cavalry general to the Duke of Wellington at Waterloo. "By God, sir, so you have," replied Napoleon's nemesis — but does not extend to the far more tactile, exuberant and volatile masses.

Facial hair is a good example. This is the most apparent and most contrived visual difference between the sexes and it is something that Canadian men cultivate. Police officers, bankers, lawyers, street kids and hockey players. The thick moustache, the gappy attempt, the goatee or even the full beard. Far more common than in Britain and far more of a statement — ask the man who gives you your next speeding ticket why he hides his upper lip behind a hedge. "Nothing significant, no, no, no." As Freud said, one "no" would have been enough.

And ask him why he spends three nights a week pushing weights above his head. The pumped-up image, the strutting of the Gym-Jims, is more than a fashion in this country. It is pertinent that the portrait of the tough guy in Canada is of a heavily muscled individual, whereas in Britain the picture is more that of a sinewy, sharp-faced hard man.

But if Canadians come off worse in some areas compared to Englishmen, they are enlightened paragons in others. The northern rock band The Mac Lads sang that men should treat women like toilets but also remember that "at least a toilet can't follow you around." They might have been speaking for a small and repugnant minority, but they did bring this song out on compact disc, did sell many copies and do have a following. It would be a different story in Canada.

At its worst this is the beer- and vomit-stained culture of the English urban pub, splashed in machismo pomposity. It is dying, but it exists. And, Canadian politicians and social reformers take note, it is changing not because of propaganda and legislation but because of the increasing embourgeoisement of the country initiated by Margaret Thatcher.

The relationship between men and women in Britain is less equitable than in Canada, but perhaps a little more exciting. British men are probably not as aware of important themes such as the crime of domestic violence and the need for shared parenting, but they are less burdened by inflated issues like suppressed memory and date rape. Britain is, of course, a far less didactic society than Canada. And that is a lesson in itself.

The Passing Parade of Sensitive Males

They are easy to spot, the arrival of sensitive and enlightened male varieties who compose contemporary Canada. Their uniforms are as distinguishable and stylized as those of any nineteenth-century regiment of the line. We shall know them by how they dress, how they act and what they read.

Hey, there's Noah. He is walking three feet behind his wife, and even though she is now holding and feeding the baby, Noah still has that blue corduroy Snugli strapped round his neck and shoulders, the zip open — just in case.

Noah wears brown shorts, white socks, Birkenstock sandals and a constant smile. He refuses to admit that a single earring is *déclassé* these days or that body piercing simply doesn't look good with thick spectacles.

Noah wishes he could have gone down to Washington a few weeks ago for the civil-rights anniversary march, but he had his men's group meeting that day and his wife thinks that Noah can only properly affirm her and share her empowering journey if he attends regularly.

Noah tells everybody how happy he is, and insists that baby Daniel is named after the great Sandinista leader and *not* after the genocidal, patriarchal Biblical character. Even so, "Mandela" would probably have been a better choice of name. He subscribes to *The New Republic* but is so busy these days with all the babysitting that he seldom has time to read it; he wishes there was a mass-circulation newspaper that told the truth about the good works of the NDP; and of course his decaffeinated coffee wouldn't be the same in the morning without *The Globe and Mail,* but he can't believe the sort of columns they're printing these days.

And here's Doug. The beard didn't come easily to Doug but it was worth the effort. At one time a beard was a sign of gauche masculinity, but radically new men now employ reverse symbolism and grow beards en masse — we owe it to our sisters to show that we can amplify our feminine self and be hirsute at the same time, he explains. Patterned and paisley sweaters are compulsory: they are sensible, and the white ribbon contrasts better with vivid colours.

Doug used to attend Noah's men's group, but he is now ashamed of his sojourn among the fellow travellers of male oppression. He just can't understand why other people aren't as empathetic as he is. Doug has studied the statistics, read the seminal works, attended the lectures. Maybe he, his father and his friends don't beat up their wives, but bourgeois veneer will always wear down to ancient habit in the long run.

Doug has seen the future and it is now, or at least it is in the one weekend a month his ex-wife allows him to see Jason and Joshua. He reads several California magazines committed to gender re-evaluation and even contributes an occasional column entitled Vasectomy Chat; and of course his herbal tea wouldn't be the same in the morning without *The Globe and Mail,* but he is hurt, angry and shaken at the sort of columns they are printing these days.

Here's Jack. He doesn't spend too much time on choosing his wardrobe, but, although he might not admit it, he likes to wear clothes that make him attractive to his wife. He shares looking after the children and the household duties with his wife, not because he is a *new* man but because he is a *good* man, not because anyone tells him to but because he wants to. Jack's father did the same with Jack's mother.

He's never attended a men's group but he does sometimes play baseball with his friends from work. He gets drunk perhaps half a dozen times a year, occasionally laughs at jokes that he wouldn't repeat to his wife and has even been aroused by the odd pornographic magazine or video.

When Jack hears about a rape he cringes, not because he is a man but because he is a human. As a friend of his once said, if every man is a potential rapist, does that mean that every Gentile is a potential Nazi? He reads whatever takes his fancy, and of course his thick, black coffee wouldn't be the same in the morning without *The Globe and Mail*, but he wishes he could find the time to make it to the columns on the back page these days.

Seeing the Light in the Forest

I received a letter recently from a man who is involved in what he describes as "the men's movement that you parody as being composed of crazy guys beating drums in the forest." Most of the letters of complaint and chagrin written to me and to this newspaper about my column have more to do with piffle than with epiphany. But this one was different.

The writer, whom we will call David (because that is his name), had taken time over his words and his thoughts, and seemed to genuinely care about what he was saying. He was moderate, sophisticated, self-mocking. Epistolary balance, a rare commodity. I agreed to meet with him.

David's experience was that many of the groups that have been established in the last ten years around the vaguely New-Age, Iron-John type of men's movement were, indeed, fatuous and redundant. "Insecurity and lack of direction, all hidden anger and uncertainty about sexual preference, bad marriages and straightforward stupidity," he says.

But David tried several different meetings until he found one that was suitable for him. He likens the search to a Christian looking for the right church or an amateur hockey player trying to find the appropriate group of men to play the game with after a hard day's work. "It's entirely natural, and entirely understandable that some people will exploit the whole thing or just misunderstand it and form groups that are counter-productive."

He considers himself to be relatively apolitical. From our conversation, I would say that he is disturbed by the masochists of the left who cry out that as men, they are monsters and dullards; and he is repelled by the sadists of the right who claim eternal male superiority and blamelessness.

For David, the position of men in contemporary society, his own position, began to lack foundation. He was almost jealous of women finding or rediscovering strength and quintessentially feminine values. He stresses that he did not resent them but admired them, that he likes and loves women. Does he protest too much? I'm not sure.

David's group appears to neither condemn nor congratulate itself, merely to discuss feelings, ideas, aspirations. What, I ask, is the difference between this formal gathering and a bunch of male friends in a bar, and why the forest retreats, wild-man emulation and the storytelling of which they so readily boast?

"There's a structure to it. The forest is an old tradition, returning to basics. Men, after all, are hunters in their most primitive form." He blushes; he says he knows what I am thinking. Perhaps he does. My mind is blurred by a vision of a very fat bureaucrat running through the trees in a loincloth and carrying a spear. Daniel Day-Lewis Senior in The Last of the Accountants.

"As to the stories, again, tradition, returning to an older purity, very influenced by native Indian culture. We are telling each other, ourselves, that we are worthy, we have roots, we are strong and independent men and don't have to swear, abuse women or get drunk to be so. We're going back to the beginning to find out who men really are. There are surprisingly few specifics discussed, more the general themes of masculinity."

There is also a particular concentration on paternity and on the dynamic between fathers and sons. It is profoundly encouraging, in that it explores concepts of continuity and emotional vulnerability that have been misplaced — if not lost — by so many men.

I ask David if those involved are in stable relationships, and whether they ever feel uncomfortable with what is, after all, a quite contrived environment. "Oddly enough, or perhaps predictably enough, these are middle-class, usually happily married men. Partly because of that sort of background yes, they are awkward with some of the openness. It mustn't be forced, though," he says. "It has to be enjoyable to be useful. We've had a drop-out rate of under 10 per cent. I'd say over half of the rest claim that their marriages, their lives, have improved. They can communicate now, express their deeper feelings."

David then asks me if I would like to attend one of his meetings. I tell him no, that my mind has not been changed but perhaps it has been expanded. I will not be banging drums in forests. I will, however, now admit that some of my friends do. And say it without blushing.

Life Through the Eyes of a "Typical" Male

A day in the life of Canadian Everyman.

It's morning. My wife makes my breakfast, making sure that she has first applied all her makeup and slipped into a suitably revealing yet responsible costume. A hybrid of harlot and madonna, that's how I like them.

The meat, meat and meat breakfast is placed on the table by my smiling spouse. I don't believe all this pinko propaganda about cholesterol and heart disease, I know what I like.

My woman is now free to change the diapers of our half a dozen sons. She's slow today, better hurry up or she won't get them to hockey lessons on time and she'd better not think that I'm going to pick them up from school because I've got that wet T-shirt contest to judge along with Wendal, Wayne, Will and Wolfgang from work. What's a guy to do, we've got to have some free time to express ourselves after working a five-day week to keep the wife and kids in the luxury they demand.

I'm like this, I've always been like this, all men are like this. I know, all those clever women columnists in *The Globe and Mail*, *The Toronto Star* and on television tell me so.

I'm home. If I say so myself I had one too many of those great new ice-brewed beers, and if a man can't throw up in his own home then where can he throw up? Wifey will clear it up, I mean what else has she got to do?

I manage to get myself into bed and she says to me she hopes I had a good time and that she understands about the mess. Then, believe it or not, she puts her arms around me. Come on! I've been celebrating. What does she think I am? This isn't even a weekend. She's been reading too many of those crazy women's magazines that tell babes to make their men more sexy. Give me a break. These clever girl writers, they might be spot on when it comes to describing how every Canadian man leads his life but they're out to lunch when it comes to the gals.

Another day at work. Doug, Doug and Doug at the office told me about a peach starting work today and, man, they weren't kidding. Yeah, working stiff has now taken on a completely different definition — hey, I better watch my sexist jokes, but then we're all like that. I know because those clever girl columnists in the papers and on TV tell it like it is.

This babe at work loves it when we whistle at her. I know it, how could she not? Doug even asks her if she'd like to come to a ball game. She says no, she prefers ballet and when it comes to sport she's fond of boxing. Geez, I'm not one to spread rumours, but you certainly wouldn't think she was one just by looking at her.

I suppose I shouldn't judge babes like that but it is normal isn't it, the human race would just disappear if we were all, well you know. I mean every day coming to the office I read another poll or statistic telling me that every man thinks of babes as sex objects and judges them by their bodies and all. I guess you can't change human nature.

Home again. She's crying. I hate that. I haven't cried since I was a kid, haven't hugged the kids for that matter since they were born, it's just not manly. It's the male way, as I say, just read those columns and those surveys, you can't argue with facts.

I ask her why she's crying, she says it might be menopause. What! Men getting it in the neck again, and just for moving too slowly. I give her a beer, tell her to pull herself together and then I go to a hotel with some of the boys. Funny, they tell me they've all had trouble with their wives complaining about them pausing too much. Wacko if you ask me, but then I'm no columnist or statistician.

So it turns out that the peach at work is not what I thought. We've kind of become friends, if you know what I mean. Now don't get me wrong, I still love my wife but then a man has urges that a woman will never understand. After all, I've never raised my hands to her, I'd never walk out and refuse to pay any child maintenance — now come on, that puts me in a minority, because most men do all that. I know because I've read it in those newspaper columns and seen afternoon TV shows about it.

Anyway, a few months later and my wife's left, the kids are God knows where and I've lost my job because of my drinking. Like, I'm going home from the pub one day. This guy comes up to me and says, "Hey, Everyman, you're not real, you're just someone else's polemic, rhetoric, overstatement."

I figure he's a nutbar, but then I feel funny. I start to disappear, I mean this, I start to disappear. My legs first, then the rest of me and all these "isms" fall to the ground. What? I can see statistics disappearing, arguments just kinda fading away. Geez, those clever girl columnists didn't tell me about any of this.

FATHERHOOD

It is a wise father that
knows his own child.

WILLIAM SHAKESPEARE, *THE MERCHANT OF VENICE*, II, ii

The Caring London Cabbie Who Was My Father

I remember the smell of the soap as he scrubbed his hands in the bathroom. Pungent. Antiseptic hospital odours, because this was for removing ground-in dirt and oil from beneath hardened fingernails and from calloused hands.

His skin was so tough, I can still recall the scraping sound of the razor on his evening stubble, still see the darkness of the water in the basin after he had cleaned his face.

He always spoke to me as he washed before eating his dinner, told me tales of his own childhood and let little drops of moral tuition fall into my lap. Simple. Prosaic to the cynical, poignant to me. "A promise is a promise." It was. He never broke one. He was my father.

He drove a London black taxi for forty years. It was a job that attracted waves of young Jews after the Second World War, a job that paid a decent wage if a man was willing to work twelve-hour days, six days a week.

When I was small and we were driving home from the weekly soccer match to which he took me he would sometimes pick up people who were hailing cabs along the way. He wasn't supposed to, not with me in the vehicle. But what the hell, I was six or seven, and sat in the hollow space next to the driver's seat where the luggage was stored. I was barely noticed.

I could never understand why the passengers treated him with such contempt, such patronizing disregard. He was "cabby" and "driver" and "you!" No he wasn't, he was my dad. But he smiled and said nothing and did his job.

And then told me more stories from his past, such as about the times he boxed for the Royal Air Force. Oh, the pride. And about how his German cousin had gone back to Berlin in the 1930s to rescue his family. The family did not manage to escape and the cousin never came back. A long time ago, said my father, and not for you to worry about.

He winked, a wink full of authority and confidence. Never again, he said. I believed him. He was my father.

He always looked so strong, so able to protect me, so powerful. Powerful enough to cry when he felt the need. I heard him weep when my grandmother died. Confusing. How should I react, what should I do? Just be there, as he was for me. He came into my room, saw the fear and apprehension on my face and recited a short prayer in Hebrew with me for my grandma and his mother. He kissed me, held my hand and then drove me to school before putting in his twelve hours. He was my father.

I remember his euphoria when I went to university, the first in his family to do so. Of course he was gauche when I graduated, took too many photographs, was unaware that the wine he was drinking was a forty-year-old classic and didn't understand the Latin that was spoken before the ceremonial meal. So what? His wisdom and sagacity were born long before the Roman Empire imposed its language on the ancient world. He felt a little out of place but it didn't matter to him. All that concerned this working man in a smart suit was that his son would not follow in his footsteps. "Do you know why I work such long hours?" he would ask me so often, as if we were acting out some catechistic exercise. "So that you won't have to push a cab around and tip your hat to people." Then he'd pause. "So that you won't have to." He was my father.

He couldn't afford to take the time off to go on holiday with me, my mother and my sister. There were no paid vacations for him. If the truth be told, there just wasn't the money for us all to go away. He'd stay on his own, work even longer hours and live on sandwiches and tea. We'd ring him from a cold British beach hotel and tell him how much we missed him. He knew. He was my father.

And when my first child was born, this extraordinary ordinary man said very little. Just stared at the baby, and then at me. He spoke through his eyes and I understood. Son, he was telling me, let him be able to say just one thing when he grows up: He was my father.

I didn't have the heart to tell him, "Dad, you're wrong. Haven't you heard, haven't you read the studies, seen the divorce-court custody rulings? There's no such thing as a paternal instinct and men simply don't make natural parents. You just didn't get it, Dad, you just didn't get it."

Goodnight, Grandpa

There was no obituary in *The Times*, or any newspaper for that matter. The death was private and so was the life. No public awards, no friends in high places. What commemorations there were came in the local pubs among his friends, in the oral, lyrical tradition of London English that Dickens, at his best, almost captured. I speak of the death of my grandpa. He was eighty-nine years old. It was time. He would have been the first to say so. Blind, unable to walk, a shell of the great man who was. What a bloody lark, he would have said. The great, untamed, kind, strong, wise, gentle man.

He worked at many different professions in his life, never settled for one and never made much money. He and his wife were cockneys and they would have had it no other way. His life was interrupted in 1939 when His Majesty gave him a gun and told him to kill the nation's enemies. He must have been reasonably good at it, because he survived for six years. He didn't talk very often about his time in North Africa or Sicily and never, ever boasted about it. If the war arose in conversation, it was usually the subject of mockery and laughter. "Me a soldier? Blimey." And he would tell us tales of one-upmanship over the officers, of innocuous activities on the black market, of how ordinary men thought and behaved. "The Krauts? Well, we hated 'em. But I tell you this, we respected the bastards." Then he stopped. I knew he didn't want to say any more. My mother remembered that every time "Long Dave," his East-End nickname, came home on leave he had another stripe on his arm.

And then one day I was looking in his bedroom for a watch he had lost and I found his medals, tucked away. So many of them. I was fascinated by the different colours and the glorious words about valour and honour. I supposed at the time that he had misplaced them, just as he had his watch.

He drank a great deal. Was he an alcoholic? No. He enjoyed it rather than needed it. And when he was drunk, he was a nice drunk. Playful, affectionate. He would dismiss men who were made brave by drinking as "not real men. Liquid courage. Easy, that." He never raised his voice when lubricated and certainly never raised his hands. He was also a smoker, sometimes swore and even told jokes that lacked sensitivity towards women and minorities. Working-class men did, do, thank God. He had no tolerance for those who were offended by his ways. Better still, he hardly even knew they existed. The ultimate insult to society's puritanical bores. He would have told them to go forth and multiply, but then he didn't read the Bible.

He gave me pocket money every Wednesday afternoon when I was little. Sixpence. Worth nothing now, worth little then. And it always seemed more important to him than it was to me. It used to confuse me, embarrass me. But I now know just how little money he had and just how resistant he was to accepting charity. Sixpence. A million dollars.

His home overlooked and overheard the railway track and when I slept on the sofa in his living room I was kept awake by trains making their way to parts of the world I had never seen, barely knew of. Adventurous places such as Blackburn or Stoke, where I was sure that people were different, brighter, more interesting. At home, in my own bedroom, I didn't feel like this. But at grandpa's place, anything was possible.

A quarter of a century later my mother telephones to give me the news. She isn't crying but she has been. She explains that her dad has left me a note and a small box. The note says, "You've never seen these before Mike, so here they are now. Not much, but all for you. Just put them away somewhere, safe keeping. They don't matter. You know I loved you, Grandpa." They were his medals.

Goodnight, Grandpa. I know that the drink and the smokes will be even better, the jokes even dirtier and more wicked, in your Heaven. Goodnight, man.

Grief and Fear as the World Changes in a Split Second

An anecdote of the extraordinary within the ordinary.

Saturday afternoon in High Park in Toronto. The sun is in one of its relentless moods, inexorable in tossing down furnace-like threads of heat. Lucy holds my hand, tightly. I can feel her pulse, her life. Her diminutive, perfect face is all ice cream and smiles. Four-year-old joy. She plays on the swings, plays on the slide, laughs at the animals in the tiny zoo, skips and jumps and asks me questions that defy philosophy and theology in single, simple bounds. When she runs she frowns and pumps her arms and, like some cartoon character, seems to make hardly any progress at all.

Her red-and-blue ball rolls down an embankment. Only a few feet. I tell my daughter to stand still. I'll get it. Just wait for me, Lucy. There's nobody about. She's safe. I rush down the hill, pick up the ball, rush back again. Only seconds. And Lucy is not there. Lucy is not there. Like submerging your head under water. Every sense — sound and sight and feel and smell and taste — instantly changes its perspective. And a father's sixth sense as well, the one that develops immediately after his child is born.

C. S. Lewis said that grief felt like fear. Well, fear also feels like grief. That ancient, emetic feeling that I remember so well just before that fight in the schoolyard, when the biggest kid shouted, "I'll see you at four, outside." Flushed, swallowing, blood racing. The first time I parachuted, I thought that I would never be as frightened again in my life. I was wrong. Lucy, Lucy! A horrible blending of anger, devotion and fear. I've told her that if she ever loses sight of her mom or dad she must look for a woman or man with children or a police officer and tell them her telephone number. Just seven digits, formal and dull, 920-4500. But not for Lucy. "Nine-two-zero-forty-five-hundred" she would chant as if it were a panacea-like mantra, and then giggle. She'd say it over and over again so as to tease us, and throw her head back with more laughter. Every time we said, "Lucy, that's enough," she would just start again. Monkey.

Now, without thinking, I am reciting it under my breath. Nine-two-zero-forty-five-hundred, nine-two-zero-forty-five-hundred. Reassurance. Like some mindless, numbing repetition of a rosary. And I realize that I am panting, and that I have been sprinting around the park for fifteen minutes. I am covered in sweat and I have also cut my leg on a sharp branch. I hadn't noticed; I'm clenching my fists. Say it, Lucia, say it, shout it, as loud as the thunder that you love so much when you are safely in your bed, so that I can hear it and come and get you. Nine-two-zero-forty-five-hundred. But there's nothing.

Fear getting stronger now. I'm not making any bloody progress. Christ, Mike, end this! Time to make a decision. Do I continue this animalistic gush or do I retreat to a telephone and call for help, notify the police? I'm usually so definite, so calm in judgment. Now I'm sinking and sinking, Somme-like, in a mud of panic and ambivalence.

And then God proves his existence. Late, as always. Standing behind a tree, so small and so vulnerable, is the puckish child whose cord of life I cut and whose existence is a crucial part of any political or social comprehension. She is crying, because the hiding was a game in the beginning but then she saw how sad and excited I was and thought I would be cross when she stopped the game. I hold her, surround her with me, smother her in me. She stops crying and says, "Daddy, you looked so funny." I suppose I did.

An anecdote of the extraordinary within the ordinary. The bond between a father and his child. An everyday event that contains within it aspects of the most significant and precious. Because something is numerically common does not preclude it from being qualitatively spectacular. Let us now define fatherhood, and let us define it with care, passion and understanding.

When It Comes to Divorced Fathers, Let's Hear It for the Good Guys

The recent court ruling about the taxable status of child-support payments is delightfully and quintessentially Canadian. It is inspired by decency and a willingness to do good; it represents yet another clumsy intrusion by the law into daily life, and it has provoked any number of comments and columns based upon a fraudulent mythology — in this context, that divorced fathers invariably refuse to contribute equitably to their children's support, and that it is always single mothers and never their ex-spouses who live on the verge of impoverishment.

There are, of course, myriad divorced women bringing up their children with little more than a few dollars and masses of courage and commitment. There are also many regrettable if not regretful men who pay little and sometimes nothing to their separated families. Yet we must not be so naïve to assume that as soon as a marriage ends, every father's paternal passions are mysteriously expunged and his love for his children evaporated like some sociological theory. Such generalizations seem of the logic of the propagandist and the wit of the zealot. Briefly, let's hear it for the good guys.

Within Canadian society there are countless well-paid men who function at financial subsistence levels because they believe their responsibilities to their children do not end with divorce. There is an added dimension to all this: Many men who scrupulously pay child support are denied access to their children by intransigent ex-wives even after the courts have awarded joint custody. Enforcement of visitation rights is expensive and difficult, and any further legal decision concerning child support must link such payments with visitation privileges. This is certainly what Donald believes.

Donald (let's call him that) is a man in his early forties who was married to Penelope for eight years. They had a daughter, Amy. The marriage had its good moments but eventually fell apart. No wrong-doing on either side, no abuse of partner or child, just an absence of love and an increasing and mutual apathy. The court awarded joint custody — Donald would see Amy every second weekend, one evening a week and half of the school holidays — and child-support payments were established. They were generous, and Donald never missed a date. He also gave extra money to Penelope when he could afford it, so that Amy could have those Levi's jeans that the other kids had, or go to the rock concert with her friends.

Penelope remarried. She and her new husband live in a fine house. Donald lives in a small apartment, but still pays for his Amy. Then

Penelope decided that Donald could not see Amy any more. "But the courts said that I can. For God's sake, she's my daughter!" Tough, says Penelope. Donald goes to court. Once again, the judge orders joint custody. And once again, as soon as Donald arranges the first visit, Penelope says no. It could cost Donald $20,000 to fight the case again. He cannot afford it, and is sick at the thought of wasting any of the money he has saved for his daughter's education on lawyers' fees.

If Donald went to Penelope's house and demanded access, or submitted to human nature and shouted and banged on the door, the police would surely be called and Donald would probably be arrested, maybe even losing his joint custody order as a result. So he drives past Amy's school and imagines her. And writes to her and keeps these returned, unopened letters in a file to show to his daughter when she grows up, to prove that he did not abandon her. He will not deprive her of support payments, because he loves his child, just as most men, like most mothers, love theirs.

Recently Donald received a letter from his seven-year-old, explaining that she never wanted to see her daddy again. Experts agreed that the vocabulary of the note was far too advanced for any child of Amy's age. It had been dictated.

Donald's hope is that his daughter will eventually wonder about her father, go to see him for herself and decide what sort of man he is. It will be a long wait. As it is for so many men, who are not indifferent, uncaring reprobates.

They are the good guys, the ordinary guys, the Donalds, the guys who think the debate over child-support payments barely scratches the surface of the problem. They would, simply, like their voices to be heard. It is, they think, only fair.

A Fathers'-Rights Group That Values Balance

In their struggle to create a paradise of equality, the policy makers and activists of Canada have won a Pyrrhic victory. Some people have benefited from the war, but so many have lost. This is particularly the case for those men who feel that their basic rights have been torn from them. Behind the advancing lines of egalitarianism there are groups of guerrillas who refuse to surrender.

There are over one hundred organizations in Canada representing men who have been treated unfairly by the legal system or by their ex-wives, who have been falsely accused of abusing their children or denied access to them. Some of these groups are bitter and misogynistic. But there are others that are moderate and responsible. One of them is FACT, Fathers Are Capable Too. It has not been established for long, but already has more than one thousand supporters and one hundred paid members. The founder is Greg Kershaw, a thirty-five-year-old computer programmer from Kitchener; the group meets every second Tuesday in a member's house. A quarter of those present are women, and meetings are often led by a woman.

"It's important, it maintains balance," says Mr. Kershaw. "Some of these men's groups are too one-sided. They're like the male-victim equivalent of battered-women's shelters, where women go for help and are told that all men are monsters. Feminist indoctrination centres. We don't want to be like that."

It is 7:30 on a Tuesday evening in Brampton, Ontario. In a corner, warming his slightly shaking hands around a mug of coffee, is Terry. He has joint custody of his daughter, and his ex-wife is now living with another man. Terry's daughter arrived at his house covered in bruises, crying to her father that Mummy's boyfriend had beaten her. Terry telephoned the Children's Aid Society. They rang Terry's ex-wife, informed her of the complaint and then made an appointment to see the little girl in three weeks. Time for the body to heal, for truth to be hidden. "Imagine if my wife had made a complaint about me," protests Terry. "Three weeks! Are you kidding?"

Bob nods his head. He has been surviving on a $1,500 monthly disability payment for some years. After his marriage ended, he lived with his parents. He tried to gain joint custody of his child but was told by a judge that he would have to first find an apartment. He did, paying $750 a month rent. His ex-wife then insisted their child attend day care and that Bob pay the $650-a-month cost. Impossible. He asked, if, as he was at home, he could look after his son in the daytime. Denied. He is now incarcerated by paradox: If he wants to see his son, he cannot pay for food or heat. His ex-wife has gone to the Family Support Plan, who intend to garnishee the day-care money from his disability payments.

Then there is Harry. He paid $70,000 to lawyers in a custody battle and won joint access to his child. It was acrimonious, and his lawyers advised him to wait thirty days before he visited his child. He agreed. When he went to collect his daughter in her Toronto home, he found that she had been taken by her mother to British Columbia. After an expensive two-year court campaign to decide whether Ontario had jurisdiction in another province, Harry was granted day-only access to his daughter, as long as the visits took place in Vancouver.

Roger isn't surprised at all. After his divorce, he was the main parent of his daughter. His ex-wife's lawyer explained to her client that if this continued she would receive less child support. Roger's access was suddenly denied. An assessor with a known bias towards women examined the case and recommended sole custody for Roger. The judge would grant only joint custody. Roger's ex-wife still denied him access. They returned to court, where the judge said that the original assessment was now too old. A new one was made, and this time the "right" answer was given. Sole custody for the mother, even though she had moved fifteen times in under three years. Roger is now almost bankrupt.

In case the skeptical among you console yourselves with the thought that some of these cases are doubtful, they are all heavily documented and represent only a fraction of the total. And by the way, when I asked Greg Kershaw the line he hears most often from new members, he replied: "I thought it could never happen to me. This only happens to other people."

Winning the Battle

This is a tale of an ordinary man. A priest. A teacher. A forty-four-year-old father of two daughters, ten and thirteen years old. A good person who was suddenly, and through no fault of his own, taken by those he thought he could love, and those he thought he should trust, into the middle of hell and abandoned there. A court order prevents me from mentioning his name. I shall call him, simply, Victim.

In 1985, Victim was asked by the National Parole Board to take into his house and help rehabilitate a former criminal. "Much as I believe in the message of the gospels, I have a wife and daughters," said Victim, "and they might be in danger." He was repeatedly assured that this would not be the case. The parole board failed to inform Victim — and have since apologized for their omission — that the criminal was a rapist, and had spent seventeen years in and out of prison.

Within weeks, the house guest began an affair with his host's wife. Shortly after this, the recidivist and the wife ran off together, taking the children, the furniture and the contents of Victim's bank account. Victim searched for and eventually found his wife and managed to obtain access rights to his children.

But after only two visits and much complaining from his wife that the meetings were too expensive, the Durham Region Children's Aid Society intervened and without consulting or contacting Victim demanded a child-protection order against him for sexually abusing his children. A social worker rang to say that the children's mother had alleged that Victim had molested his daughters and that until he confessed his crimes and sought psychiatric treatment he would not be allowed to see them.

"I couldn't believe it. I begged her to see me, to listen to me. I told her that in my profession I have counselled marriages, intervened in disputes and know that you have to hear both sides of the story," says Victim. "The social worker apparently knew better. She said she didn't need to see me or hear me and that was that."

For one hour every two weeks, he was allowed to be with his children. Three men watched him through a one-way window to monitor his activities. The social worker never left the room. At the end of the hour, the girls were, according to witnesses, "ripped, screaming, from his arms."

Yet Victim refused to surrender and took the case to trial to prove his innocence. Almost a year later, the society admitted privately to Victim that they had made a mistake and asked him what he wanted. "Three things," he answered. "Write a letter to my bishop; let my daughters decide where they want to live; and pay my legal expenses." The society agreed to only the first request. Victim said he would fight them. Fine, they replied, but if you do we will proceed with the court-protection order as if you were guilty.

Eventually, the court decided that there was overwhelming evidence in favour of Victim, dismissed the Durham Children's Aid charges and ordered it to pay Victim's court costs of $92,000, eventually settled at $60,000. Though proved free of guilt, Victim was still being punished. He was "treated like a leper" by many members of the Anglican hierarchy and barred from appearing in numerous Toronto pulpits.

Shortly after this trial, Victim's wife was herself arrested and charged with assaulting her daughters. As a consequence she signed a recognizance order giving up all further contact with her children.

Now reunited with his daughters, Victim sued the Durham society in the Supreme Court of Ontario. The trial resulted in Justice William Sommers completely exonerating Victim and ordering the society to pay him in excess of $200,000, plus legal fees. The judge also found that the Durham society's position was "utterly unconscionable" and its actions "reprehensible."

This is the first time that a man has successfully sued in such a context and legal history has been made. Durham Region Children's Aid Society intends to appeal the ruling to the Supreme Court of Canada. This will cost a great deal of time and money. It would surely be easier and cheaper if they fell to their knees and screamed mea culpa.

Is the case unique? Yes. As unique as human malice, organizational arrogance and straightforward injustice. Abuse is a terrible thing. So is wrongful accusation. Victim is an articulate man who managed to find help. Others do not.

Fathers Subjected to Witch Hunts When Sexual Abuse Alleged

Last week I wrote about an Anglican priest who had been falsely accused of sexually abusing his daughters. The children were taken from him, and this wretched man was humiliated by both his wife and the Durham Children's Aid Society. He was eventually proved innocent in two courts of law and the welfare organization in question has been ordered to pay him almost a quarter of a million dollars in compensation.

I had intended to say more about this man today, but due to the number of letters and telephone calls I have had from lawyers representing victims of false accusation in similar circumstances, I am obliged to widen my net of coverage.

How, for example, could I not write about George, who lives just outside of Toronto? George's marriage broke up and he and his wife argued over custody of their two children. After a hiatus of many months, and with no previous reference to the issue, George's wife alleged that her husband had sexually abused their six-year-old daughter. The girl was examined and interviewed. During the first such meeting she could not even identify where a boy's private parts were situated; by the third interview she claimed that her father had penetrated her and asked her to touch his penis. It was later revealed that the child's sister had said, "Mommy helps us remember."

Two widely respected psychologists gave George thorough examinations and found that there were no indications that he was a potential abuser. The SCAN (Suspected Child Abuse and Neglect) unit in Toronto's Hospital for Sick Children examined the girl and concluded that no penetration had, in fact, taken place. George took and passed a lie detector test. The case then went to litigation. Six days before the judge at the Ontario Court's General Division was to make a ruling, the local Children's Aid Society suddenly placed George on something called the Child Abuse Register, informing his wife and her lawyer that they had done so. The register is confidential and inclusion on it requires no conviction or proof. George was not given a hearing or trial. So weak was the evidence, however, that the judge still found that the case was insufficient. George is now fighting to have his name removed from this scroll of the unclean.

Such incidents are far from uncommon. They often occur during acrimonious custody battles and bitter divorces. And when a man is accused of sexual assault there exists an assumption of guilt. The pointing finger appears to be sufficient. Frequently, if the accused man asks us to look at the hand, the arm, the heart behind that finger, we scorn him, snidely questioning why he is protesting so much. There can be no smoke of accusation, some people believe, without the fire of abuse.

The situation reaches almost hysterical proportions as we enter further into the age of the dictatorship of the social worker, when too many Children's Aid Societies define themselves not by the number of families they sustain but by the number they dissolve. The claim that "we helped one hundred families work it out" is less impressive than "we saved fifty children from sexual abuse from fathers." They are also loathe to admit error, out of fear of subsequent censure or financial punishment by their political overseers.

The point has been made before but it is worth reiterating: Sexual abuse cases represent a contemporary Salem. Indeed there is now an international computer network, known as witch hunt, composed of men fraudulently accused of these crimes. The monomania of the seventeenth century also involved a gender-biased law, often relied on the evidence of emotionally unstable people and was built heavily upon the manipulation of children. Today accused men have to face not only the plaintiff but a wall of tendentious statistical material and an atmosphere that susurrates with rumour and innuendo.

For those who think that I am ignoring the horror of sexual abuse, I am certainly not. It has happened, is happening, will happen. It is a putrid reality rather than a fashionable chimera. Yet murder and assault are also terrible crimes. The difference is that when someone is accused of murder or assault, the balances of the law give them an equitable chance of proving themselves innocent and require a massive degree of proof to find them guilty.

The wrong that is sexual abuse, the righteousness and justice of the law and simple human decency require that the innocents are protected, in all of their forms, child or adult.

A Social Worker Willing to Speak Out

Dennis Pringle is a social worker. Following a brace of columns I wrote recently about men — and one man in particular — falsely accused of sexually abusing their children and the manner in which many social workers refused, sometimes maliciously, to hear a man's version of events, Mr. Pringle decided that he had had enough.

As a man, as a social worker, he concluded that he had to speak out, to talk about his experiences in London and Thunder Bay as a child-protection worker, a crisis counsellor and a family-support worker. Very few people in Mr. Pringle's position would have the courage or the opportunity to speak openly to the press about the gaping fallacies and errors of the social-work industry. Mr. Pringle is able to do this only because he has left the Children's Aid Society to set up a private practice.

At thirty-seven with long hair, half-a-dozen earrings and a red bandanna around his neck, Mr. Pringle looks more like a cerebral rock musician than some fustian government employee. But he has dedicated his life to helping others, to trying to put things right, wherever they materialize.

"The number of false accusations of sexual abuse against men is significant, particularly when it comes to custody battles. But not only custody. I had a case recently where false allegations were made against a man because the woman wanted more children in her custody so she could claim more welfare." He pauses, grimacing when he recalls the incident.

"What angers me is that when these allegations are found to be false, men don't even get an apology. Their lives are ruined. They have been stigmatized, they are broke because of the expense of using lawyers, and we just ignore them, let them bleed. There are so many cases coming forward now where social workers have believed one side's story and have not carried out any proper investigation.

"When they are proved wrong — and often the accused men don't manage to achieve that, because it's incredibly difficult — the Children's Aid Societies skirt the issue entirely. They defend themselves by claiming that if they are made accountable under law they won't be able to do their job. No!" he says, angry now, annoyed by what he has seen.

"It should make them do their job properly, find the truth. Hundreds of men are coming forward, wanting justice after their children were taken away from them or they were charged with abusing their kids. It'll be an incredible backlash. Children's Aid Societies are terrified that the public might find this out."

Part of the problem is the social composition of the army of social workers in this country, Mr. Pringle says. He believes that too many of them come from privileged, unrepresentative backgrounds and have no experience of the street and of its grim, grimy realities. This produces a naïve credulity, an eagerness or even a lust to believe stories of oppression that support their prejudicially formed political and economic theories.

"If the accuser is poor, or a woman, there's far more chance that they will be believed. Even if the father does accuse the mother, the chances are that social workers will believe the woman and not the guy. We're encouraging more false allegations because we refuse to believe that women would lie, that kids would lie." This is a perverse denial of feminism: that women are somehow less sophisticated and more childlike than men and hence cannot or will not utter an untruth.

Yet there is surely a necessary corrective of an ancient imbalance here. Women had few legal rights in the past, a situation now being repaired.

"Yes, and I don't think men would go into social work unless they believed that," Mr. Pringle says. "But men are under siege by a feminist thrust throughout the system. There's a bias to do as much as possible to convict men accused of sexual offences.

"If they've committed the crime, then they have to be convicted — I've seen what abuse does to a family. But a lot of men feel as if they're being treated unfairly. Look at what happens to people who make false accusations. Women are thought to be distraught or damaged so they go unpunished. The system is favouring injustice with select people. Unacceptable."

An ambivalent conclusion. The bureaucratic hierarchy of Canadian social workers may be in a primitive state of denial; that is cause for despair. But many ordinary social workers are not; that is cause for hope. And the latter part of the equation always triumphs in the end. Dennis Pringle still believes that. He has to.

Don't Fathers-To-Be Have Rights, Too?

Martin was going to be a father. He and Janet had been lovers for more than two years. Both of them were journalists, both in their late twenties, both apparently wanted a family. They didn't live together but had considered it. They were happy. Janet telephoned Martin at work and explained that she had seen the doctor and that there was no doubt, she was definitely pregnant. Martin was ambivalent but evinced only excitement. How curious, he thought, that Janet was surely excited but evinced only ambivalence.

Martin fell into cliché and predictability with ridiculous ease. He offered to marry Janet. A little archaic, he knew, but it was a spasm produced by good motives rather than bad thinking. Janet said that she needed time to think about that one. Sure, said Martin, and then added, laughingly, that she shouldn't wait until the grandchildren came along.

He began to tell people about the baby. Janet told him not to, and he understood why, but what the hell, he was proud and he'd never felt this way before. Friends asked if he wanted a boy or a girl. He didn't mind, he replied. But he was lying. God, he wanted a daughter more than he'd ever wanted anything in his whole life. Sally.

He rang Janet too often now, left messages on her answering machine asking her how she felt, sent greetings on her modem. They embarrassed her. Embarrassed him, too, if truth be told. He knew that he'd seen caricatures of expectant fathers in movies and books for years, knew that he didn't want to act in that way. Also knew this was exactly the way he was acting and, Jesus, it felt good.

Sally. What a name. He'd always wanted that name. Janet had often said that she also loved it. Sally.

A week later, Martin received a second telephone call from Janet, at work. She had made two decisions, she said, and she hoped so much that neither would cause Martin too much pain, because she cared about him and would always care about him. She wanted to end their relationship, she explained, and she wanted to have an abortion.

Martin didn't pause. Pause? In fiction people always pause after they receive bad or shocking news, particularly on the telephone. But no pause here. What?! Why are you saying this/What has changed between us/We have to speak/I love you/Just hold on/Think about it/This can't be real/I love you/You're not serious/Don't I have a say in this/I love you. And then he began to cry.

The usual scenario developed. Numerous calls from Martin to an increasingly hostile Janet. I needed space, she said, and you couldn't give it to me. It's over. He accepted it. Had to. But there was more now. What about Sally, he said. Stop calling it Sally, shouted Janet. It's not even a baby yet, we don't know its sex and it's never going to exist. Odd — there was a long, long pause this time.

Martin considered his options, spoke to male and female friends about the situation. Get a lawyer? Are you kidding? That was for misogynists and old-fashioned men who didn't understand. Martin had always believed in a woman's right to choose. I mean, it's her body.

And it's my child. My child. If it was allowed to be born, I'd be financially responsible for it for at least twenty years, but before its birth I am treated as an irrelevance. This isn't fair. This isn't bloody fair. What about my pain, my agony, my body! I want my child to be born and nobody will or can help me. Human rights, gay rights, minority rights, animal rights — what about my rights as a father? What about Sally's rights?

The baby was aborted. Martin cried a lot. Had some therapy, joined a support group composed of other men whose unborn children had been aborted. He was surprised how many of them there were. He saw Janet at a party last Christmas. Didn't speak to her. Wanted to. Wanted to tell her that he had never been concerned with esoteric questions about when life begins or what we define as valid human existence. Just wanted his child to live or even, if there was no option, to be consulted about its death. All quite prosaic, really, and in so being, rather profound. Beautiful name, Sally.

The Story of Fathers and Daughters

An episode from a volume of wisdom that began its first chapter before Bible, Talmud or Platonic treatises were even contemplated: It is called the story of fathers and daughters.

In 1993, I took my three-year-old daughter to see *The Nutcracker* at Toronto's O'Keefe Centre. She had never been to any live theatre before. She counted down the days, and when the morning of the long-awaited evening broke, Lucy asked me, as she crawled from her bed and while her eyes were still slits in her brown, puckish face. "Are we going now?"

Soon, I replied. Soon.

She was ready two hours before we had to leave. Party dress, party shoes, party coat, party smile. But first there was dinner with Dad. One of the jewels in the crown of infancy is the way in which children are so impressed with what are in reality acutely commonplace things. They comprehend and appreciate the extraordinary inherent within the ordinary. This is what *makes* them young; and it is what might, if they are very lucky indeed, *keep* them young as adults. A hot dog and a few

French fries in a New York–style hamburger bar are suddenly transformed into the consummate creation of a Parisian chef with two generations of culinary evolution under his tall, starched hat.

Oh, how protective I feel towards my Lucy. I could fight and defeat armies for this small one, conquer mountains and wrestle tigers. Or at least spend $10 on a meat-and-potato meal. Pray God she doesn't ask me to teach her ballet; my build is more that of a sugar plumbous fairy than any ethereal Nureyev.

And then to the theatre. A miracle happens. In that hiatus of crepuscular majesty as the curtain begins to rise and my daughter's sight becomes accustomed to what is before her, she manages to utter, "They're real people, Daddy, they're real people." This television- and cinema-accustomed tot has felt the breeze of a much cleaner wind than has ever blown from the electronic media.

From the opening stanzas of Tchaikovsky's genius, this daughter of mine is embraced by the experience. She claps with the rest of the audience at the end of each vignette, every scene. No prompting, no self-consciousness. The intermission is merely an unwelcome interruption; the strutting rodomontade of the mouse does not frighten her a bit. Brave, as well as brilliant. As for me, I have become a vicarious observer, and though I have watched this ballet so many times before, I am seeing it for the very first time.

We leave the theatre and drive home. My wife and my five-year-old son are waiting up for us. Lucy rushes into the house and her mother asks her all about it. Did they wear costumes? "No," says Lucy. "They were real."

A perfect evening. Yet within twenty minutes of arriving home, this miniature in a floral dress is sobbing uncontrollably, hugging me with all the strength that her tiny body can muster. She is shaking.

"What is it darling, what's the matter?" At first she says that she has a tummy ache — that perennial explanation for tears, temper and tantrum offered by children the world over. And then she pauses in between gulps of air to enlighten her obtuse father as to why she is so upset.

"When I take my party dress off [tears], when I take it off and put away my special shoes [tears], then, then it will be all over [tears], the ballet will be all over," and a head buried in my chest and a sea of weeping to break the heart of all and every.

Eventually, I convince her that there will be more outings to the ballet, more dressing up, more deluxe junk-food dinners. But this is far too meagre a solution. What I couldn't express to her but what I believe to the very depths of my being is that the magic need never end, the mystery and mystique need never be concluded.

Because even though some people doubt, misunderstand or are even indifferent to this unique love — that which we call the story of fathers and daughters — it is in fact a dance that will continue forever.

Fathers and the Delivery Room

Our first two children were born around dawn. Not this one. Oliver added his nine pounds to the world at 11:21 on a grey, soggy morning. But what am I talking about? It is always dawn when a child is born, the greatest of dawns, the only dawn. And always a time of supreme ambivalence for a prospective, cogitative father.

In the past we were second-class citizens in the republic of childbirth, segregated in waiting rooms of panic where we were supposed to wipe sweat from our creased, manly brows, furiously pace the floor and then smoke cheap cigars when an avuncular doctor or, more likely, overworked nurse, rushed in and announced: "Mr. Smith, you've got a bouncing baby boy." Try smoking a cigar in a hospital today — you'll never have children again.

We are all umbilical cavaliers now, reciting our prenatal-class lessons like some battle cry or medical mantra and reminding everyone present in the delivery room that we want to cut the cord, that grey-white piece of sinewy matter that tangibly links child to mother.

The hospital staff indulge us and smile, knowing that when the time comes to do the cutting our hands will be trembling, we won't be able to distinguish the cord of life from Arthur Sullivan's Lost Chord, and an obliging professional will have to put the scissors in our hands, guide us forward and tell us what to do. Yet the symbolism is still there; and more important, the grand intentions. It is a laudable impotence.

The whole thing is terrifying. As men and fathers we are to a large degree spectators, and spectators often see more of the sport. Not disinterested voyeurs, but loving and loved onlookers. On the one hand, the birth is pure and unvarnished James Herriot, all animal reality and primordial grace. On the other, it is supernatural, ethereal, holy. Fear and passion, incredulity and devotion, shock and euphoria. We become early, ancient man, mere children ourselves. It is as it is supposed to be.

Of course, the extent of a father's contribution to an observation of the event is all about the whims of fashion. Men did not ask to be left outside in the past and they don't particularly insist on being privy to it all now. In this case the trend is for the good, but it is still a dynamic that is dictated from above, by those who claim to know better.

Another trend is developing at the moment, one that is less encouraging. Some young women are asking close female friends to be with them for the birth of the baby. How I hope that this does not become accepted wisdom. The logic is strained. Will we then have mothers-in-law and high-school chums present at the conception — "You're doing wonderfully dear, be brave now. Almost finished. Soon it'll all be over and then you can have a nice cup of coffee and a sandwich."

The greatest bonding experience in the world for men and women, for a man and a woman, for two people in love, is to be together when their child is born. When my wife, enduring agonies I can never comprehend in a three-hour labour without anesthetic, shouts, "I just want my Michael," I begin to weep. I weep. I am weeping. We are holding each other and looking into each other's eyes and I am praying for some of this pain to flow into me but know that ultimately all I can do is tell my wife that I love her.

To be candid, I do not want her platonic friends there. Is this selfish or simply appropriate? I opt for the latter, but then it is easy for me. Bernadette did not want anybody else to be present. If she had, what would I have done? Don't know.

All notions are passed through the prism of an individual's experiences, opinions and beliefs. Some people claim that the birth of a child should be the direct concern of the extended family or the community — this, indeed, was the view of the early Christians — but I reject the idea.

I believe that the creation of a third life is the apotheosis of the love between two people and two people alone. Not the most miraculous of miracles, but the most common of commonplace — it is not the uniqueness but the very frequency, the regularity and, yes, even the banality of childbirth that makes it so timelessly extraordinary and beyond the dusky limitations of human understanding. And as a mother it belongs to my wife. As a father it belongs to me. To me. It is mine.

The Arts

All great art is the work of the

whole living creature,

body and soul, and chiefly

of the soul.

John Ruskin
The Stones of Venice, vol. I ch. 4

Censor Perceptions

The paradox of literary censorship has been tackled before, and the trends are easy to recognize. Ostensibly open-minded liberalism and socialism are prepared to grant freedom of voice and freedom of publication only as long as the view or the material falls within certain severely defined wavebands of acceptability. Every philosophical argument concerning liberty seems to evaporate when a directly contrary opinion is expressed. We live in the age of liberal prejudice, where books are rejected before they are even read, arguments eschewed before they are even heard. And the consequent censorship often takes a more subtle and arguably more insidious form than straightforward banning. How do I censor you? Let me show you the ways.

Reviewing is one of the sharpest of sharp ends of contact between a book and its potential readers, and a form of very good publicity. Every society, every city, has an incestuous literary community, whether it be the giants of London or New York, or the less heavily muscled Toronto or Sydney. And in spite of, or sometimes because of, the efforts of books editors at newspapers and magazines, books are sometimes given for review to people who have a known regard for, or friendship with, the said book's author. Or, more to the point, they are given to someone who the editor knows dislikes the said book, its subject, politics or author.

The quality of the review is not all that matters. The size, placement and timing of the critique are also extremely relevant. Reviews can sometimes be inserted in newspapers months after publication, so that the all-important initial sales drive is hindered. Reviews can also be very short, indicating that the reviewed book does not deserve a full treatment. A studied and tendentious neglect. On the other hand, in some extreme situations authors can be so friendly with an editor or so supported that their books receive not one but two reviews, providing publicity too generous to ever be purchased. Yet disliked books can have their reviews tucked away in pages full to boredom with advertisements or hidden between non-literary items deep within a newspaper.

Another vehicle of censorship is exclusion from media coverage. Part of this phenomenon is due to lack of inclusion in the "loop" — that group of radio, television and newspaper people who live by a system of media symbiosis — but then this itself is an aspect of control and censorship. There are several key radio and television programs that help book publicity and sales, and if authors are not invited to appear on these their books will suffer. If the authors manage to be invited onto the shows, they may still be subject to disapproval, which can manifest itself in two ways. The first is straightforward hostility and criticism, but the second is more interesting. It is the so-called "objectivity" approach, where a producer or interviewer will claim that the book under discussion is of such a nature that a "balancing voice" is required. Whereas only two people — host and author — are usually involved in the equation, suddenly a third, outside commentator is introduced to give an opposite view to that articulated in the book. An author advocating full abortion rights or homosexual marriage, for example, does not require a critic, but an author arguing the case for abortion controls or the sanctity of traditional marriage most certainly does.

We also have the less palpable but equally damaging attempt to marginalize an author. Canard and innuendo about the undesirability of a certain book and a particular author can take many forms. It could be talk encouraged among librarians about the author's racism, misogyny, homophobia, conservatism, fascism, devil worship (insert favourite accusation here). Or words of advice and warning given to buyers who purchase thousands of books from publishers for hundreds of stores, or simple derision and abuse at fashionable and important parties about a book's politics — this last one much more significant than you might imagine.

For further information about all of this, ask any number of writers. Try talking to William Gairdner in Canada, Rush Limbaugh in the United States or Paul Johnson in Britain. All of them, and so many more, experienced the sort of treatment I have described, yet all of them wrote books that became national bestsellers because of the genuine popularity they enjoyed amongst the ultimate and best arbiters of quality and importance, the book-buying public. And please remind yourself that the view expressed in a book is as irrelevant as the colour of its dust-jacket — anybody can tolerate a friendly opinion, it is the toleration of that which angers and offends that defines you as a supporter of freedom or a fan of oppression. It is increasingly time to take sides. Do please choose.

Let the Children Speak

Consider this: a man knows what a woman likes to read, he knows as well as she does what a woman appreciates in literature and, in fact, is probably better able to judge women's literature than a woman herself. It is not that he intends to be insulting, provocative or even patronizing, it is just that he does, after all, know better. A man is capable of supreme empathy, of unlocking his soul and his mind to the aspirations and understanding of women. Again, he knows better.

This at least appears to be the logical extension of an argument that was initiated and then propounded by others in the letters pages of *Books in Canada*, and one that has been pursued for many years in the publishing and reviewing industry. This little battle is fought within the context of children's literature, with one army claiming that books for children and young adults should be reviewed not by children themselves or perhaps vicariously by their parents but by professionals, individuals who are librarians, booksellers or writers of children's books.

As was said in one letter, one that represented a case of worrying myopia if not of epistolary blindness:

"Professional reviewers in the children's-book world know what is being done by a wide range of authors and illustrators. They know the history of children's books and of the work of the creator being reviewed."

The correspondent goes on to ask: "Why . . . has *Books in Canada* decided that children's books must be reviewed by non-professionals, whose primary review technique seems to be canvassing their children for their opinions? This is the equivalent of asking adult book reviewers to make sure they consult their neighbour and include his or her views in a review of the latest Canadian novel or political work."

Is it? I don't think so. I believe it is more like a Gentile critic who has been asked to review a book about the Holocaust speaking to a Jewish friend before writing on the subject, or a heterosexual man questioning whether he can fully appreciate a gay coming-of-age novel. In fact, neither of these examples is sufficiently similar or complete to make the point adequately, for while an adult can with a careful sensitivity and directed reading construct an understanding of another adult's life, no mature man or woman can authentically recreate the emotional, the artistic, the visceral understanding of a child. It is not a question of whether it *should* be this way, rather that it *is* this way and *has* to be this way.

When C. S. Lewis was working on arguably the greatest children's story of the last fifty years, *The Lion, the Witch and the Wardrobe*, he showed the manuscript to his friend, J. R. R. Tolkien. The author of *The Hobbit* was not at all impressed and advised Lewis to abandon the story, being particularly angry at the inclusion of Santa Claus in a chronicle of a non-earthly world. Yet the very success of the book was due to the fact that within its pages Christian metaphor swam with meaty anthropomorphism in a sea of ancient legends and atavistic mythology. To his eternal credit Lewis remained unconvinced by Tolkien's rejection, showed the work to the young daughter of a friend and on her advice changed nothing at all of the first of his "Narnia" books.

Surely this entire argument is really about humility and compromise. Children do not always know what is good for them, but they invariably know what is fun for them, what pleases them and stimulates them, what makes them want to read more books and form their own creative and critical sensibilities. Critics who possess a refined and considerate knowledge of children's literature are essential, but they can only benefit by opening themselves to the opinions of those for whom children's literature is actually written in the first place. The best critics, of course, know this already. They also know that to do otherwise is to commit an appropriation not of voice but of taste, opinion and judgment. The literary views of children may be unvarnished but they are also untarnished. Rather than reacting with suspicion, we should be delighted by the endless possibilities and dazzling avenues of exploration they offer.

Who Stole Reviewing?

I waited for a long time before writing this column. I wanted to give the larger Canadian newspapers and magazines sufficient time to review Christina Hoff Sommers's book *Who Stole Feminism: How Women Have Betrayed Women.* Time's up. This seminal work has been out in Canada for the better part of a year and has been given insultingly little coverage, after initially being ignored altogether. A similar phenomenon occurred in the United States, where the book was not given its appropriate place in the review sections of the press.

Because of the size of the media in the United States, however, the book did at least get a certain amount of attention. But north of the border it has, with a few noble exceptions such as the *Ottawa Citizen* and a non-books column in *The Globe and Mail,* been largely ignored. Or should I say rejected. The silence is deafening.

I have written about the effective censorship of books that challenge the liberal status quo. Step forward, Ms. Sommers. She is a philosophy professor at Clark University in Massachusetts, and a contributor to the *New Republic* and the *New England Journal of Medicine. Time* magazine described her book, vulgarly but not inaccurately, as arguing that "feminism has been derailed by a bunch of neurotic, self-indulgent intellectuals who have a direct personal interest in grossly overstating the woes of womankind."

What this feminist author does is to tear away at the foundations of victimology, that chimera upon which the entire industries of fraudulent statistics, false accusations and radical political agendas are so frequently based. She analyses two central studies, one by the American Association of University Women (AAUW), that allegedly proved that girls suffer an enormous loss of self-esteem at the age of eleven and from then on they are treated unfairly by schools. Because of this, Washington initiated the Gender Equity in Education Act at a cost of $360 million. The studies also influenced many legislators and educators in Canada. In Toronto we now have the ludicrous situation where a "woman centred" school has been created, where for $6,000 a year the sensitive wealthy may send their daughters.

Sommers shows that both of these studies relied on the highly problematic ideas of the gender feminist Carol Gilligan and her obsession with the moral differences between the sexes. Sommers also points out that the definition of lack of self-esteem consisted of girls at eleven realizing that they were not going to become rock musicians or movie stars, while boys continued with this fantasy. She argues that self-esteem is impossible to quantify or measure, that the AAUW has been taken over by extremists who detect patriarchal murder around every corner and that they severely distorted the truth in their studies. In fact, girls remain on a par with or do better than boys in school. Fifty-five per cent of students entering university are women — the percentage is higher in Canada.

There is more. The etymology of the phrase "rule of thumb" was perverted by radical feminists. They simply made up the story that the saying was derived from the idea that men were once allowed to beat their wives with a rod no wider than their thumb, and that this was then incorporated into British and later American law. This was repeated without doubt or challenge in the *Washington Post*, *Time* and many mainstream publications. Yet the phrase has no such origin. In reality it applied to carpenters who knew their trade so well that they did not require a ruler; in this case, the only violence being done is to the truth.

Then we have Naomi Wolf claiming that 150,000 American women die of anorexia every year. No, says Sommers. The figure is actually less than a hundred. Or what about the "fact" that on Super Bowl Sunday domestic violence increases by 40 per cent? This conclusion was ostensibly the result of years of research, and led to calls for legislation and advice to women to arm themselves or leave home on this particular day; but when the findings were analysed and the academics concerned were interviewed it appeared that it was all nonsense. Women's shelters, hospitals and police stations were all monitored — no change on Super Bowl Sunday.

Sommers claims that our universities are under attack, that our literature is being ripped apart and that our regard for truth is under siege. Her book is new, fresh, objective and revisionist, and it deserves maximum coverage. Which leads me to ask once again why it has not received more attention from the vast majority of Canadian publications. Conspiracy? Surely not. The usual idiots doing the usual damage? Perhaps. This I do know. Christina Hoff Sommers might want to title her next book *Who Stole Reviewing?*, and base it in Canada.

Winds of Change

I once wrote a column attacking the recent wave of revisionist biographies that are committed to nothing other than making as much money as possible for their authors and publishers. I condemned the recording of irresponsible and unfounded rumour as if it were fact, and I said that such books did biography and literature a bad service. But that was only one half of the equation. The other is more positive. At its centre is the idea that intelligent, open-minded and objective biography is not only a very good thing but is also quite inevitable.

The practitioners of the genre, these locksmiths, these spies who peep through the paper curtains of a literary life, have always been around, but it was Lytton Strachey at the turn of the century who transformed the art. If there was a pivotal moment, it was when Strachey revealed that an English nobleman had passed gas while bowing to Queen Elizabeth I. Humiliated, the man retreated all the way to France. On his return, many years later, the poor wretch went to see the queen and the monarch's first statement was that she had "quite forgot the fart." Nothing would be the same again; or to put it another way, the winds of change began to blow.

Since then literary biography has dealt for the most part with revealing previously unrevealed truths. Whether it be the details of Hemingway's suicide, the fact of D. H. Lawrence's homosexuality, the way in which F. Scott Fitzgerald wrote his fiction or some of the details of Graham Greene's personal and professional life, we have been told a great deal more about literature and as a consequence have a greater appreciation of its content and of its creators. The two, of course, are intertwined. A biography sets a work in context, places its author in time and space. A novel such as *To the Lighthouse*, for example, cannot be properly understood by a reader who is not familiar with Virginia Woolf's definition of feminism, with Edwardian attitudes towards women and, indeed, with Bloomsbury's ambivalence towards Virginia Woolf.

The vitality and the importance of biography also concern the fundamental direction of modern literature. If fine writing and fine reading are to survive we must oppose and defeat those critics barking out like little *Obergruppenführers* that the written word is all that matters and that we should not, must not, study the life of the author.

Of course, it comes as no surprise that it has become fashionable to criticize literary biography. I once heard a rather sad, under-achieving young man ask Andrew Motion, the biographer of Philip Larkin, why he wrote biographies, adding "after all, you've got a life." The question may have been ill-informed and pompous but it did reflect the views of those who know no better: biographers live vicariously, they are unable to write fiction or poetry themselves, etc. In essence the usual and tired complaint levelled against critics, that they are eunuchs who envy the lusty. Not true. Many biographers also write novels and some, Peter Ackroyd being a consummate example, have reached the highest levels as both biographers and novelists.

The issue is even more germane in Canada, where there is no strong tradition of literary biography. Most of the authors who write biography do not attempt another and only dip their toes in the tidal waters of this swelling sea — *The Toronto Star* books columnist Philip Marchand's life of Marshall McLuhan and former *Books in Canada* editor Paul Stuewe's book on Hugh Garner are two appropriate examples. There are reasons for this. I well remember a widely known Toronto literary figure proclaiming that it was wonderful "that at the Harbourfront Reading Festival the writers got on so well with the biographers." By "writers" he meant, of course, novelists.

Yet it is vital that Canadian writers are chronicled. Why, for example, haven't we heard about two or three rival biographies of Morley Callaghan being written, with publishers trying to outbid each other for the rights? The reason is that it just ain't happening. The same is true of most other Canadian writers. There is a biography of Lucy Maud Montgomery and another is currently being written, but you can be sure that an American or English author of similar success would have been the subject of at least half a dozen biographies.

Yet Canada requires and desires more rediscovery of its cultural heritage than larger, more secure countries. Even now there are writers from the past who are slipping into that twilight zone of distant memory and will soon be forgotten. Pearls of Canadian culture will be lost, and the necklace simply isn't sufficiently long or ornate for us to let this happen.

Ultimately it is not a question of whether we ought to have biographies but whether we could survive as a culture without them. I cannot imagine a governor general explaining that he had quite forgot the fart, but I can well imagine future Canadians regretting the day that the original incident was not recorded.

Double Standards

I have just returned from Britain, where it has happened once again. This time it concerns Alan Paton, the South African novelist, author of the international classic and plea for racial equality *Cry, the Beloved Country*. Paton was the president of the South African Liberal Party and was long revered for his opposition to apartheid and oppression. The white crusader pleaded for Nelson Mandela when the ANC leader was on trial, he was welcomed by liberal-minded people everywhere, given platforms in the best universities, churches and assemblies in the world. A new biography by Peter F. Alexander, however, reveals that Paton was not the knight in shining armour that we had thought.

Paton was, in fact, an authoritarian father bitterly disliked by his children. At the reformatory where he taught, he administered 2,000 strokes of the strap and cane a year to the inmates. They were terrified of him. He was also chronically unfaithful to his wife, seeking out prostitutes wherever he could find them. As a teacher he used anything to hit his charges, including cricket bats. The girls in the class were victims of his cruel, relentless and brutal sarcasm. When he was injured in a chemistry experiment in school and driven away in an ambulance, the pupils threw their hats up in the air and cheered.

So, as I say, it has happened again. Yet another radical, liberal, socialist or leftist author has been shown to be hypocritical and dishonest, writing books that preach and propound one type of ideal, but in their personal life and private utterances demonstrating quite another set of attitudes. I encountered this in sickening doses with H. G. Wells, whose novels and works of non-fiction earned him the reputation of a revolutionary socialist and feminist. In fact, he was a racist and an anti-Semite, an abuser of women, an uncaring and manipulative father, a plagiarist and a fraud.

Wells's sometime friend, sometime enemy George Bernard Shaw was another hero of the left because of the views he expressed in his plays and essays. Yet when the playwright returned from one visit to his beloved Soviet Union and a reporter asked him about the forced starvation in the Ukraine (millions were murdered by Stalin's commissars), Shaw responded by throwing a tin of Russian meat at the journalist.

Both Wells and Shaw were, of course, inspired by Karl Marx, father of the modern concept of class struggle and revolution. "The Jewish Nigger Lassalle fortunately departs at the end of this week," Marx wrote about a visitor. "It is now completely clear to me that he, as is proved by his cranial formation and curly hair, descends from the Negroes . . . The obtrusiveness of the fellow is also Nigger-like." Marx went on to defend slavery in the West, claiming that there would be anarchy without it. As for Jews, this self-hating monster asked, "What is the worldly religion of the Jew? Huckstering. What is his worldly God? Money." The list goes on.

It is not only writers on the left who operate by such double standards, of course, but it is hard to avoid the conclusion that they do make a habit of it. One of the reasons for this is that authentic conservatism is founded on important notions such as natural law, instinctive correctness, order and structure, and old but never tired beliefs such as consistency of word and deed. The Marxist dialectic and its less extreme little siblings separate our personal from our political life and hence give us more room for moral manoeuvre. Thus, when Lenin told H. G. Wells that he "did not care" how Wells treated his wife as long as he wrote books that advocated feminism, he personified the attitudes of those who separate personal morality and political ideology.

Brecht knifed a mistress and threw her down the stairs, but championed East Germany and proletarian drama — he was forgiven everything. The lionized Jean Genet made remarks about women and Jews that were murderous in intent. But Genet advocated world revolution, the Black Panthers and the Palestinian cause, and so was somehow considered to be on the right side. There is a double standard at work, and not only in literature. President Kennedy's immoral actions were hidden by a liberal press corps for decades; we know that a Nixon or a Reagan would not have received such generous treatment.

In Canada the situation is not fundamentally different, but it is painted in a brighter, friendlier colour, less red than pink, less black than dark grey. Which brings us to those Canadian novelists, poets and playwrights who applaud socialism, liberty and reform in their writings but act like utter reprobates in their personal life. Hypocrites. Should I name them? Come on now, be serious. One hint of such an accusation and this venerable publication would be awash in libel suits. History, however, will judge; and if you are really curious, just ask around.

Anti-Semitism Has Many Lives

The body may be moribund, but it ain't yet a corpse. Every time the thinking classes assume that the issue of anti-Semitism in literature is safely incarcerated inside a sealed container, up it pops like some perverse and sepulchral jack-in-the-box. In the past, of course, discussions around the issue have been based as much in histrionics as in history. Every zealot who screams about the iniquity of Charles Dickens's Fagin has clearly not read *Our Mutual Friend*, in which the Jewish Mr. Kiah is a paragon. Those who accuse former governor-general John Buchan of being an anti-Semite may experience difficulties in explaining why the author of the Richard Hannay stories is honoured in the Golden Book of the Jewish National Fund. G. K. Chesterton and Anthony Trollope anti-Semites? Wrong. H. G. Wells and George Elliot friends of the Jews? Wrong. Wrong. Wrong!

The perception of the Jew in literature is bound irretrievably to the wider perception of the Jew in the Diaspora and, of more importance, of the state of Israel. After 1967, Israel lost its victim status, or rather saw it forcibly withdrawn by an eagerly judgmental Gentile world. No longer handsome young paratroopers fighting for liberty, but hardened occupiers, shooting at children. That the images are equally false is irrelevant. Jews are now fair game for those who would attack them; these ghouls have never gone away, but simply lowered their heads. The Holocaust, as one *Times* of London critic said last month, was a very long time ago.

Gore Vidal saw fit in a recent essay to characterize Jews in negative light because, as he explained with some risibly broad and inaccurate brushstrokes, there were many Jewish people in the ranks of neoconservatism, and many neoconservatives were homophobic. Generalization, the blood-soaked banner of the bigot down the ages. Children's author Roald Dahl stated in 1984 that "Hitler was a stinker, but there was a reason for what he did, you know. Jews talk about the war all the time, but they weren't keen to do any fighting, were they? My bad characters are often based on Jews, yes." Some people urged a boycott of Dahl's works, demanded contrition, requested a discussion. Nothing. And Mr. Dahl, his publishers, his agent and all concerned went on to do extremely well indeed, and the matter was conveniently deposited into the wastebin of anti-Semitic history. It is surely axiomatic to say that if such words had been uttered by an internationally respected author about another ethnic minority, the outcry would have provoked resignation, legislation, even the odd *fatwa* [a religious edict].

Dahl is dead, and was never part of the literary establishment. Martin Amis is very much alive, and is the breathing quintessence of modern English literature. His novel *Time's Arrow* tells of a Holocaust doctor, an Auschwitz torturer. The literary merits of the work need not concern us here. The intrinsic ugliness of the volume lies in its treatment of Jewish suffering or, more to the point, its lack of the same. The protagonist's life is portrayed by Amis with an emetic apathy for those under the man's knife and his clamps. They are stage props, toys with which to play and then discard. From the first page of the book, Amis is entertaining his readers with alleged humour: "Consider the Jewish joke," says Amis's murderer, "with the old lady running distractedly along the seashore: Help! My son the doctor is drowning." No voices for the wretches in the camps, no identities, no humanity. In *The Spectator*, diarist Julie Burchill eloquently pondered, "Can it ever be right to perform a party trick on a mountain of skulls?"

This is not to say, of course, that there are certain no-go areas within literature. If there are, there shouldn't be. It was an unwritten law in German writing after 1945 that no Jewish character could be depicted as unsavoury or malicious. This sensitive and empathetic pact has been expunged in the past five years, particularly in Austria, and it is probably for the good. The issue can be taken too far — within some Israeli universities the writings of Jewish author Philip Roth are considered to be anti-Semitic. But the issue is one of fashion and double standard. It has once again become permissible to caricature Jews; more visible minorities have taken their place in the hall of the abused. A symptom of a greater vulgarity and callousness? A blurring of sensibilities in this jejune age? Or a signal that, as Europe unfolds and atavistic tensions re-emerge, the Jewish people ought to once more put out the sentries?

Runners-Up

Did quixotic and somewhat absurd gym teachers actually mean it when they told generations of their charges that "it is not the winning but the taking part that is important"? Surely not. Most of us would commit every crime in the canon to triumph in our chosen race. I worked for some years with the screenwriter Colin Welland, one of the most honest men in the British literary community. When he won an Oscar for writing the script of *Chariots of Fire* he evinced virtual euphoria. The press condemned him. When he failed to win the U.K.'s equivalent of the Academy Award he exhibited regret and chagrin. The press condemned him. Prizes are a conundrum.

It needs to be stated at the outset that there are several positive aspects to literary prizes, especially within the Canadian context. They bring a fresh and particularly necessary spotlight to the literary community; they increase awareness of new books and new authors; they increase the sales of a particular book; they award money to authors at a time when the Canada Council is being savaged by a parsimonious and antediluvian government.

Yet there are also less attractive factors involved in the equation. The Canadian Book Marketing Centre is currently compiling a directory of the literary prizes open to Canadians. They have listed 116 thus far, but are still working on the project. We are all aware of the Governor General's Award and the first-novel prize co-sponsored by *Books in Canada*, but what about the Ann Connor Brimer Award, the McNally Robinson Award, the Harold Adams Innis Book Prize, the Aldo and Jeanne Scaglione Prize, the . . . ?

There is an extraordinary proliferation of literary awards, and we have to ask ourselves whether there is a sufficient number of Canadian writers worthy to be laureates. It is possible that Canada is more blessed than other countries when it comes to gifted authors, but surely there are limits. If we are not vigilant, literary awards will begin to resemble the Order of Canada; so devalued by the quantity of its recipients — and the quality of them — that those who have not actually been given the damned thing now constitute a statistical minority and might consider applying for government assistance.

In Britain literary awards are not as numerous as in Canada but are often much more fatuous. The pinnacle of pointlessness is the Arthur Markham Memorial Prize, for the best book written by a manual labourer who has been injured when working in or around a coal mine. The judges must spend tens of moments on that one.

It is worth recalling, however, that the staff of *Books in Canada* once discussed initiating a "Second Novel Award." They were in jest, but only just. There is some logic to awarding a prize to the best second novel; most writers will agree that second birth is far more arduous than first and that it far more accurately represents a novelist's capabilities and direction. As to the argument that younger writers require financial assistance, two of the writers on the SmithBooks/Books in Canada First Novel shortlist this year are forty-six years old, and all are over thirty — hardly novices in dire need of a monetary boost.

The select group of actors who have refused to accept an Academy Award propound that it is invidious and insidious to compare different performers in different productions. G. K. Chesterton once pronounced on a not dissimilar theme that it would be akin to comparing the colour black with the shape triangular.

Is it equitable to tell one author that he is superior to his rivals; fair to that writer, fair to his comrades? And who are the judges and whom do they represent? It is still genuinely staggering that Mordecai Richler's *Solomon Gursky Was Here* was not even nominated for the 1994 Governor General's Award. Do we seriously have such an abundance of novel-writing talent that someone of Richler's stature and abilities can be left from the list of the best of the year? It was, in fact, the very stature that probably kept him off the list. Nobody dislikes a winner more than a loser.

To respond to your charge of hypocrisy, yes, I would accept a nomination or a prize; I have done in the past, on several occasions. The Nobel Prize–winning economist Milton Friedman lived in a rent-controlled building but lambasted the policy of rent control. He justified what opponents condemned as a crass double standard by arguing that his taking advantage of rent control would not aid rent control, while refusing to take advantage of it would do it no harm. By the way, the literature division of the Nobel Prize has been won by the likes of Paul Heyse, Carl Spitteler and Pearl Buck; no James Joyce, no F. Scott Fitzgerald, no Graham Greene, no Margaret Atwood, no Robertson Davies.

Sabre Clashing

Britain has never seemed so Greene. The Graham of that name, that is. The incompetence of Prime Minister John Major, the peccadillos of Prince Charles and even the antics of cheating cricketers have been pushed from the front pages of the country's newspapers by discussions concerning the best novelist never to have won the Nobel Prize, the author of the *Power and the Glory*, *Brighton Rock*, *Our Man in Havana* and the rest.

The reason is that three biographies of the man have been published almost simultaneously, and two of them, by Michael Shelden and Anthony Mockler, are solidly revisionistic, digging away at the foundations of Greene's character and achievements and presenting a flawed, intensely difficult and even immoral man who allegedly managed to fool most of the people, most of the time.

The defence against this barrage of literary grapeshot is provided by Greene's official biographer, Norman Sherry, whose second monumental and Boswellian volume is now out, and by Greene expert and researcher Christopher Hawtree. The latter stated publicly that Greene had always considered Anthony Mockler to be "unspeakable" and that he, Hawtree, shared the opinion. But these are the British literati and such an insult did not go unnoticed or unforgiven.

Mockler tried to physically attack his detractor at a *Spectator* magazine party and, when he failed, wrote to him, threatening to "knock off your block and pulp the remainder" the next time he got the chance. The diminutive Hawtree took the correspondence seriously and requested and was granted police protection.

Then I heard that at a *Private Eye* magazine luncheon in London's Soho, a highly respected magazine editor announced that her journal was about to host a grand and lucrative book prize, and that she would do her best to seat Anthony Mockler and Christopher Hawtree at the same table. "Should cause something to happen, I think," she said, giggling. Hilarious nastiness all around. Again, these are the British literati.

Shelden has remained relatively quiet throughout all of this, probably intent on letting his book speak for itself. It does. Although the Greene estate refused the author permission to quote from any published or unpublished sources, the work is still 500 pages long.

In it, Shelden makes the extraordinary claim that Greene murdered a woman whose body was found in a trunk in Brighton station in 1934. He alleges that his subject was a chronic copulator who was unfaithful to his wife and sought out teenage girls; that his early novels were peppered with anti-Semitism; and that he had a penchant for depicting violence towards women. Shelden also says that Greene spied for MI-6, and was homosexual — for God's sake, the man was an upper-class Englishman, are we meant to be surprised by these twin revelations?

Yet this is relatively mild and moderate compared to the claims of Mockler's book. Here we have Greene offering to spy for Ireland against his own country, passing on secrets to Kim Philby leading to the execution of British agents, harbouring incestuous feelings towards his sister and perhaps indulging in plagiarism.

What Mockler lacks in evidence he tries to make up for in assiduity, sometimes of the most inappropriate kind. He pushed notes to Graham Greene under the door of the room in which the author was dying. Greene placed an injunction on the book, preventing publication while he lived.

Mockler also wrote to various literary editors asking that they not give his book to poor old Hawtree for review purposes. A rash and clumsy act. Once again, these are the British literati. Hawtree was given the book to review for the *Evening Standard*, whose literary editor A. N. Wilson revels in the sabre clashes of such in-fighting. Hawtree went so far as to quote Mockler's letter about him in the opening paragraph. He then eviscerated the book for its poor prose, inadequate research and fanciful allegations.

Hawtree wrote that the attacks made by both Shelden and Mockler were complete nonsense and that a good biography is still to be written.

It could be argued that Hawtree is myopic when it comes to criticism of his hero, viewing everything said about the man through Greene-tinted glasses. Whatever the truth of the matter, however, the debate continues, and might even extend to Canada, what with Shelden speaking at the Harbourfront Festival of Authors, and Louise Dennys, Greene's niece, resident here as the publisher of Knopf Canada.

In part, this is all rather a mess, an example of the most base type of voyeurism and of the biographer playing the role of the bloodstained vulture. But it also demonstrates how the genius of a dead white male writer can still vibrate through the cultural world, escape from the ghettos of the books pages and dominate the news. And in spite of, or perhaps because of, the inherent pugnacity and vitriol, it really is such a lot of fun.

Words on Film

The movie *Shadowlands* is about the life of the novelist and philosopher C. S. Lewis and his relationship with the poet Joy Davidman. Anthony Hopkins, who plays Lewis, and Debra Winger, who plays Davidman, are probably about to appear in other films, playing serial-killer cannibals, love-sick war criminals, feminist lawyers and butlers who either did or did not do it.

Lewis himself would have been sickened by the thought of his work and his views being portrayed on the screen by an actor. He simply would not have understood the reason for it. If you want to know about me, know me, read my books, he often said. Lewis was more correct than he knew. Indeed, in the entire two hours of *Shadowlands* we do not see Clive Staples Lewis writing anything at all — he does, however, smoke a pipe quite a lot; and all authors do that, don't they?

There is a vehement contradiction, an inherent oxymoron, involved in films about authors. Writers' lives are invariably, and, in fact, almost must be, relatively dull: literary creation involves tedious, isolated weeks, months and years in a study behind a desk, in front of a word processor, putting words on paper. The more one talks about it the less one does it.

Oscar Wilde might have been involved in witty conversations at the Café Royal and a nasty court case, Dylan Thomas might have drunk himself across two continents, Malcolm Lowry might have killed a man and Robertson Davies might even have had a budgie called Derek. But none of this is particularly important. What matters is not the costume and the packaging, but the body and the contents. Authors are authors because they write. For a movie to authentically recreate the life of a writer it would have to devote at least half of its time to the image of fingers holding a pen or of hands typing at a keyboard.

Some films that have portrayed writers have been entertaining in themselves — one thinks, for example, of Jeremy Irons as Kafka (*Kafka*) and Ian McKellen as D. H. Lawrence (*Priest of Love*). They were successful, however, precisely because they wallowed in the flummery rather than the reality of a writer's life. The often stultifying boredom of writing is eschewed by movie-makers, as it should be by any director or actor who knows what is good for his or her career. At their worst, movies that feature authors as their main protagonists are marvellously bad. You know the sort of thing:

Scene: Paris, 1864, July. The summer mansion of Napoleon III. There is a sound of knocking on the huge doors. Exit the royal door-opener to ascertain who it is. He returns, carrying a heavy French accent.

Servant: "Your Highness, there is a man at the front of the palace with a book under his arm. He says that his name is Flaubert."

Benign Dictator: "Aha. Show him in, I wish to patronize an author of promise and with any luck this might just be the man."

The penchant for the authorial biopic also says a great deal about contemporary sensibilities, about a world where only an estimated 10 per cent of the people who purchased Stephen Hawking's *A Short History of Time* actually read the thing. We like our literature in sound-bite chunks, predigested, effortless and, of course, available on video cassette within the year. The problem with books, particularly with good books, is that they require more than a couch, a bag of popcorn and a television converter. We use one part of our brain when we watch a screen, a different part of it when we read a book — a much larger part of it, at that. Yet effort is out of fashion in a society where instant and facile gratification is at the core of a multinational, billion-dollar industry.

One cannot help recalling the immortal conversation that took place in the Oscar-winning film *Chariots of Fire* between the athlete Harold Abrahams and his lover. "I won't run if I can't win," from the sprinter. "If you don't run you can't win," from his guru-like partner. Imagine the National Film Board's bilingual production of *They Called Him Mordecai*. "I won't write if I can't win the Booker," from our hero. His agent responds: "If you don't write, you won't even win the G.G., Mr. Richler." God help us, God help us all.

Letter from Coronation Street

This must be a dream; a Jungian reaction of an expatriate with a hidden longing for his homeland. There is an English street, an English pub, an English sweet-shop and English houses. But it is all slightly too small, in grand miniature, as though the whole thing was built for thirteenth-century Celts who, we are told, seldom grew to more than five feet. It can't be. Mediaeval Welshmen didn't buy the *Daily Mail*, chew humbugs or drink Newton and Ridley beer. Did they?

So it's no dream, unless it's one that has come true for the millions of fans, many of them in Canada, who are addicted to the British soap opera *Coronation Street.* We're in Manchester, at Granada studios, where this sophisticated television show has been made for over thirty years. Members of the public are allowed to tour the studios and see where their champions and their devils do their bit each week. Thousands come here, pay their money, take photographs and buy mugs, beer mats, key rings, videotapes, anything, everything. A gullible but endearing suspension of disbelief. And after all, that is what theatre is all about.

That leap of trust is made a little easier because it is raining. It is always meant to be raining, metaphorically and otherwise, in this part of the world. There is a greyness, a griminess about these big Northern English cities in which the denizens take a veritable pride. And "The Street" is the natural manifestation of all that. There is no artificial glamour here, no shoulder pads, ostentatious wealth or absurd and contrived plots involving inheritances, princesses and oil.

In fact, there isn't very much at all. As critics will tell you, there are no gay romances, no abortions and no rioting, hardly any black characters, little talk of politics and a severely limited representation of what is too often the dangerous dowdiness of inner-city life. There is perhaps a time warp, but one conceived by outstanding writers and performed by accomplished and subtle actors. Unlike American soaps, the success of *Coronation Street* is not about audience fantasy but audience identification. Empathy as opposed to envy.

Doreen and Harold from Mississauga empathize three afternoons a week, when the show is broadcast on the CBC. So much so that on their holiday to Britain they've put aside Shakespeare's Stratford and the Lake District so as to visit The Cabin and The Rover's Return. "If you look at the counter in the store, there's a tiny Maple Leaf badge. And Jim sometimes wears a Blue Jays T-shirt," says Doreen.

Jim is a regular on *Coronation Street*, his character a former soldier with a Belfast accent whose marriage broke up but is now repaired and whose sons are doing nicely but you never really know and whose wife lost a baby but is okay and . . . Just as Harold is in full flow, along walks Jim McDonald. The icon has stepped down from the wall. Gasps.

Doreen holds her husband's arm tightly. Harold comforts her. "It's okay, dear, it's okay," he says.

Jim walks with long strides. He smiles, all confidence and roguishness — still in character. They're not filming today, so we don't know why he's here. Perhaps he likes hanging around and being noticed. He's approaching Doreen. She's breathing heavily. "All right, are ya?" he asks, loudly. If Doreen had leprosy, she'd be cured by now. Harold takes charge — he was in the war — and arranges autographs and photos of the three of them. All done, and Jim strolls off. Close encounters of the third kind — that's when you meet them.

What is so noticeable about the crowds here and the things they are encouraged to see and do is the decency, sense of balance and the appeal of all concerned. The appearance of a television star can be overwhelming, but nobody screams or does anything too ridiculous. They appreciate good entertainment and they've come to see where it is all produced. They want to smell the place, feel it, almost taste it.

Not so bad, that. A delightful eccentricity. And as soon as Jim has left the area, people are making jokes about him and speculating as to whether he will remain on the show. That sort of cynicism is very *Coronation Street.* Very *Coronation Street,* indeed.

A Frank Magazine in "Nice" Canada

Some time ago I wrote my last fictitious diary in *Frank,* the Ottawa-based satire and gossip magazine. I had written the column for almost four years; at one time it was a joy but had become a chore. It was time to end it. And it was time for me to consider again whether this country needed or could sustain a publication such as *Frank.* To both questions I believe that the answer is in the affirmative. The reasons are less connected with the exact nature of *Frank* and its particular successes and failures than with the general need in Canada for a satirical and revelation-committed magazine, and because there are several precedents in Canadian history for such a phenomenon. The established wisdom, that Canada is a nation rooted in "niceness" and cannot tolerate unbridled satire, is in this case completely unfounded.

In the last century there was J. W. Benough's *Punch in Canada* and a harsh, acerbic journal called *Grip* (1873–1894), named after the raven in Charles Dickens's novel *Barnaby Rudge.* In the 1920s came the more gentle and humane *The Goblin.* Then there was the Yukon satirist E. L. Stroller White, who operated in the late nineteenth century right up until the first two decades of the twentieth. Most important of all was Bob Edwards, whose *Calgary Eye Opener* (1902–1922) specialized in an eviscerating style of journalism and exposed some of the real (and occasionally imagined) wrongdoings of Western businessmen, politicians and celebrities. The paper was repeatedly sued but managed to hang on to existence and arguably liberated the nature of the province and its journalism.

In the years following the Second World War, there were occasional bursts of satirical energy but nothing that seriously rivalled the shenanigans of the prewar years. Then came a series of magazines attempting to survive on a soup of satire, gossip and exposure. *Cow* magazine lasted for around a year in Toronto, *Zed* and *Uranus* did not even make it past the drawing board but did have some good and caustic plans. Then came *Frank* in 1988, which is no surprise to E. Graydon Carter, the Canadian who edited *Spy* and now edits *Vanity Fair* in New York.

As he told me in a recent interview, "Countries need to be confident of themselves, and countries like Britain and France most certainly are. North America is different. The United States still has problems with its identity and Canada certainly has. So with a satirical magazine on this continent it's like making fun of a child, before it has become a man. It's seen as unseemly. But it's changing. I could see it happening when I lived in Canada. I think satire, gossip, is liberating. It certainly can be if it's done properly."

There are foreign comparisons, in Ireland, France and Germany. In Britain, *Private Eye* magazine has existed for three decades and has become an essential element of that country's media. Its legal costs are enormous and it is often obliged to appeal to readers, more than

120,000 of them, to pay for litigation. Those readers are loyal, and they respond because they have grown to maturity with the magazine. The front half of this raw, poorly produced organ contains gossip and short news items, interspersed with humorous columns often modelled on conventional newspapers. Further to the back are serious investigative articles. There is also an implicit but undoubted xenophobia in the humour, which Canada, to its credit, would refuse to tolerate. Yet it can also be bitingly funny. Auberon Waugh wrote a column for *Private Eye* for a decade. "Most of the people who claim to write satire are simply telling jokes," states Waugh. "Satire is about more than that. It involves commentary and parody and showing up faults. *Private Eye* held on by its fingertips for years, but the effort was worthwhile."

The history of Canadian journalism demonstrates that in this country the effort has to be determined, because when the establishment feels at all threatened its full-fed knights will charge forward to defend their cause. Bad taste, they will shout, as they did when *Frank* mockingly called for the "deflowering" of Prime Minister Mulroney's daughter. Well, yes. But as Malcolm Muggeridge said, "Good taste and humour are a contradiction in terms, like a chaste whore." It is also true that many of the loudest critics of gossip magazines are the loudest gossips. They merely desire to control the flow of the gossip and nominate its victims. Nor must we forget that in ostensibly egalitarian and classless Canada, elites and elitism are less abashed than in most other western countries and they guard their position fiercely. Their stature is conferred not by family name or place of birth but by knowledge of information and immunity from criticism. Thus their apprehension.

Satirical magazines also have to champion an increased public access to significant information. This is in a country that tolerated the media reporting ban on the Teale/Homolka case. At their best, such publications will also act as relief valves for information considered too sensitive by the mainstream media. A delicate flower, then, and there are a great many people who would break it at the stem before it has been given time to blossom. Yet the roots are deep and thick and it just might be that the garden of Canadian culture is a greener place because of it.

Not for Comfort

I have said before that if magazine and newspaper columns were CDs they would be tucked away in the Easy Listening section of the music store. The Perry Comos of Canadian journalism. Anodyne, asinine and slavishly discreet. Their writers, concerned that they might not be invited onto "Morningside," receive another government grant or be mentioned in the "Noises Off" column of *The Globe and Mail* alongside Stuart McLean, Ian Brown and Stephen Lewis (sorry about the juxtaposition, Ian).

I use the phenomenon of the column as a yardstick because it indicates just how free and feisty is a country's journalism, and by extension a country's culture. Lament, oh Canada. The most noxious are the coy ones, mostly retreads from the sixties. With these we might assume the influence of dinner-party and "Of course you can have a column, darling" styles of hiring. Bronwyn Drainie wishing her important, famous friends at the CBC a Merry Christmas in the *Globe* is a fitting example. Or Marni Jackson writing in *Toronto Life* about removing avocado stains from her futon, or about other hilarious antics of the comfortably off Toronto WASP. All to be collected in a book entitled *The "Only in Canada Could This Person Be a Journalist" Zone.*

Both columnists, and many others, are part of the literary family compact. They are related to others in the media by blood, by marriage, by their school and college days, and by political affiliation. One of the reasons that they are allowed to get away with such a travesty is that Canada is a country ruled by a nasty concoction of fear and reverence and few people are prepared to point out that the emperor is naked. This dull acceptance should come as no surprise, as what we now call Canada was founded by refugees from revolution. They were either patrician Anglicans or militant Presbyterians with a penchant for authority and decree. And thus the Canadian media are the poodles of the status quo rather than the watch-dogs of the nation. The United States, on the other hand, owes its modern foundation to Anabaptists, congregationalists, people who were innately suspicious of secular and religious government. Australia is Irish, Canada Scottish, which accounts for the former's delightful contempt for the powerful. Britain has long been a cynical, sardonic country and its columnists are similarly sharp and virile.

Canadian political columns are little better than the apolitical varieties. In a country with a liberal establishment, hierarchy and media, a leftist column is nothing if not conformist, and so many of them are indisputably of the left, and indisputably conformist. There are a few good ones — I seldom agree with Carole Corbeil in *The Toronto Star* but she does make some original points — but most of the breed are boorish and pusillanimous. Their socialist lustre amounts to refusing to wear ties at dinner parties where they receive newspaper awards from their friends.

Of the humorous columns, *The Toronto Star* offers what seems like dozens; but Joey Slinger is the only writer of the kind in any way worth reading, with most of the others being of the "Please love me, please. I'm sensitive. Look, I'm going to make a joke about rednecks" ilk. Humour requires a willingness to outrage. Niceness is rarely amusing, particularly a politically correct niceness. We also have that most Canadian species, the Doolittle columnist who is part fiscal conservative, part social liberal. There are several of these creatures about, loath to lose their chances of an Order of Canada or a seat on a Canada Council jury.

Then there are a handful of columnists who write for the *Sun* chain, *Maclean's* or *The Financial Post* who refuse to tread the accepted Canadian line, and one or two other writers spread out in the West and in the Maritime provinces who occasionally restore one's faith in individuality and principle. Sadly they are few, and they do themselves no good with those in the media with money and influence.

Somebody once wrote to me about my column in *Books in Canada,* complaining that I was tendentious. The belief that columns should not be calculated to promote a particular cause or viewpoint is astounding. My correspondent, who is probably far from untypical, thinks that columns have to be objective, in the centre, balanced. What nonsense. I have suffered petitions against me at *The Globe and Mail,* threats of murder, attempts to have me fired from magazines and television stations. It is how it is meant to be. I am succeeding. The worst fate for any columnist is to be ignored, the second most dire is to have myriad letters of support sent to the editor. The job of the columnist is not to comfort. John Wilkes, he of eighteenth-century sedition, was obliged to flee England to protect his life. His sin was to write that liberty was everything. He'd barely get an immigration hearing in modern Canada.

We'd do well to remember the sneering advice given by the Duke of Wellington to a would-be blackmailer: "Publish and be damned." Advice to any self-respecting columnist: publish and damn them.

No Such Thing as Writer's Block, Just Blockheads

Say hello to Ron, Mr. Average Canadian Writer. He sits at his word processor and contemplates just how vital he is to the evolution of the national identity and the preservation of the Canadian way. Actually he has little else to do, for on this particular morning the words will not come. Poor Ron, he is suffering from writer's block.

The fruitless monotony is interrupted by the noise of the mail arriving. No grant cheque today. How annoying. Ron is entitled to state subsidies; he is, after all, a writer. Still, with his applications to three different funding organizations he's bound to be rewarded before the end of the month. And there's only an hour until lunch and his meeting with Bob, another writer without whom civilization would collapse and who is also as blocked as a public toilet at a British soccer stadium.

Ron spends the hiatus sitting patiently, waiting for the muse to come and sit on his shoulder and whisper sweet, melodious suggestions into his ear. The trouble is, the volatile entity in question may just as easily perch on Ron's shoulder and dribble down his back. But today there is no muse at all. Just like yesterday. Poor Ron, poor Canada, poor literature.

Ron telephones me. "I suppose you've never known what it is like. I mean, you're so prolific," he says, "what with all those books, columns, reviews. So prolific." Ron is employing a euphemism, one that may well be motivated by envy, by sloth, by ennui, by lack of talent. What he is attempting to obfuscate is the simplistic and fatuous belief that industrious and productive writers are not to be trusted and are somehow betraying the rules of the breed.

Better to stagger into launch parties with a creased brow and a haggard grimace and compete with one's peers in the time-honoured sport of boasting of artistic constipation.

Roughage and relief should come in the form of need and desire. Bills to pay, mouths to feed. But need and desire also manifest themselves on a more esoteric and sublime level: the lust to create, to write. I can say without a tincture of the affectation or pretence that I am not fulfilled if I spend a day without having written something, albeit merely the notes for a piece of work to come.

Not for Ron. He tells me that he is prepared to lie low and wait for his flash of insight. "If a thing is worth having, it's worth waiting for," he says, sinking into the quagmire of cliché. What, I reply, like the cure for cancer?

I continue that in my experience there are two types of people who describe themselves as writers — those who talk about writing, and those who write. If you can't stand the heat, get out of the study. Or, as George Orwell said, "Writing is a job, not an excuse. If you can't do it, find another one."

Consider G. K. Chesterton with his sixty major books and plethora of weekly columns, Hilaire Belloc with his biography of James II written in three weeks, George Bernard Shaw writing play after play and then replying to almost every letter he received in gorgeous and witty detail, the legion of late nineteenth- and early twentieth-century authors who wrote, wrote and wrote again. Quantity needn't blemish quality, and paucity certainly does not guarantee excellence.

The phenomenon of writer's block is, with some noble exceptions, a chimera, invented by underachievers to create a miasma of mystique around their vocation, to help them pretend that literary creation is more important, more complex and less penetrable than other professions.

In some ways it is, but for the most part it is not. It is tiring, difficult work, it requires discipline and concentration. Inspiration, when it comes, is invariably the product of determined thought and an intelligently directed effort.

The solution to writer's block is straightforward — stop suffering from writer's block. We do not become precious, ethereal beings when we pick up the pen, merely workers toiling in a privileged environment.

My father was a London taxi driver who left home at eight in the morning and returned at eight in the evening. The odd thing is, I can't recall him waving his silk scarf and his broad-brimmed fedora in the air and exclaiming to his wife and children, "My darlings, I am simply too, too distracted by the beauty of the lilies to go to work today." I wonder why. I suppose he was one of that small but fortunate handful of men who just didn't suffer from cabbie's block.

Incorrect Again

Damn it, I want to be a contemporary novelist. I want to be one of those clever young people who write a fine novel and present it to a grateful and artistically esurient world. I want to indulge in creative catharsis, push back the frontiers of cultural acceptance. The firmament of modern fiction, so lustrous and fulfilling, so necessary, so original.

But can I do it? I am doubtful. I have to confess that for a nineties novelist I come from a deprived background. You see, I was an abundantly happy child; I loved my parents and was loved by them. Mum and Dad, curse them, stayed together when I was a youth and have stayed together now that I am an adult. They didn't hit each other, they made each other laugh, they loved and love each other, they showed me time and patience, provided stability and as much material comfort as they could — the bastards, how dare they ruin my chances of literary celebrity like that?

Didn't they care, didn't they know, didn't they realize what they were doing? I begged my Auntie Ethel for just a tincture of abuse, physical, emotional or sexual. Selfish woman, holding my hand, telling me sanguine stories with happy endings and buying me toys and chocolate, how could I have a chance? As to the grandparents, with their cuddles and devotion and smiles, they'll have a lot to answer for in the great New Vision Publishing House in the sky.

My sister was no better. She got married, had children, is employed, loves her husband, thinks life is quite a lot of fun. And she reads books with ethical and moral conclusions, thinks Dickens is more honest and pertinent than most of the living authors put together. Cow! Jesus, the woman should be incarcerated.

None of my friends dresses in black or cries in public, my children aren't deformed, and my wife is beautiful, talented and, I am so sorry, believes in God. I'm in deep excrement here. Come on, Mike, think, think.

What about homosexuality? It's no good, I'm also smitten with that plague of the would-be literati, I am not gay. God I've tried, but I just can't do it. I'm not a homosexual, I can't write a book of liberation about discovering my sexuality and coping with oppression, discrimination, prejudice. Worse than this, as a man I can't even pretend to be a lesbian. No purple passages about stolen kisses with teenage girlfriends from my private school — I didn't even get to private school! — or beach cuddles with my soul sister and gentle, gentle, oh so gentle hands speaking to my skin and charming my senses and sensibilities. It had never been like this with boys, never embraced the wildness and the sensual serenity of . . . and so on. So many Sapphic-experience novels now — where have all the hetero women gone, gone to magazine-writing every one.

What about a novel of colour? Well, the dust-jacket could be coloured, but the author is dangerously pink, fair-skinned even, red-haired, with some drops of Jewish blood but otherwise an imperialistic Celt, the deaths of millions daily on his conscience. Even the Jewish stuff is pretty useless these days. A minority out of fashion and out of favour, they've got their own country as well and have, rather annoyingly, refused to be slaughtered for half a century. Richler, Roth, Mailer, Bellow, Malamud, you are as dead and white and male as Rudyard Kipling.

So if my family wasn't dysfunctional and I'm white and straight, I'll have to settle for second best and splash about in a bit of dual-text fiction, some experimental prose, deconstructed neo-plagiarism, or even avant-garde, new-form writing so that my novel will appeal to award juries, grant committees and fashionable critics. "Yes, #th+66rrt. Yes Yes YES. Shakespeare's scrotum man. $*11=+#. Oh Yesss." You see, even with this I am too positive, too content with life. What's wrong with me, am I unhinged?

That's it. I am unhinged. Traditionally handicapped, culturally challenged. I even have the title. *Crazy Brit* — a novel of growing up smothered by orthodoxy and convention. "A biting indictment of fascism's influence on the education of white, heterosexual youth." (The *Village Voice*) There we are, a happy ending. Christ, a happy ending . . .

Eat My Launch

I have lost track of how many book launches I have attended. I am in my mid-thirties now and have been a part of the literary community, first in Britain and now in Canada, for around a decade. So we are into the hundreds. Hundreds of glasses of wine, hundreds of cardboard plates of cheese and fruit, hundreds of exchanges of courteous and perfunctory humbug. Nor am I a regular at these events, unlike some writers and literary journalists in Canada whose maxim appears to be "Now is the time for all good men and women to come to the aid of the launch party."

As a spectacle, book launches are unique in their peculiarities, their façades of interest, their rigid and regulated mores and moves.

Over in the corner, talking earnestly with the owner of the bookstore, who only opened the place on a cold Thursday evening because he was guaranteed extra sales and a mention in the "Noises Off" column of *The Globe and Mail*, is a dramatically embarrassed publicist. She is speculating why nobody has turned up from any of the major newspapers and why there are only seventeen people in the place. She wears a now well-rehearsed look on her face, as though she has just heard tragic news, perhaps of a death, over the telephone. She has employed it five times this month alone.

"I know there would have been a line fifty yards long if it hadn't been for the snow (Montreal)/ earthquake (Los Angeles)/ indifference (Toronto). And I just can't understand why Harbourfront, The Idler pub, the U.B.C. Bookshop all decided to host readings on the same evening as our launch. It's entirely their fault. I'm definitely going to talk to my publisher and I know he'll be very, very pissed off."

In the opposite corner is a knot — tight, coiled and unoriginal — of lugubrious young poets who write about the mystical sanctity of the clitoris and are published by White Nostril Press. They are competing in the playoffs for the "nonchalance and contempt for establishment success" competition. They discuss a figure holding court in the middle of the room.

"That talentless bastard over there has just got another bloody grant from the Canada Council. Sickening."

Talentless bastard approaches and holds out a hand in friendship.

"Hi, man, how are you? Loved the last column. And congrats on the grant, well deserved. Yeah, *mazel tov*."

And then there is the poor author. Was this such a good idea? Was the head of publicity correct when she said that launch parties don't sell books and that the money would probably be better spent on an advert or an airplane trip to other cities?

Perhaps. But she did admit, speaking in academic terms and thinking of other authors who were nothing like him at all, that launch parties do bolster the egos of notoriously insecure people.

The cynosure of the hour knows that some of his peers, other young novelists, spend hours, days, on the telephone inviting and then reinviting people to their launches. These tend to be the same people who are obsessive about blurbs, hunting down celebrity authors with the assiduity of a safari leader ordered to satisfy a royal visitor. "I've done it. I mean, I've really done it. Jonathan Tedious has not only agreed to give me a 'brilliant young writer, with promise aplenty' but has also agreed to come to my launch." His friend is cynical. "Darling, he comes to every launch. And he hasn't read a book in years."

But just as our Galahad in the authorial wilderness is wishing that he was indeed appearing somewhere in Halifax discussing the relevance of his book to the rape of the fishing industry, God rises from his slumber, smiles down on him and directs his heavenly flashlight towards the tower of unsold copies.

Lights. Lights. They are illuminating his efforts and his creative panache. He is transformed by the piercing exposure of television. Yessssssss. It has all been worthwhile. Quickly he evinces apathy. TV is a sell-out, he'd rather have an extract in *Why* magazine or the *Onanism Review.* Honestly. Still, the cameras are here so he might as well do the interview. "Relax, honey," from one of those annoying poets, who have scattered like a bunch of mall rats being approached by a security guard, and now buzz around the floor babbling at anything that moves. "It's Cable 10 doing a piece about the owner of the bookstore. Apparently he has an interesting collection of hockey memorabilia."

So it ends. Really enjoyed it . . . See you at mine . . . I don't think reviews matter anyway . . . Are you going to Banff? And the author moves gradually towards his publicist and asks ever so quietly, "I didn't sign too many copies, did I?" No, dear, not at all. Not at all.

Hints on Self-Defence

The Arthur Markham Memorial Prize is a British literary award — it could originate from no other nation on Earth — and may be won by manual workers who have spent their employment in or around a coal mine, or have been injured when so labouring. The shortlist of candidates is very short indeed.

Soft of hand and soft of belly, I have never been considered even as an outside possibility.

Those qualified to deliver the annual Chesterton Lecture in London seldom have experience of the mining industry, but they are similarly select and few in quantity. The happy band numbers biographers of G. K. C., media celebrities who have shown an interest in Chesterton and the Chestertonians, and, some four years ago, a cabinet minister and prime ministerial contender with a fine set of first editions — the investment initiative qualifying him as a Thatcherite, the artistic content proving his scholarly credentials. These people are invariably even softer of belly than I; hence my invitation to be the man of 1990.

Westminster Cathedral is, like so many things English, not quite what it seems. The epicentre of British Catholicism may appear to be soaked in mediaeval prayer, but it first saw the light of stained glass during the last century. Its conference centre, where Chesterton lectures take place, also boasts the occasional façade. At 7:00 on an August evening the assembled crowd consisted of tweeded dons, collared priests, interested intelligentsia and five young men with cropped hair and bellicose tattoos, wearing Doctor Martin boots, bomber jackets, cross of Saint George badges and the grimace of lads who would not feel overly comfortable participating in a Forest Hill seder.

"I've been out of the country for a year or two," I tentatively explained to my blithe chairman, "but surely the large types in black aren't typical Chestertonians?"

A pause. "Actually, I think they're the North London branch of the society," said my host.

My concern transformed into worry, tinged with fear. Could it be the paradoxical nuances of Chestertonian prose that had attracted these young Fascists, or was it that the subject of my talk was "Chesterton & Anti-Semitism"?

I eyed the heavy decanter to my left, calling to mind the chapter in *Self-Defence for the Intellectual* on glassware and drinking vessels. Scanning the room for potential allies in this possible conflict with the sons of the Axis, I experienced a disturbing ache in my stomach; or was it lower down in my anatomy? The octogenarian Monsignor in the corner had been a handy rugby player at Cambridge, but was no pugilist today; the pro-life zealot in the third row had not even a placard to hurl in my defence, and the Oxford Professor of Anglo-Saxon had not raised a limb in anger since he lost two of them to a crazed combine harvester in Norfolk. How long, I pondered, would it take the boys in blue to make it to the building, run through the doors and rescue democracy, public speaking and the British way of life? About twice as long, came the answer, as it would take the Mosley boys to sever one of my more important arteries with a razor or broken bottle. A stiff upper lip is all very well; it tends to lead, however, to a fat one.

The contents of the talk are largely immaterial. A defence of Chesterton: friend of the Jews when it mattered . . . many intimate Jewish friends . . . passionate anti-Nazi . . . mourned by Jewish leaders after his death. Rounds of applause, perhaps not perfunctory. Gratitude of chairman. Questions. Baby Himmler, biceps distending his "Blood and Race" tattoo to enormous proportions, stands up to ask the first question.

"Ah. If, like Chesterton would 'ave lived till na-ow, what would he 'ave fort of the Jewish conspiracy?" he inquires, his accent a poisonous hybrid of base cockney and a vain attempt at oratory — doubtless learnt from *Teach Yourself Goebbels* (New Phoenix Press, Alabama, $25.95. Mail Order Only).

The black-shirted clod continues: "Like, Jewish terrorists killin' British soldiers in Palestine, the Zionist control of the media, Israel suckin' the weld inta anuvver war, ya know."

Indeed I did. Know, that is, his meaning and the aetiology of his bigotry. A long, long — wish it could be longer — glass of water.

"You are absolutely correct my friend. More than this, the World Jewish Conspiracy not only exists, it is conducting a meeting this very evening. Further, it is taking place in the McDonald's across the road, and if we hurry over there, en masse, we might just catch the buggers plotting another economic depression."

Laughter. Laughter. More laughter. Hands clap and voices of joyous sanity shout "Hear, hear." I smile, nervously; and await the response of the political ghosts from North London. They blush, but do not move. The decanter is still within reach, and that aged Roman priest may at a pinch be capable of rabbit-punching Heinrich; the Oxford professor possesses power in that electronic wheel-chair — will he use it for good? And then . . . nothing happens. More questions, gentle banter and no further comments from the lad with the twenty-inch neck. I am still, of course, warmly wrapped in the cloak of a public meeting. What about when the assembly disperses? Inevitably, it does. The gang rises, as one muddy scrum; the light, in deference, fades. They approach. They reach out their hands.

"We bort your book. Will ya sign it?"

Never have I attached my signature to a volume of my prose with such relish and euphoria. Is the pen mightier than the sword? Of course not. The blackjack is good, the baseball bat is better and the decanter best of all.

Ain't We Got Funds

There are few spectacles as repugnant and, ultimately, pointless as cultural or political polarization. Such extreme division is usually formed by two ignorant and splenetic solitudes sustained by a refusal to realize and accept that there is a middle, moderate and correct path. A perfect example of this is the debate over state funding of the arts, and of literature in particular. The issue is in focus once again, with both sets of champions polishing their rusty swords.

The literary critic John Metcalf's heavy-handed and notorious condemnation of grants and grant-supported writing has reappeared in *Freedom from Culture* (ECW), a collection of his work. Metcalf is supported by those quixotic advocates of the free market's invisible hand, whose knowledge of economics is dwarfed only by their ignorance of the arts.

Opposing this position we have the CBC-friendly defenders of the status quo, seemingly determined to subsidize even a sneeze or a cough from the writers of *This Magazine* or the authors at McClelland & Stewart as long as these involuntary expirations are in the interest of Canadian nationalism. Such people have a great deal for which to answer.

Between these positions lies something both horribly dull and undeniably glorious: a balanced, intelligent financial support for potential or inchoate excellence, and even a little helping along of a few gutsy mediocrities. If Canadian letters are to continue to enjoy the benefits of state support there must be a judicious reform of the funding process.

First, we cannot continue to pour money into hopeless causes. If the government continued to support an industry that was a perennial loss-maker there would be a massive outcry. Similarly, authors who fail to produce viable pieces of work for which they were given grants should not receive any further grants. There are a number of such writers, who specialize in applying for money for projects that will never come to fruition; projects that they had no intention of completing, or in some cases of even starting.

Second, in line with the above, we have to be more selective in whom we support. Funds are severely limited. A friend of mine, a respected and talented author who is partly in the grant-giving business, told me that "some of the people we help are literally unsure where the next meal is coming from." I am sorry for them. But not very. If they have been in this position for some years it should have occurred to them by now that they are in the wrong profession. A young poet with ambitions is allowed to starve with romantic dignity; a middle-aged novelist with children and responsibilities really ought to know better.

Third, we should consider the idea of a payback scheme. If writers make sufficient money from a book for which they received government support, they should perhaps repay the grant-giving body, which in turn could help another struggling author.

Fourth, all juries should be blind. That is, not appallingly myopic, but unaware of the names of those applying for financial support, as currently occurs in only one major grant contest at either the Ontario Arts Council or Canada Council. This would prevent most of the subconscious or deliberate corruptions that occur at the moment. Examples are legion.

Fifth, we must wash from us the stains of politically correct jaundice and judge applications according to their merit. There is now an almost tangible degree of bitterness felt by many writers who do not belong to officially identified "minority groups" at what they see as the impossibility of their receiving major grants when they are competing in a system that discriminates against them. If we analyse the list of those receiving writing grants at a federal, provincial and municipal level this anger does seem to be justified. A writing career curtailed due to lack of money is just as dreadful for a white writer as it is for a Native or black author.

In conclusion, grant-giving agencies, liberal grandees and radical interest groups can fiddle while Ottawa burns if they like and reject my views out of hand. But they ought to know that the dictates of the economy and the rise of the Reform Party will necessitate fundamental changes in the near future. My proposals are merely cosmetic in comparison to what may be looming on the horizon.

Oh, and I know you're asking. Yes, I've done fairly well from grants. And always completed the projects for which I have received support. If I ever become wealthy I will, of course, refrain from applying for further financing. Mind you, even now, for some strange reason, some left-leaning juries appear less generous towards me than in times past. Extraordinary. See point four.

Hypocritical Fundraiser for Freedom of Speech

In early 1995, 1,200 Canadian writers and their friends gathered together for a fund-raising concert for PEN, an organization supposedly committed to literary freedom. They managed to raise more than $100,000. Various authors took to the stage to read works about liberty, tolerance and truth. They heard about imprisoned writers and particularly about one, the Nigerian author Ken Saro-Wiwa, and how he had been arrested for publishing material displeasing to the status quo.

One of the entertainers fighting the good fight for freedom of expression was Mary Walsh from *This Hour Has 22 Minutes.* Walsh is a tax-funded performer in that she earns her living from the CBC and hence through the largesse of the Canadian public.

She thought it amusing to announce to the crowd that "some writers ought to be in prison, don't you think?" She then suggested one particular taxpayer, the author and columnist David Frum, as the main candidate. At which the full-fed princes of the literary ruling class laughed, cheered, applauded and showed their vociferous approval. If there was dissent, it was not heard.

Now Frum needs help from nobody in defending himself. He is also, I must stress, a friend of mine. But these two factors are immaterial. What occurred at the PEN benefit was a sickening example of dishonesty and cannot be allowed to stand unchallenged.

Frum's conservatism is unpopular with some members of the chattering classes, people who make up the intellectual establishment in Canada. Fair enough, and I am sure Frum does not write love poetry about them either. It should end there, and in intelligent and healthy debate. But no. Frum holds a certain philosophy about, for example, the free market, arts subsidies and the positive influence of the U.S., hence it is permissible to make wisecracks about putting him in prison for his views. I'm sorry, I just don't get the joke. I do, however, get the sheer hypocrisy and lack of logical thought.

The chatterers evidently do not realize that many of the persecuted writers for whom they cry their public tears are similarly unpopular with the literary power blocs in their own countries. Perhaps a Nigerian, funnier version of Mary Walsh stands up on an African stage and makes jokes about Ken Saro-Wiwa. I hope not. Good God I hope not.

Freedom of speech is not about tolerating friendly views but about allowing the coexistence of opinions with which you fundamentally disagree.

Liking friends is easy; respecting enemies is harder — and it is the latter that defines us as either civilized democrats or clumsy authoritarians. This was not merely a comedienne making a joke. This was a rally, a nasty and infectious rash of mass histrionics and support for censorship. I used to be a member of PEN and I used to be a member of The Writers' Union of Canada but I will not re-join either until I am convinced these organizations are committed to the well-being of all writers, irrespective of their political persuasion. In 1994 I hosted the biography section of the Harbourfront Authors' Festival and I began every session by pointing to an empty chair, and explaining that in a perfect world it would have been filled by the incarcerated writers of the world.

The difference between the left and the conservative right is that the former believe only "some" people should be locked up for their views, the latter believe that nobody should be thus treated.

Voltaire's comment on the subject is still the definitive treatment of the issue. "I disapprove of what you say, but I will defend to the death your right to say it." Not "I hate your politics and I'll beat the life out of you if I get the chance." But then Voltaire was not a member of PEN Canada. Grants and literary prizes all round please, all paid for by people, well, people just like David Frum.

Do Salman Rushdie a Favour and Give Him Some Bad Reviews

Salman Rushdie's *East, West* is reasonably good. Many reviews claim that it is startlingly brilliant, and Canadian critics in particular hail it as a masterpiece. This is ridiculous.

Within the field of literary appreciation there is enormous room for subjectivity and individual perception, but there are also certain objective standards of excellence. Again, this is no masterpiece, and the reception of the thin, surprisingly meagre collection of short stories is indicative of Salman Rushdie's predicament. Rushdie is a prisoner not so much of the *fatwa* levelled against him by the Ayatollah Khomeini more than six years ago, but of the way the event has changed our understanding of the man. No critic can review him honestly, nobody can even discuss his work, without submerging himself in what made this man the most famous writer on earth. Salman Rushdie is no longer an author, he is a cause.

To his credit Rushdie is the first to lament this state of affairs. When we spoke shortly after the publication of *East, West* he was bleakly philosophical. "Most famous writer in the world? Well, it just goes to show that being famous isn't all it's cracked up to be. I'd settle for being a much less famous writer and being able to walk down the street. There were one or two reviews in England that said, 'Gosh, isn't it amazing that he writes anything at all?' Do me a favour, I thought, and spare me this form of patronizing; read what's on the page and just tell me if you like it."

It is now impossible to discuss Rushdie and his work with any sense of balance. More than this, we no longer discuss the cause either. Certainly writers should not be threatened for what they write and freedom of speech is a cornerstone of any democracy. But there are many authors who will explain off the record that Rushdie is to the battle for literary freedom what AIDS fundraising is to charity. That is, one issue becomes so fashionable and so predominant that other deserving causes are neglected. There are countless authors and journalists from Third World countries who are incarcerated in real prisons, beaten, tortured and murdered. Some would say that Rushdie illuminates their plight, others that he obscures it. He himself has had enough of the entire debate.

"I know that some people are very hostile to me, but there's nothing much I can do about it except to know why I think what I think, why I did what I did, and why I'd do it again." A pause. "Really, no really. I'm getting on with being a writer and to hell with everything else. I have no regrets about the novel I wrote and frankly I'm no longer interested in getting into those discussions. I don't care a button, I don't care a fig, as Edward Lear would say."

But Lear wrote about owls and pussycats and Rushdie wrote nasty things about the founder of a world religion.

Rushdie has tried to establish a compromise with his Islamic opponents, and even reverted to the religion of his birth in a well-publicized but ultimately fruitless attempt to alleviate the situation. He is less willing to compromise now, more strident.

"There were a lot of people who seemed to be willing to become fellow travellers of this kind of censorship in the name of some spurious definition of community values. It's sort of stopped. People have lost interest. The political establishment doesn't seem to have much interest in this case any more."

He reflects for a moment. "Look, *Satanic Verses* was published over six years ago, I started writing it over eleven years ago, when I first thought about it was twelve or fourteen years ago. For me now to be asked to discuss and justify artistic choices that were made in my mid-thirties, when I'm approaching fifty, is just peculiar because I don't remember. I have no idea what the day-to-day creative choices were. It becomes a kind of fiction when I talk about it, I have to make it up. So there. It's an old book, here's a nice new one, and there will be another one along in a minute."

I am being gently criticized for prying. But it has to be said again: all that Rushdie has become, every way that he is perceived, is the result of the *fatwa. Midnight's Children* was a superlative book, *Shame* was a most impressive work, but a new generation of readers and writers has established a different Year One for Rushdie, and it is the year of *The Satanic Verses*, Iran, ayatollahs and hiding.

Thankfully, he is doing less of the latter than ever before, meeting friends in England and going out. "I'm no longer living in a box," he says, "I do recapture elements of everyday life, being around, going out. These are in ways I can't discuss, you understand. But one doesn't have to cower. I want to be a writer, to be funny and scatological and irreverent. I was proud to have carried the banner of certain principles, but no longer. I don't want to be a great abstract figure. I'm a person."

Rushdie did some of this "being around, going out" in Canada in 1992, when he appeared at a PEN benefit in Toronto. When he came on stage the audience was genuinely shocked, delighted, incredulous. It was a special moment. Rushdie remembers it even now as being particularly significant. "It had an enormous emotional impact on me. The degree of affection and sympathy was unforgettable. Nourishing, moving. It meant a great deal."

After this event it became fashionable to wear "I am Salman Rushdie" badges. I wonder how many of these people, however, could also have qualified to wear "I've Read The Satanic Verses" or "I've Actually Spoken to an Insulted Muslim" badges. We would also do well to consider just how committed are the literary politicians of this country. When the Canadian university professor Philippe Rushton published an academic text concerned with race and intelligence he was censured, threatened with professional persecution and, yes, with death. Some found his views to be emetic. Fine. Some, evidently, find Salman Rushdie's opinions to be equally vile and are prepared to kill him. Is the core of literary freedom about the individual issue or about the greater principle? And would all those PEN activists who defend Salman Rushdie have stood up for a professor from Ontario whose writings are less comforting to the contemporary liberal mind-set?

Rushdie's time in Canada demonstrated the dilemma of his fame and the dichotomy between the personae of international martyr and working author. Necessary though the visit was, the possessiveness evinced by some people towards Rushdie was absurd. This wretched man became a victim of territoriality. One prominent literary journalist recalls trying to arrange an interview with Rushdie when Adrienne Clarkson was minding him in Ottawa. Forget the RCMP, the Special Air Service and the CIA, nobody was going to take him away from that good lady, even if it was for his own good.

"People have got to stop reading my work as a message in a bottle. It takes a long time to get out of a pit like this, I suppose," he explains. Long pause. "Look, I'm not trying to say that what has happened hasn't had an effect but I'm not all that clear what that is. It's not linear, not clear. Maybe readers can tell, I'm just doing the stuff. I keep a diary, have been throughout this time. I didn't in the past unless it was a particularly important time like a special journey. But with this, with this thing, it was so complex, moving at such a speed, had so many different aspects to it — well, just the day-to-day aspects were so interesting and peculiar and unforeseeable that I needed to write them down or I'd forget them. One day it will be published in a more literate form. I'd like to tell this story. If as a writer you have the misfortune to develop an interesting life you have to write about it. But before I write it the story needs to be over, no secrets any more. There are still things I can't talk about, things that are not known, and I'd like to take the lid off. Can't do that until there's no longer any problem. You know, most of all I'd like to thank those people who've remained loyal."

Rushdie has to realize, though, and perhaps already has, that the normal life is as lost as Mohammed's magnificent green cloak. Moreover, we can attempt to restore some sense of normality only when commentators and critics can do their job properly. When *The New York Times* or *The Globe and Mail* can give Rushdie less than the lead review, honour him with less than hyperbolic praise, even say that the emperor is sometimes completely bloody naked, Rushdie will be a much freer man. He remembers the journalist Christopher Hitchens telling a story of a British trade-union leader replying to a piece of irksome government legislation. He said that he was responding to it with a "complete ignoral."

"This is now my position towards the *fatwa*," says Rushdie. "I'm treating it with complete and utter ignoral, with the ignoral it deserves." Interesting. He really should tell his friends.

The Colony Strikes Back

Whenever I fly to London from Toronto I reflect on those original settlers who made the contrary journey, by ship and with ideas of empire in mind. There is no doubt that colonialism is indeed an egregious thing and that Canada, and its arts community, is still suffering as a result of British ravages. I am making this particular journey for the launch of my book, a biography of H. G. Wells. The British author was helped enormously, ironically enough, by a Canadian, Lord Beaverbrook; yet a biography of the owner of Express Newspapers dismisses his Canadian origins with a contemptuous and insulting alacrity. How typical and how sad.

My contemplations about this fact are broken by a flight attendant who kindly offers me a British Sunday newspaper to read. I accept two. The *Observer* is in good form, particularly its columnist Michael Ignatieff, who spearheads the publication's opinion pages. The elegant and eloquent scion of the great Canadian diplomatic family waxes lyrical about matters of British interest. The *Observer* done with, I set about the *Sunday Times*. Interesting. Particularly a coruscating and provocative column by Barbara Amiel, where this highly intelligent journalist advises Prime Minister John Major on how best to salvage the British economy.

When I disembark at Heathrow airport I make straight for my old haunts in London and visit some friends in Covent Garden. The flight is beginning to have an effect, however, and I need a drink. The nearest pub is in Maiden Lane, an inviting venue known as the Maple Leaf. Hockey sticks, Edmonton Oilers shirts and Canadian provincial flags adorn the walls and on a large television screen an episode of TVOntario's "Imprint" is being aired. This is all a little too much, and I take a taxi to my parents' house, picking up the magazine on the seat next to me. It is the *Spectator*, bursting with its usual eclectic jumble of witty essays and stylish reviews. It is owned, of course, by one Conrad Black, and this issue features a thrusting article about Canada and Black himself by John Ralston Saul.

The family home at last. A cup of tea, an armchair and British television — still the best in the world. Michael Ignatieff again, this time on "The Late Show," an arts program featuring in-depth discussion and intellectual jousting. Ignatieff announces that a forthcoming episode will include a feature about Margaret Atwood. On another station is Mordecai Richler holding forth about Quebec, Canada and anti-Semitism. And so to bed, with a much-read copy of *Joshua Then and Now* that was on top of a heap of books in the spare room.

A new day. Lunch with my editors at Bloomsbury Publishing, one of the busiest and most accomplished publishing houses in Britain. Across the quintessentially Londonesque Soho Square and into the offices of the company. An enormous poster of Michael Ondaatje stares down at me from the wall and newspaper cuttings interviewing "The Canadian

Booker Prize winner" cover the doors of the building like some extraordinarily literate wallpaper. Juxtaposed with the Ondaatje material is an advertising picture of Barbara Gowdy and a few copies of a literary compilation published by Bloomsbury and named after its location, Soho Square. It is edited by Alberto Manguel and boasts articles by Robert Fulford, Marq de Villiers, Timothy Findley, Jane Urquhart and Ronald Wright, among others. Bloomsbury's publicist informs me that with any luck the busy and increasingly influential Noah Richler will do something on my book for BBC Radio.

Lunch. A good meal, a passable bottle of wine and a newspaper. I opt for the *Daily Telegraph*. This is one of the success stories of British journalism in recent years. It is owned by, well, Conrad Black. The ambience of the restaurant is slightly soiled by the television being on. Only four channels in Britain but a fifth is on the way. One of the people in control of the new station looks certain to be Moses Znaimer. There is also a feature about the Canadian entrepreneur who owns Toronto's City TV in that day's newspaper.

My final task in promoting my book. A discussion about literature in Kensington Library. A middle-aged, middle-class lady asks in suburban tones whether I have "ever met Robertson Davies?" I confess, to my chagrin, that I have not.

Back to Canada, to Toronto, to my office. A friend telephones and confides that a CBC-Radio producer has reservations about me. I am, he advises, simply too British. Only in Canada, you say? Pity.

The Media

The media themselves are the avant-garde of our society. Avant-garde no longer exists in painting and music and poetry, it's the media themselves.

Marshall McLuhan, 1973

Debatable Propositions

An extremely interesting letter appeared in a recent edition of *The Toronto Star*'s television magazine. A certain Ken Baker wrote that he was most upset with what he perceived as the CFTO journalist and commentator Mike Duffy's "anti-immigrant bias."

We are all, one assumes, still entitled to our opinion and the truth or falsity of this accusation is not the point here. What is significant is the manner in which Mr. Baker continued. "I was discussing this with my friends recently and we've had it," he wrote. "From now on, our families will boycott any product advertised during the 6:00 newscast until Duffy is removed."

The specifics of this attack are important and indicative of a worrying attitude towards literary and journalistic expression. This man was not saying that he would no longer watch Mike Duffy — on the contrary, he would make sure that he always watched so that he and his comrades could assemble their boycott list — or that he would refrain from watching other CTV shows as a form of protest. Nor did he refer to specific comments from Duffy or give examples of this alleged bias. What Mr. Baker did promise was to do his meagre bit to damage the revenue of companies and individuals advertising with CFTO at a specific time, hoping that they would decide to divert their advertising dollars elsewhere. So Mr. Baker was trying to punish independent business people, in the hope that CTV would be angered or hurt by this and thus reprimand, censor or fire Mike Duffy. That the boycott will have no great effect is immaterial. It is the intent that says everything. It shouts it, screams it. It is a jarring, awful noise.

This is yet another example of how too many Canadians believe that they can control opinions that they find distasteful or merely contrary to their own political positions. Rush Limbaugh's show was removed from Canadian television because fewer than 300 people complained about it and accused it of "homophobia." Yet hundreds of thousands of Canadians were registering their approval of the show by watching it, and not in prime time but well after midnight. Limbaugh was breaking no law, moral or civil, and those who did not like his views were not being pressured into staying up till the early hours of the morning so as to be provoked. It was almost most unlikely that any children would have been watching and, anyway, Limbaugh is no Power Ranger. Yet a handful of zealots and bigots had their way. Powerful television executives submitted to tiny, vocal special-interest groups, leading one to ask where the real owner in Canadian society lies.

Nobody is going to take Mike Duffy off the air, because he is an experienced and gifted journalist with a faithful audience. But if the target of this smear campaign had been a junior reporter in the early stages of his career, a Ken Baker, or a few friends of a Ken Baker, might well have had an effect. How regrettable, and how dangerous, that we have allowed the country to get into this frame of mind, where attempts to stifle debate are considered acceptable and feasible.

It happens at every level and in every manifestation of the media. There are no-go areas in publishing, subjects that are considered unacceptable amongst respectable literary people. What nonsense. In addition to writing a column for *Books in Canada* I used to be a columnist at *The Globe and Mail.* On one occasion, one of my articles did not appear because a journalist from a separate department of the newspaper, a senior editor, initiated a petition against me. Only five people signed it, but with most of the senior staff absent an acting editor went along with the protesters and dropped the column. If journalists, people who are meant to be committed to notions of freedom of thought and word, would rather prevent contrary speech than engage in intelligent debate, we are in a dire situation.

Instead of engaging in argument, even heated or at times a little acrimonious, we try to incarcerate the mind, the thoughts and the speech of those with whom we disagree. And like it or not — and please don't dig up some frenzied fundamentalist who wants to ban half of the contents of the local library — it is not the right that usually does this but rather the left, those very same people who would be the first to demand government boycotts against nations where there is no "freedom of speech."

It's rather like being a little bit pregnant. We either believe in freedom of speech or we don't. There are laws prohibiting incitement to violence and racial hatred, so we are protected against the outer borders of lunacy, and of course we must never forget the difference between freedom and licence. But every day we see the edges of the intellectual and political envelope reduced and curtailed — if we are not careful there won't even be any room left for the address.

Facing Off with the Media

Last week I spoke to the Reform Party conference in Ottawa on the question of media objectivity. I am not a member of the Reform Party, nor have I ever voted for it. This was a paid speech, something I do for numerous organizations, discussing many journalistic subjects. Unlike some columnists, I have no party allegiance. Yet a handful of media friends wondered if I was somehow tinging my neutrality. Would you really ask that, I replied, if I were speaking on such a theme to the New Democrats or one of the myriad left-of-centre groups in this country?

I spoke to the Reformers about various cases of the media being unfair to conservative causes. I mentioned, for example, a recent episode of the CBC Newsworld show *Face Off*, where the producers had wanted a debate between Svend Robinson and Judy Anderson, former president of REAL Women, on the subject of sexuality and the law. Anderson agreed, but Robinson refused to appear on television with her. Instead of telling Robinson that they could not be blackmailed, the producers cancelled Anderson. They then changed the show's structure, eliminated the usual format of two guests and instead held a debate between guest Robinson and co-host Claire Hoy, with Hoy's fellow host and combatant Judy Rebick acting as moderator. Extraordinary. This has never happened in the history of *Face Off*'s U.S. elder sibling and inspiration, *Cross Fire*.

I explained to the Reformers that this was crass media manipulation and another act of marginalization — where anti-conservatives push their opponents out of the media loop. It is instructive to note, I concluded, that before she became a television host the same Judy Rebick had in the past refused to appear on air with the same Judy Anderson. But I was also sanguine in my speech. I argued that the majority of journalists are simply doing their jobs to the best of their abilities and have no political axe to grind. Reformers, I stressed, are entitled not to positive coverage but to fair coverage. It is not as bad as it all seems. And then I came home and read the newspapers.

On the Sunday of the conference *The Toronto Star* ran a large photograph of an aged Reform delegate with his shirt gaping open at the neck, sleeves rolled up and suspenders distended. He was bald and was called Werner Greitz. Behind him was an enormous television screen provided so that the 2,000 people at the conference could see the rostrum speakers. In the *Star* picture, a Reform official appeared in shadowy image on this screen. The caption beneath the photograph began with "Big Brother." Let us be direct. Surely this delegate was chosen from so many others in Ottawa because of his bellicose and working-class appearance and his Teutonic name; and surely the term Big Brother was used because it is pejorative and conjures up an Orwellian nightmare.

Monday's coverage by the *Star*'s Rosemary Speirs explained that the "delegates in vote after vote had moved their party even further to the fundamentalist right." Now even allowing for the recent drop in standards of education and in the use of English, surely a working journalist knows that the unqualified noun or adjective "fundamentalist" has no meaning. Fundamentalist what? There is no such thing as the fundamentalist right because the right is profoundly disparate and divided and, by its very nature, has no fundamental and literal truths to which one may adhere. The word was used because it raises grotesque images of suicide bombs and foreign, alien extremism. Well played, Rosemary.

Other journalists wrote of this apparent move to the right. Yet on the three central issues of the abolition of the Charter of Rights, control of trade unions and the "three strikes and out" policy towards serious crime, the convention moved to the centre and not to the right at all. Canadian Press was still concerned. "What's not clear is how the Reform leader will expand public support after four days of passing policy resolutions that push his party further right." A strange conclusion.

Reform is the fastest-growing party on the continent, and while the centrist Conservatives and the left-wing NDP struggle for federal existence, surveys reveal that Preston Manning's party is remaining steady or increasing strength in almost every area. Perhaps all of their supporters voted Reform in the first place on the misunderstanding that the party isn't actually right-wing at all. And all Canadians are, naturally, liberals or social democrats.

Canadian Press did reveal signs of hope in what it described as "dissidents" in the party, who opposed the leadership. Dissidents? Perhaps these struggling fighters could join up with their "fundamentalist" enemies and stage a re-creation for charity of the siege of Beirut. If they had the stamina. As *The Toronto Star* explained, "most of the delegates" were "middle-aged or older." Unlike all of those youngsters at the other political conferences.

The odd thing is that I spoke to a great many students, young people, working mothers, teachers and former members of other parties who were looking for change. Dissidents all, I suppose, hiding from Big Brother as they move indefatigably to the right and towards inevitable failure and obscurity. So very sad.

AIDS-Day Reports Dodged the Truth

It was undoubtedly moving, as any listing of the dead must be. I write of what occurred in the arts sections of many of Canada's larger newspapers on World AIDS Day. A great deal of space, sometimes pages, was devoted to poignant rollcalls of artists who have died of AIDS. "Imagine: A Day Without Art" pondered *The Toronto Star* on the front of its arts section, adorned with a twenty-centimetre-high red AIDS ribbon. "The names say it all: 128 Canadian artists whose hands and hearts are now silent."

The Globe and Mail wrote that few groups have been as hard hit by HIV — the virus that leads to AIDS — as the artists of the world, "dancers, painters, photographers, musicians, actors, designers, writers." All of this is irrefutable and all of it undeniably sad on more than the obvious level. Because it represents a gross oversight, in the shape of a redundant euphemism. What binds these people who have died of AIDS is not only their contributions to the arts but, for the overwhelming majority, their sexuality. They are homosexuals. And many of them — though not, it would seem, Canada's editors and journalists — would have wanted us to know it.

Which poses the question of why hardly any mainstream arts publication refers to this fundamentally important aspect of the tragedy in their coverage of the AIDS crisis. It is not, of course, that these highly informed media people are unaware of the fact, it is not that they assume that readers already know of it (restating truths is, anyway, part of the job of journalism) and it is not, surely, that they believe that sexual inclination is irrelevant. If it were the latter, it would be a contradiction of all of the efforts and gains made by the gay community since the 1960s.

No, the answer lies in well-meaning liberalism and in straightforward obfuscation. We have been told interminably by expensive government advertising campaigns, by health activists and by news organizations that AIDS is not confined to one group and can kill anybody. This is certainly true. But the reality of the situation in North America and Europe is that the only community AIDS has devastated is that composed of gay men. The consequences are clear. Because of the cultural fecundity of so many male homosexuals and because of their quantitative and qualitative triumph in the arts, that field has been dented as never before. There are no listings of deceased businessmen in the business sections, no scrolls of dead sportsmen in the sports sections of our newspapers on World AIDS Day. A basic truth, axiomatic to the honest and also something that should involve a bitter pride; one group doing so much to help create certain elements of an artistic culture.

This pointless game of hide-and-seek is conducted because of a fear that AIDS funding or sympathy might be reduced if the virus is associated with homosexuality. There exists an understandable dread of marginalization, of being stereotyped or caricatured. But it is the duty of journalism to report the truth, not to pursue a particular cause or try patronizingly to understand what a specific community might desire.

Here we should think on the recent *Vanity Fair* article about the new cultural establishment in the United States. The piece managed to discuss a group of immensely talented and powerful people in great detail, without once mentioning that most of them were Jewish. In Britain the *Spectator* did point this out, albeit in a callow and somewhat offensive way, and was immediately denounced as anti-Semitic.

Vanity Fair as well as the *Spectator* were wrong. The former seemed unaware of the paradox of its coverage, typical of the reporting of minorities that has evolved in the past twenty years and one that stresses sameness rather than differences. Those Jewish directors, producers and writers in the article have not succeeded because they are Jews, but their Jewishness has done much to make them what they are. It is not, or should not be, a matter of shame or of disguise but of profound satisfaction. Yet far too often the oppressed are shaped by their enemies, those who would have them be quiet and go unrecognized. The tragedy of Jewry is that too often they, we, are defined by the anti-Semite, and even in how supposed friends write about Jewish issues and Jewish people.

Vanity Fair thought that it might offend its subjects if it mentioned their religion, yet religion and race as well as sexuality are foundations of being and no person can be properly understood without due reference to them. Arts reporters on the newspapers of Canada believe, at best, that mentioning the homosexuality of the artists who have died of AIDS might cause grief to the victims' memories, their relatives or the greater public. This is doubtful and, though purportedly benign, it is not at all noble. The truth comes first. If not, it dies first. But then the truth, just like individuals, can also be shaped by its opponents.

Media Coverage of Gay Rights Unfairly One-Sided

Let us temporarily put aside the actual issues concerning the recent Supreme Court decision about homosexual couples and instead concentrate on the media coverage of that ruling. The highest legal entity in Canada has maintained the established definition of marriage.

Last year a similar statement was made by the Ontario legislature when it rejected Bill 167. So both the democratically manifested voice of the people of a province and the law of the land have spoken.

But there is another estate of government in Canada. Immediately after the Supreme Court declared its decision, the media began their work as a less than loyal opposition. Lawyers, politicians, church leaders and ordinary Canadians who applauded the ruling were virtually ignored as the rollcall of interviews with anguished homosexuals began to be aired and printed. We were told of the sheer cruelty of the majority, those wretched people who simply refuse to understand that things have to change, whether they like it or not.

On the Saturday following the decision, *The Globe and Mail* published a one-and-a-half-page story. Two large photographs of smiling homosexual couples — one male and one female — dominated an inside page while the front of the newspaper was headed by a picture of a wedding ring being exchanged by two hands: both attached, one assumes, to nurturing and enlightened same-sex bodies as the caption beneath read, "Vowing to change the traditional family." A photograph of a Canadian soldier chained to an ammunition dump in Bosnia as a hostage against NATO airstrikes was half the size. We do not know his views on homosexual marriage.

The paper argued that when "an Ontario judge granted four lesbian women court orders to adopt children born by their partners, there was no public outcry" and quoted a lawyer as saying, "If the politicians said Ontario wasn't ready for this, where is the backlash? There were no demonstrations in the streets."

This is rather like an old Soviet diplomat assuring us that the Russian people were happy because they did not write letters of discontent to the editor of *Pravda.* The media have led a concerted campaign to isolate and marginalize opponents of radical social reform, painting them as ignorant bumpkins and tossing the meaningless term "homophobic" at anyone who disagrees with legislation concerning the group rights of homosexuals. It then wonders why more people do not make a "public outcry." Would the media be balanced and respectful? The question is rhetorical, the answer is tragic.

The Vancouver *Sun* covered the story by interviewing the couple who had tried to change the law, Jack Nesbit and Jim Egan, a homosexual United Church minister and the executive director of Equality for Gays and Lesbians Everywhere.

"When the couple heard the news from their lawyer," wrote reporter Neal Hall, "Nesbit suffered three angina attacks from the stress." Still able to speak to the press at some length, however, Nesbit explained, "I think when the media leave, we'll both have a good cry." He could be dry-eyed for some time. As to the *Sun*'s lack of interviews with supporters of the Supreme Court decision, that *was* enough to make you weep.

I hosted a two-hour long radio show on Toronto's CFRB, the largest private station in Canada, following the Ontario ruling on lesbian adoption, and almost every caller told me they opposed the decision but felt that their views were not being represented in the public arena. They believed that the traditional family was being forced into a corner it could not defend without being given some of the weapons possessed by its enemies.

The media coverage of this case represented an unbridled attempt to influence public feeling about a ruling for which some journalists felt contempt. The view of one homosexual lawyer that "we have to be saved from the majority, from mob rule" has been accepted by many newspapers and, it would seem, by the CBC. It should not surprise us. When Ontario's Bill 167 was defeated, demonstrators at Queen's Park screamed "Shame, shame, shame." One radio reporter opined that the bill's defeat was "indeed shameful." Her comment and the antics of the ill-informed and jaundiced Canadian media have been worse than shameful. They have been hateful of the Canadian people.

Liberal Media Unfairly Trash Conservative Opinions

Last Saturday, *The Globe and Mail* devoted the cover of its television magazine to American commentator Rush Limbaugh. The article within was written by Shirley Knott, who made her detestation of her subject extremely clear from the beginning of what was supposed to be, I can only assume, a balanced review of a soon-to-be-aired PBS show entitled *Rush Limbaugh's America.*

In the pristine tradition of Woodward and Bernstein and the bravest and best frontline war reporters, Knott told us, "Make no mistake, Limbaugh is selling hate. He makes hating liberals, poor people, gays, feminists, intellectuals and immigrants easy for his fans, because he makes it funny." Evidently most upset now but determined to do her job and enlighten the public, Knott then described Limbaugh as a man who launches "tirades" and indulges in "distortions, slanderous rumours and outright lies."

The pain is almost tangible at this point but Knott will not yield to her tears of empathy and suffering. She summons her tenacity, grits her teeth and calls Limbaugh a "trashmeister," a man who speaks "slander and venom" and is loved by "middle-aged men with doughy faces and the women with fly-catcher hairdos who populate white, middle-class, small town America" without whom Limbaugh would be just another "overpaid gasbag." Marvellous, award-winning stuff.

Now I could respond in similar vein by saying that too many Canadian journalists are suburban mediocrities who embrace knee-jerk liberalism because they do not have the intellect or courage to think for themselves. But I shall not, because it would be a caricature. Yet I will say that some journalists in this country appear to have a profound difficulty with anyone who expresses a conservative opinion. And hatred, in their eyes, consists of taking up a contrary position to the liberal status quo and the leftist establishment that is so powerful in Canada.

Columns labelling virtually all men as rapists, all white people as racists and all conservatives as uncaring monsters are, according to some, simply informed essays. Articles condemning parents who smack their children as being inhuman, dismissing all people who smoke cigarettes as being white trash and characterizing all men and women who live in small towns as being morons are, apparently, not hatred at all but reasonable opinion. Whereas television pundits who describe

U.S. President Bill Clinton as being creative with the truth, who refer to employment equity as inverted racism and who condemn abortion are simply hate-mongers. Interesting.

The magnificent Shirley Knott concludes her article by waving the flag of Canadian sainthood and telling us that "Here in Canada, the *Rush Limbaugh Show* came and went on two TV stations with little more than a whimper in the programming departments. You might say that, collectively, Canadians decided to give TV trash-talk the bum's rush."

How sweet. A delicious cross between Pollyanna and Stephen Lewis. We're just too noble, too sensitive and too sensible up here to listen to Rush Limbaugh. But reality deserves a hearing. Limbaugh was aired by CFTO television in Toronto until early last year, when a small but organized letter-writing campaign aimed at the station and at the CRTC led to the show's cancellation. Another victory for censorship. Limbaugh was aired at an impossible time, between 12:30 and 1:00 a.m., yet he still achieved audiences of over 100,000. More than 600 people telephoned CFTO to protest Limbaugh's removal. "I told them to write in," said executive vice-president Joe Garwood. "I also think it was wrong to get rid of Limbaugh. I think the letters represented an incredible intolerance of other people's views but we really had no choice."

In fact, if Limbaugh were aired at a reasonable hour he would probably do very well in this country, far better than many of the CBC shows that the taxpayer is currently obliged to subsidize on a daily basis. More than this, a Canadian version of Limbaugh would likely be extraordinarily successful, and that is a terrifying prospect for the old red guard who like their populism cleansed and controlled. Are we brave and democratic enough to try it? I think so. But don't worry Shirley Knott, you and your friends really don't have to watch. Even in Canada.

The Military

There is a right kind and wrong kind of victory, just as there are wars for the right thing and wars that are wrong from every standpoint . . .

Harry S. Truman
Memoirs, vol. II, ch.19

No Dishonour in Fighting to Protect What You Love

They have taken us off for centuries. Men, that is. To war, that is. Sometimes we volunteered, sometimes we were conscripted. By a twist of bellicose irony, my great-great-grandfathers might have met on fields of battle. One was a Jewish peasant in Ukraine who was kidnapped by Cossacks and had a ring inscribed with the words "Property of the Tsar" through his ear. He served in the Russian army for fifteen years.

Another was a career soldier from Cardiff. Unemployment obliged him to take the Queen's shilling and he lost an arm at Balaclava. The two men were on opposing sides during the Crimean War. Did they fire upon one another? Who knows? It is both romantic and revolting to imagine that they did. They had little in common apart from their tryst with the future. And their gender.

A facile yet effective socialist slogan during the 1930s announced that "a bayonet is a weapon with a worker on both ends." The propaganda was wrong. A bayonet is a weapon with a man on both ends. Warriors famous, infamous and anonymous. Different nationalities, different ages, different causes. All men. On Remembrance Day we put aside a few seconds, a brief hiatus of solemnity, to remember, so that we can continue with our forgetting. From Sedan to Vimy Ridge to the Falklands to the killing fields of Gettysburg.

Gettysburg. How deliciously appropriate that a four-hour film depicting that battle was playing in 1993 at the precise time that we commemorated our own fighting men. And how illuminating that so many North American male movie critics tried to outdo one another in their efforts to flagellate the piece for glorifying this decisive battle, for being pro-war, for not making Gettysburg sufficiently emetic, vile and grotesque. Little liberal lemmings.

I went to see the film. It is without doubt flawed but also something of an achievement. American films seldom run to such length, what with our sound-bite sensibilities and television-raped concentration spans. Some reviewers thought that the speeches in the movie were far too rhetorical and the acting inflated. I think not. It is a faithful recreation; the words spoken by the military leaders are recorded as fact by those who were actually present, and the intensely literate and passionate 1860s produced language that shames our vapid age, splashed as it is with ennui and cerebral sloth.

No, what these critics were trying to do was to expunge from their hands what they perceive to be the blood of their fathers. They believe that war is only about degradation and pain and that a movie that presents military conflict in any other manner is egregious and to be condemned. How dare we make a film that shows battle as containing elements of courage, commitment and selflessness, they say. Our credentials as new and reconstructed men could be lost forever, they imply. To be ashamed of what one is. How wretched, and how typical.

Warfare is part of our history and our heritage. Wars have frequently been unjust, but they have just as frequently been about justice — the Civil War most certainly was, and only a fool or a charlatan would claim that the Second World War, for example, was merely a set-piece slaughter designed to satisfy the male psyche. There have also been atrocities in war, but only a tabloid historian would argue that this was common. Decency remains decency even when tested under fire, and men do not automatically become monsters when they don a uniform.

To misunderstand and blithely censure the acts of heroism shown in the film *Gettysburg* is to indulge in a filthy act of anachronism and obfuscation. The fact that 15,000 Confederate volunteers were willing to march towards the enemy knowing that half of them would not return cannot be dismissed with puny reactions or intellectual spasms. As men we have repeatedly fought for what we knew and loved. And even if the cause was wrong, that does not necessarily diminish the honour inherent within the act. There is nothing for which we need apologize.

Those wonderful old men, those conduits through which past glories are passed down to us, who hold out their wrinkled hands and ask for a few coins in exchange for a poppy stained with symbolic red, are no different in essence from the men of both sides who fought at Gettysburg or from the men who have offered and given their lives in other conflicts. They were simply men.

Canadian Vietnam Vets Derided and Ignored

There is a group of Canadian men who fought for a cause, who risked their lives in defence of what they perceived as democracy, against what they saw as bellicose imperialism, and who are not officially recognized by their homeland and who do not receive pensions from the country of their birth and of their residence.

They are not fashionable, nor is their cause. Not chic, like, for example, the men who fought for the Republicans in the Mac-Paps during the Spanish Civil War and now are championed by the lords and ladies of the cocktail party circuit.

These ignored and derided warriors are the Canadian men who volunteered to fight for the United States during the Vietnam War. More than 12,000 of them went, more than a thousand died. The latter group included Richard Dextraze, son of General Jacques Dextraze, chief of the Canadian defence staff from 1972 to 1977. Most of the volunteers, however, were ordinary; part of that glorious ordinariness that has provided the workers, the builders, the creators, the blue-collar men for every country for millennia. Many were natives, most were from Ontario, some had served in the Canadian army. Ordinary.

Canadians fought in all areas of the U.S. military, and did so for various motives. Some sought adventure, some believed that Canada ought to help a friend across the border, others possessed a wide detestation of communism.

It has been alleged that there were a great many mercenaries involved, and hence they do not merit our sympathy. If this is true, they were ill-advised. The average wage of an American soldier in Vietnam would be laughed at by any self-respecting soldier of fortune. When these men returned they found that it was advisable to obfuscate their past. Canada had made up its mind about Vietnam and had decided that everybody who fought there was a murderer. Including Bill, from a small town in Quebec.

"We thought we would come home as heroes. What fools we were. We were despised. I'd listen to the radio and hear middle-class guys from down south who had deserted, who'd run up here to Canada, telling Canadians what it was all about. I found that I was — still am — less welcome in my own country than an American who broke the law and deserted his country.

"People challenge me, demand to know how the hell I could have volunteered for Vietnam. I could talk for hours about how the North Vietnamese invaded the South and how the Americans were bound by treaty and decency to aid a victim. Or how communism proved itself to be a horror — just look at the boat people. Or how Canada benefited from the American military umbrella but played the game of neutrality. But what it really comes down to is that I believed it was the right thing to do. Understand, the right thing to do.

"And I'd like to know why we don't challenge American draft-dodgers more. Were they all motivated by some higher morality, or could it just be that there was a bit of self-preservation and good old cowardice involved? Who are we kidding? It's become a no-go area. They're saints, we're sinners. Crazy."

For Bill and his comrades, the lack of recognition and acknowledgement has had deeper repercussions. Whereas American veterans have worked through a massive national catharsis composed of monuments, pensions, movies and books, the Canadian experience has been left raw and bloody.

"There are men walking around out there who are dealing with memories, with anger, with pain, all through a bottle. Hey, buddy, you should have held up a store, you'd get more sympathy from social workers and the government." He lights a cigarette, his hand shaking with passion. "Things are getting better. We've been allowed into the Canadian Legion now, there's some opening up of people's minds. But it would be better just to talk about all of this and try not to condemn us. A few months ago somebody in *The Globe and Mail*, an American, one who dodged the draft, said that he had to apologize for his countrymen the way young Germans had to apologize for the Nazis. Nice. Really intelligent and balanced. I'll tell that to the parents of the Jewish kid who died next to me in Vietnam."

So what does Bill want?

"Not money, not a Canadian medal, not a movie about us, forget all that. Just understanding. That's what I want. Understanding. Jesus, it's like water in the desert. Men are out of fashion, so what chance do men have who actually volunteered for battle? Don't answer that . . . please."

Two-Faced Army-Bashing

In a country where the armed forces have been pushed constantly deeper into decay and irrelevance for the past thirty years by an aggressively pacific government and liberal culture, it is extraordinary to see the present predicament and future state of the military discussed on television and in print at virtually every turn.

It is army-bashing time. The cause is a tragic one. Canadian soldier Elvin Kyle Brown participated in the fatal beating of a Somali civilian and was sentenced to five years in prison for his crime. The young paratrooper's actions were repulsive, and justice has been done.

Yet this was far too fertile a crisis to be ignored. Within months of the case, the privately funded but government-friendly Canada 21 group issued a report saying that Canada's armed forces ought to be tailored and structured specifically for peacekeeping purposes. We were given an entire beach during the Normandy landings, but our fighting men are now to become a picturesquely armed pack of Boy Scouts.

The Airborne Regiment has attracted particular venom. Elvin Kyle Brown was, of course, a member of it, and others from its ranks may well have been involved in the Somali disaster. There are calls for the paratroops to be disbanded and for all commando and special forces units to be investigated with a view to curtailment or possible dissolution.

What is at the base of all of this is a fundamental confusion about military elites and about the military in general, which means a confusion about men — like it or not, men fight wars, even when they don't want to, even when they don't start them. Men will also fight wars in the future — it is not a question of desirability but of inevitability and even necessity. Thus, an attack upon the armed forces is directly pertinent to contemporary males and to masculine self-perception, to men who have been raised with the belief that sacrifice in combat is "a sweet, noble and glorious thing."

The state recruits groups of young men into fighting organizations and then sponsors their careers for the specific reason of killing, of using deadly force against the enemies of that very state. It is all a matter, in a civilized country, of national self-defence. Young men who are especially good at this job are moved further up the military ladder or placed, again by the state, into crack units. Such groups are welcomed and lauded during times of great need — surely the War of 1812 in defence of Canadian borders and the war of 1939 in defence of civilization were such times — but are more difficult to deal with during periods of peace. That same state is now a little embarrassed by the record of one of its creations. A servant has shamed his master and mistress.

The men involved in the Somalia affair are only minor members of the household staff, however, and do not represent the bulk of the men who are members of the Canadian Armed Forces. But instead of questioning the accepted wisdom of the Canadian presence in Somalia or the rationale of peacekeeping, a scapegoat is found. It happens to wear a uniform, is made up of men and has no political or public voice. It is a case of crass hypocrisy and gauzy argument. First take your man and train him for your purposes. When one of his comrades does something wrong, tell that man that everything he is about, everything you have turned him into, is wrong, impious, even un-Canadian.

There is and has to be within the armed forces — and particularly within a chosen regiment, such as the Airborne — a bellicose mind-set, an untamed willingness to fight, a combat spirit and a tribal pride. We encourage it, we insist upon it. We cannot train a man to kill with a knife and then wonder why he does not act like a member of a sandal-wearing commune; cannot tell him that he is the heir to the military campaigns and victories of centuries and then become puzzled when he does not empathize with the editorials in *Cosmopolitan* magazine.

The hypocrisy and double-thinking offered to us at the moment on this subject are untenable and unworthy. Men who have for reasons of long-held ambition or economic need donned Canadian uniforms are being left in a no man's land, or should we call it a no-nurturing-yet-violent-individual's-land? I hope not.

Distressing Undercurrents in Military Hockey Game

Recently I gave a lecture to the cadets and staff of the Royal Military College of Canada in Kingston, Ontario, on the subject of "Is Soldiering Still an Honourable Profession?" I told them that it was. And if I thought it before visiting the academy, I was certain of it afterwards.

Those intelligent, courteous, tough, decent young Canadians before me demonstrated what this country could be, perhaps what it once was.

But then I received a telephone call from one outraged and emotional cadet. He explained that a hockey game between the RMC and the shortly to be closed Collège militaire royal in Saint-Jean had taken place in Kingston on March 25. Because of the internecine tension, because of the French-English rivalry and because, simply, boys will be boys, there were many penalties and a great deal of fighting. It happens. The match was watched by, among others, the Commandant of the Royal Military College, Brigadier-General Charles Emond, and his wife.

Both were distressed at what they had seen. At the end of the game, Lucie Emond left her place as a spectator, approached one of her husband's charges and struck him. Incredulity. Later that evening Emond gave the entire RMC team a dressing down.

Cadets at the college claim the youth was struck on the face but Emond insists that "it was a tap on the behind because of the trouble. My wife was extremely upset."

He went on, however, to explain that when he spoke to the RMC team he joked that his wife should have been given a two-minute penalty for roughing. This seems rather a harsh penalty for an innocuous, playful tap.

The atmosphere at the school is now vibrant with rumours of repercussions, of comparisons between this incident and General George Patton's slapping of a soldier and with comments about why a French-Canadian Commandant and his wife behaved in such a manner towards a cadet after a game against the Quebec college, one where Emond had been commandant until fairly recently. There is much talk of honour, and of shame.

Some context is important.

One does not have to search very deeply to find people at the RMC who will complain about the new, somewhat inappropriate bilingual signs placed beneath paintings of imperial soldiers. Or chagrin at the clumsy alteration of an English-language plaque donated by a graduating class. Or complaints that experienced soldiers are passed over for promotion by bilingual pen-pushers. Or anger that there were attempts to remove a reference to empire from the memorial archway at the entrance of the college — as though Canadians suddenly did not die for this cause and did not regard themselves as being linked to Britain. How ludicrous.

History does not adapt to keep pace with modernity.

Perhaps we should argue that Canadians in the First World War actually gave their lives for the CBC, multiculturalism and Margaret Atwood.

So we already have dissent and dissatisfaction. Now this severe lack of professionalism shown towards a cadet from the wife of a man with enormous authority, who is supposed to be a father figure to the young people at the college. Boys fight in hockey games. Military boys fight in hockey games. Even English-Canadian military boys fight in hockey games.

If cadets misbehave at RMC there are numerous and effective methods of sensible and judicial punishment.

I want to know a great deal more about all of this and I want an explanation as to why a young man was thus humiliated and deprived of his honour.

No need to abolish anything, no need to single out a cadet. Just a responsible reaction from the people concerned.

Soon please. Because I also want to continue believing that soldiering is still an honourable profession.

Live by the Gun, Die by the Gun

Billy is a man of violence. Extreme violence. He is an active member of a Protestant paramilitary organization in Northern Ireland. He has killed people. He may well continue to kill people; unless, of course, he is killed himself. In the short hiatus between my meeting with him and the appearance of this article, one or both of these things might have already happened. He who lives by the illegally imported Czech machine gun will die by the illegally imported Czech machine gun.

Billy is twenty-five years old and has spent one-fifth of his life in prison, one-third of his life involved in terrorism. He is quite handsome, dark-haired and blue-eyed and with the build of a middleweight boxer. He speaks with that rich, heavily nuanced Ulster accent that many find harsh but is actually seductively melodic. Vowels lose their severity and curl, bend and meander. It is not the dialect that matters, of course, but the words.

"When I placed one hand on a Bible and one hand on a gun and swore to give all for my cause, I took an oath that I will never break," he says, fingering a heavy ring on his finger. It is a six-pointed star. Not the Jewish symbol, but a representation of the counties of Ulster: a common symbol this side of the Northern Irish divide.

"Since then, I have been a soldier in a war that demands certain things. Most of what I do is peaceful but, yes, on occasion, I have had to shoot."

I force this one. Had to?

"I'm under authority. I get a phone call telling me to be at a certain place at a certain time. I go. I receive more orders. Told what to do. I do it. I trust those above me."

I tell Billy that I can comprehend, if not condone, hot-blooded combat between two armed tribes and that I am not concerned with the politics of the situation for this interview. But what about Loyalist paramilitaries killing ordinary Roman Catholics, people uninvolved with armed conflict?

"Mistakes have been made, no doubt," he says. "But we target legitimate enemies of this country and active supporters of the IRA."

Stop. This is wrong. The most ardent Unionist will admit that there have been sectarian murders of apolitical people. I push him, and then stop.

"It is so, so easy for those not involved with violence to speak as if they know about violence," he says. "Shall I pretend that I can tell you things about writing biographies or journalism?"

I am more surprised than I can say.

And then I move closer to him. I become a voyeur, even the journalist as vulture, although I prefer to think that this is reporting rather than prurience.

"What's it like when I pull the trigger? It's like one of those dream scenes in a film. Everything slows down, but edges are hard and images are in clear focus, as though the only thing happening in the entire world is me, the gun, your man in front of you. And you know, I haven't been scared in years." He's showing passion for the first time, swearing more and raising his voice. "People who write about this stuff and tell you they puke or they shake or they piss themselves, they're making it up. No way. It's not like that. Not after a while. It feels different. It feels like you're in charge."

Feels good? I'm pushing limits now, and I'm concerned. But Billy has seen through me, recovered his position and abandoned his passion. "It's a job. Soldiers work when there's war. Stop the war, make me unemployed."

Which is precisely what Billy's Roman Catholic counterparts just a few hundred metres away would say. They are so similar to Billy, so alike, so akin. "Maybe that's why we're killing each other," he says, biting a thumbnail and allowing the sleeve of his leather jacket to slide up so as to reveal an "I.F.L." tattoo. The letters stand for Imprisoned For Loyalty and reflect the Protestant paramilitary incredulity that the British would arrest and incarcerate them.

"Of course we're similar," he says. "Don't you think I know that? I know that to an outsider it looks like brothers having a fight. Funny that, but when you think about it, people always say it's easier to hate and hurt people you don't know. I'd say it was the complete bloody opposite. Now isn't life full of little surprises?"

And he smiles. I will remember the smile for the rest of my life. And for the rest of his.

War Toys

"If we do sink, then it's women, children and reconstructed men first," cries the captain of HMCS Sensitivity as it rides the waves of new male contrition. I'd like to climb aboard, but the life jacket simply won't fit me. I am forced to remain on the dockside, wrapping myself in a cloak of guilt as I hold on to the last few months of the 6,000 years of male dominance that my gender has enjoyed.

Damn, I hardly even noticed it was taking place. More than this, what do I tell my son? In particular, how do I advise, instruct and influence him when it comes to those most important of moulders: toys? So, traditional man takes his four-year-old child to Toys "R" Us.

The problem is that conventional wisdom, the new orthodoxy, has been that any toy with a military, bellicose or even vaguely violent connotation will lead directly to your son becoming a mass murderer. My little Daniel appears to be a singularly empathetic and gentle boy, but I am sure that the handful of inch-high British paratroopers I brought him back from London last Christmas has had its deleterious and irreversible effect. Even now we have an inchoate psychopath playing soccer in the back yard.

Still, we try our best. Daniel is not allowed any toy that is too explicit, too clumsy in its depiction of any kind of reality. Hence we do not buy our son toy guns. In response, or in compensation, he constructs tiny shooters out of Lego, ice-cream cones, his fingers, anything. "Stop it, Daniel!" we his parents cry, "you're halfway towards becoming a killer and a sexual monster." The poor wretch does not respond — oh, if only he knew.

Nor is he allowed any Batman or Mutant Ninja Turtle toys, not because of their violent nature but because of their commercial repercussions. We have even less desire to transform our son into a product of the California cinema industry than we do to make him an appendage of the Pentagon.

As to military uniforms, he has never asked for one and if he does we will refuse. This time because of the aesthetically displeasing sight of children dressed in Gulf War outfits parading around their junior kindergarten playground. It is vulgar, it is thoughtless, it is crass. Will it make the child more violent when he grows to maturity? I very much doubt it.

There is not, of course, any plausible evidence that exposing children to war toys has any genuine effect on them whatsoever. The statistics and surveys are by their very nature subjective and jaundiced. We cannot really argue that no German child in 1923 would have become a National Socialist apparatchik or an SS storm trooper if it hadn't been for the market being flooded with the equivalent of GI Joes and "F-15 bargain packs with real flashing lights and Baghdad-style attack missiles."

A child is shaped by genes, environment, schools, peers and, above all, by parental example. It is time and patience and values rather than the absence of war toys that bring out the best in any child. And why should we call them war toys in the first place? As good Canadians, should we not describe miniature armoured personnel carriers, midget artillery pieces and troopers of restricted growth as peacekeeping toys, or overwhelming-commitment-to-the-United-Nations toys? Patriotism and the Canadian way demand it.

In fact there are few war toys in Toys "R" Us that are in any way suitable for my son. When he fights out his battles for civilization I would like him to be aware of the history of his re-enactments, of the course of the Roman Empire, Napoleonic ambitions, the genuine necessity of the Second World War, rather than the struggle of All American Hero with Death Destroyer.

So we bring him back more sophisticated toys from Britain, and I also gave him the collection of medals won by my grandfather during the Second World War. Grandpa was a working-class man from the East End of London, taken off in 1939 to fight in the front line, set free again in 1945. He was given grown-up war toys, and used them in situations that I can only imagine. He sometimes discussed his experiences, but only with humour and never with glee. His awards, and an intelligent purchase from the toy store, will suffice for Daniel. No damage, no appalling influences, no long-term horror inflicted on a child. Even when a grant-supported Canadian toy company is producing all-moving action dolls called Social Worker Sally or Crisis Counsellor Pete I will still not change my mind. Because truth is always truth, fashion is always fashion and panic is always panic.

No Choice But to Bomb Hiroshima

It is the near future. A little child gazes up at his father, a new, sensitive man who has read the right books about male guilt. He wears a blue corduroy baby-harness around his neck . . . all of the time.

"Daddy, what happened in the Second World War?" asks the boy.

"Bad things," replies Mr. Beard-and-Sandals. "We dropped a bomb on the Japanese and killed innocent people. Never forget."

August 6, 1995: fifty years ago to the day an atomic bomb was dropped on Hiroshima. Ever since, as the memories of Japanese war crimes began to fade, some people have tried their best to use Hiroshima, and Nagasaki, as political vehicles, through which to promote disarmament, a doubtful pacifism and, more often than not, anti-Americanism. Peace parks, ribbon-wearing, breast-beating and breast-baring. It is all so familiar now. As are the cries: Japan would have surrendered anyway; we should have given a warning; we should have bombed a deserted island; ordinary Japanese people weren't responsible for their government; and so on.

Let me state my case immediately. Atomic bombs are not good things. Wars are not good things. The rape of Canadian nurses, the mass murder of civilians, torture, medical experiments on prisoners of war, beheadings, starvation are not good things. But they happen. We cannot live by moral equivalents and we have to make ethical judgments, particularly in times of acute and bloody conflict. The Japanese and their allies in Germany represented a dark age, one that had to be defeated. In comparison the Allies were beams of shining light.

Were the Japanese about to surrender? Almost every credible historian without a political agenda agrees they were not, even after both bombs had been dropped. The Imperial War Council of Japan was divided on the issue, with Army Minister General Korechika Anami stating "that we will inflict heavy losses on the enemy when he invades Japan is certain." He was supported by many in the military and it was only the unprecedented intervention of Emperor Hirohito that managed to make any contemplation of surrender at all possible. More than this, the armed forces were still efficient and determined — six days after Hiroshima the Japanese sunk two American ships — and on the home front the Japanese continued to execute captured American airmen. When peace was first considered, a group of officers led by a Major Hatanaka plotted to murder the "traitors" and push the war effort forward.

As to the Americans giving a warning before the bomb was dropped, the determination of the Japanese was such that the bombing of an evacuated city would certainly not have led to surrender and the same argument applies to the suggestion that a deserted island off of the Japanese coast should have been used. Yet another alternative offered, then and now, is that a Japanese delegate should have been invited to the testing of an atomic bomb in the U.S. Yet if the bomb had not exploded — always a strong possibility — the humiliation to the Americans and subsequent increase in Japanese morale would have been disastrous. The Japanese intelligence services were also aware that the Allies were incapable of making more bombs very quickly.

What about the defence that the Japanese people should not have been made responsible for the monstrous actions of their government and armed forces? Partially true, but then nor were all of the Germans responsible for genocide. They still had to be defeated. Perhaps American, British and Canadian soldiers should have taken Japan island by island, town by town, street by street. And who would be campaigning for their widows now, who would be funding museum exhibits in their memory?

The question is rhetorical. Hiroshima is fashionable; the Japanese POW camps less so. I am sorry for Hiroshima. But not that sorry. The war is over. The good guys won. Tell that to your son Mr. Beard-and-Sandals.

Religion

Religion in its humility restores man to his only dignity, the courage to live by grace.

George Santayana
Dialogues in Limbo, ch. 4

A Community of Brothers

We met when we were teenagers. Paul was a high flier in a squadron of high fliers. After university he became the assistant to a cabinet minister and had a seat in Parliament safely tucked away for whenever he was ready for it.

But he had discovered God. At the age of twenty-seven, he decided to enter a monastery. He had been to stay at a golden, grey abbey on a small island off the southern English coast, first for a weekend and then for increasingly longer periods of time. He told me that he had a vocation.

We had been so similar, had so much in common. Yet only a few years later I was married and had three children, while Paul was a celibate Cistercian submerged in the contemplative life. It was like having a privileged glance into history, being given a unique guided tour into a hidden life. Paul was a monk. And my first question was so predictable, so coy and so framed in embarrassment that this young man in a dark habit smiled.

"Do I think about sex? Do I masturbate? Yes, sometimes. I try not to. I try not to do many things, try not to become angry, become annoyed with another brother, despair about the world. Yet I do all of those things, sometimes. And do I think about women? Yes. I wasn't a virgin when I entered the monastery. Some of the men were. Is it really that important?"

He had turned the question around to me, and I became uncomfortably aware that compared to this sexually naïve fool who lives with a bunch of old men, I am ill-prepared to discuss lust and sexuality.

Within Roman Catholicism, the priesthood is a sacrament, but there are no sacramental privileges attached to becoming a monk. Nor are there, by the insular nature of the position, the same social advantages that some priests might enjoy.

"I'd find the priesthood far too lonely," says Paul. "Remember, I'm part of a community here, probably not alone enough, if anything. Always friends and companions. In some ways, we as monks were precursors of the current fascination with male bonding and returning to our roots."

The uninitiated and the jaundiced assume that monasteries are retreats, venues where men flock when they wish to leave mainstream society. From the evidence of subjective experience and objective analysis, this seems to be untrue. Monasteries were established, often built on high and prominent places, to be lights unto the populace, to set an example of Christian, cooperative and peaceful living to the maelstrom beyond.

There are, of course, young men who for reasons of alienation, fear or mental instability want to withdraw from greater society into what they perceive as the comforting walls of a monastery, but they are invariably detected and rejected. More often than not, they reject themselves.

"They might imagine that it's a nice, quiet, easy life, but we work longer hours than most people on the outside, and there is nothing more difficult than living so closely with your God, knowing the expectations and being aware that you are usually failing to meet them . . . Sometimes a little amorality would be terribly refreshing and a hell of a relief."

Of course, the social dynamic that shapes contemporary manhood — the equation linking and dividing men and women — does not exist in a monastery, "which is why I'd never comment on the gender relationship in society," explains my friend. "But surely to refine that relationship, both parties have first to understand themselves. At the risk of sounding proud, I'd say that almost everyone in this place knows himself pretty well."

Some men would mock and pity Paul. And many of these critics will continue to work in lifeless, nine-to-five jobs, continue to watch television in the evening and take annual holidays at tourist traps. And Paul and his people will say good morning to God every dawn in a hymn first sung by eighth-century ancestors, illuminated by natural light, enlivened by the smells, sounds and sights of the farm and forest only yards beyond the chapel door. Paul will live and die with a group of men who genuinely love him and care for him. He will seldom be lonely or neglected. Mockery and pity: how odd, and how terribly out of place.

Anglican Leadership Out of Touch with the "Ordinary" People

What astounds me most is the arrogance of it all. The assumption that what this branch of the old liberal establishment thinks and says is in any way important or significant.

I speak of yet another slice of lunacy served up from the heavily curdled cake that is the leadership of the Anglican church. There have been bishops denying the Virgin birth and the resurrection, another episcopal loon explaining that infidelity is fine, homosexual scandals from Great Britain to Canada and the Church of England synod arguing that marriage is no longer necessary and that "living in sin" is not sinful at all but actually quite a good thing. Funny if it wasn't so sad.

Now we have a new politically correct Canadian Anglican hymnbook with "Onward! Christian Soldiers" removed because, according to one prominent Anglican, of its "extreme militarism." Not only does this man evidently not understand the true meaning of the lyrics but he clearly has not come to terms with the words of the Bible. Instead we have new gems such as "Strong Mother God" and "Faithful Wisdom: Partner, Counsellor, Comforter." God give me strength.

While these archaic liberals tamper with the people's beloved language they remain ambivalent about abortion, ambivalent about homosexuality, ambivalent about right and wrong, ambivalent about almost everything except gin and tonic. Their fashionable radicalism can surely be traced to what C. S. Lewis described as people who are skeptical about everything "not on moral grounds but from an ingrained habit of belittling anything that concerns the great mass" of their fellow humans.

The supreme, inspiring Book of Common Prayer was thought too complicated and arcane for "ordinary" people so the Anglicans brought in a nasty mixture of New Age rubbish and bland theology in *The Book of Alternative Service.* It was supposed to bring back the crowds. It was expensive and time-consuming and entire congregations are now fleeing to Roman Catholicism or embracing Evangelical Protestantism. But somehow the Anglicans are convinced of their righteousness. They assume they know best, because of their class, race and traditional power.

This is sad for me to write. I spent the first twenty-seven years of my life in England and loved the gentleness and beauty of the Church of England. But the modern church is not that of past times. There are some wonderful individuals and parishes still fighting the good fight but, as a whole, the Anglican church, particularly in Canada, has become part of the problem and not the solution. The dazzling curtain of our moral and social fabric has been ripped down the middle and all this group of ostensible Christians can do is fiddle while the country burns.

None of this should surprise us. There are any number of precedents in Canada, from other churches, from the federal and provincial governments and from public institutions such as the CBC. Extremist, erratic decisions made by a small, privileged hierarchy against the will of the unconsulted and contemptuously treated majority. The attitude is achingly familiar and usually hides under names like paternalism, feminism or social democracy.

The Anglican leaders are like so many members of the middle-class generation who were politicized during the 1960s. With a laughable gullibility they embraced the new ideas and the new morality and now try to impose those aberrations on a population that is often less wealthy and less educated than they are, who trust their leaders and assume that all is done in their interests. "Ordinary" people often love the old hymns and believe in the traditional ethics but they are told they "must change with the times." Of course, the last thing any religious organization should do is change with the times, any more than it should change with the weather or with the day of the week.

The Anglicans' former model, Jesus Christ, would be dumbfounded by all this but their founder, Henry VIII, must be smiling. He murdered dissidents, married six times and killed two of his wives. But then murder is a relative term and not really about sin at all. Pass the strawberries and cream, dear, I think there's a jolly little gardening show just starting on the television.

This Way for the Holy Water

In mediaeval England, pilgrims to the holy shrine of Canterbury exchanged bawdy tales involving flatulence and infidelity. Three centuries later, the country's monarch, Henry VIII, walked barefoot in penance for a mile to the religious centre of Walsingham, then proceeded to close the place down and murder its occupants when the pope refused to let him divorce his wife.

In other words, shrines and pilgrimages are not always perceived with the appropriate degree of respect and reverence. Who can forget, for example, Vincent Price playing a cynical, atheistic doctor in that groaning and unctuous movie *The Song of Bernadette*, dismissing the villagers of Lourdes as mere peasants who were the victims of an elaborate church hoax? Price's doctor may have had a point; it is uncanny how the Virgin Mary appears only to small children, illiterate farm labourers and crazed clerics.

For all this, Lourdes remains the shrine of shrines or, as some would have it, the vulgarity of vulgarities. I still have my battery-operated "Mary Talks with Santa Claus" statuette to add weight to the latter opinion. Portugal has its anti-Marxist Mary at Fatima, Chartres its Our Lady Underground, and in Goa the Virgin has appeared alongside Saint Francis Xavier, whose entombed body has no toes. Guides explain that the reason for the dismemberment is that "a nun bit them off in a state of religious ecstasy."

No such masticatory antics at Lourdes, where Saint Bernadette and her Pyrenean town reign supreme in the good-shrine league. I begin my pilgrimage in Madrid, in a train compartment Babel-like with the French, Catalan, Basque and English languages competing for the services of the only genuine linguist on the train.

The cheap plonk available in the luxuriant borderland between France and Spain is packaged like orange juice in cardboard boxes, yet it is superior to some of the best Canadian wines sealed in glass. Its effect on this long and increasingly languid trip is to guarantee a dignified peace among the European nations, or at least among their inebriated representatives crammed into a piece of Spanish rolling stock.

As we arrive at Lourdes, any questions about the wisdom of my journey evaporate like some vacuous element of a kindergarten catechism. Lourdes is beautiful, exquisite, a painting of a place. If the Virgin Mary did appear here in 1858 and tell a young girl to live a Christian life, she was obviously a judicious traveller.

The town is soaked in prayer but also soaked in pathos. The sepulchral line of children's crutches leaning against the grotto is part Dickens at his most maudlin, part advertising stunt and part profoundly moving spiritual exercise.

Yet if tears are near, they will not last the day. Just yards away from where crippled children claim to have been cured is a scrum of Polish and Italian women dressed entirely in black, resembling Sherman tanks camouflaged for a night attack. They are arguing, increasingly volubly, and then they begin punching each other. I am shocked. They are competing with devout enthusiasm to reach the fount of the Holy Water and fill their numerous plastic containers with the stuff. One Polish woman screams at a Sicilian rival. I ask a friend from Warsaw what the woman is saying. "If you're the better Catholic, how come the Pope is from Cracow?" he says.

Is Lourdes the site where a divine doctor graciously expunges disease and moribundity from believers, or are the apparent cures merely the result of a wave of euphoria temporarily submerging their pain and anguish? We will never know.

What is certain, and what is quite ironic, is that one can witness the presence of God in Lourdes. To do so, we must lift our eyes from the dross of commercialism and gaze at the Pyrenees and the natural, inveterate beauty of the land. If God is anywhere He is there, laughing at the credulity of the faithful and wondering why they are staring in the wrong direction.

The Pope's Choice

"My fellow bishops tell me I'm too frigging pessimistic," says Aloysius M. Ambrozic. "Pessimistic about what? Pessimistic about the Church, what will happen, the future of the Church."

He is wearing a black suit, gold-rimmed glasses and an interview smile that is not in keeping with this professed pessimism. Sitting in a polished wooden chair, he turns the heavy ring that symbolizes his position within the Catholic nature of things: English Canada's premier prelate, appointed by the pope, who is the direct descendant of St. Peter, made head of the Church by Jesus Christ while he lived and was present here on earth among us. "A responsibility I try not to consider too often; otherwise I'd be overwhelmed," he says, and fingers the only other jewellery on his person, a silver cross around his neck.

Ambrozic's frigging pessimism certainly isn't eased by the "all-knowing posture and cheap stuff" coverage of the Church by members of the secular media, who criticize him for being ultraconservative and divisive. "They get so much wrong," he says. "And they don't like to be told they get things wrong. No, I'd never write to the editor. But I do write personal letters to the people who write the articles."

He shakes his head in splenetic incredulity when I mention a story by Judy Steed in *The Toronto Star*, which appeared shortly before he took office in March 1990. In it, she said, "The archbishop is regarded as a rigid, authoritarian, provocative hard-liner who may win the church new enemies in the long run." She also quoted one Catholic teacher who said Ambrozic wanted to "return the church to the Dark Ages."

Ambrozic again twists the heavy ring that links him to the Saviour of humanity. "Never mind Judy Steed," he says. "She just wanted to sic the bitch on me . . . pardon my French." His press secretary, Suzanne Scorsone, a Catholic activist who resembles Kim Campbell with braided hair, is recording the conversation, as am I. She blushes, leans forward and asks if she should "turn the tape recorder off." She doesn't. Nor do I. Ambrozic keeps smiling.

It is ironic, or perhaps indicative of the besieged nature of the city's

Catholic Church, that the Church Street building in which Ambrozic works is in the middle of Gay Toronto. The walls in this area are cluttered with posters announcing AIDS demonstrations and homoerotic parties. But inside the archdiocesan offices there's an unnatural tidiness: a big photo of Ambrozic, a large coffee table but no coffee, jarring ceiling lights that illuminate three books (*The Pope in Canada*, *Our Lovely Croatia* and *Modern Europe: The Decay of the Ancien Regime*) and photographs of the pope embracing native children.

"We should be kind to homosexuals and understand their problems," says Ambrozic. "The poor devils, they're their own worst enemies. But all my sympathy for them will not allow me to say, 'you can go ahead and have relationships.' "

A patchwork of images of Catholicism before and during the reign of Archbishop Aloysius Ambrozic:

A rainy morning at Bloor and Dundas West. Outside a large grey building a scrum of teenagers gather, smoking ostentatiously. With their gaudy, badly applied makeup, the girls resemble those cut-price toy dolls made in Asian factories. They laugh uproariously at the most banal comments. The boys are less imaginative, all macho strutting. They swear a great deal. So do the girls. "I'm so f—— glad I'm on the pill," says one. "S——, Mom'd be mad if I had a kid." More furious smoking but, just like President Clinton, limited inhalation. "You screwing him?" All scream and laugh. "Yeah, f—— right, man." One boy explains to his girlfriend: "F—— teacher asked me for a note, wanted to know where I'd been for two weeks. S——, I told her my parole letter would have to do." And then it is time for the children to go inside the building, because Bishop Marrocco-Thomas Merton Roman Catholic school is beginning its day of instruction in Christian education and a lifestyle modelled on the example of Jesus.

Twenty-four kilometres west in Port Credit is another grey building — this one situated in luxuriant countryside. Inside the Queen of Apostles Renewal Centre, a marriage preparation course is underway. The chunky priest of Polish extraction who leads the session tells thirteen couples about a widow woman whose lawn he mowed. She had intentions not in keeping with his vow of chastity. Because of this experience, and because of his commitment to the concept of marriage, the good father decided to help engaged people through the basics of married life. The hope is that these courses will bring down the divorce rate, which is about 40 per cent among Catholics. One cannot be married inside a Catholic church now without receiving a certificate from such a course. On this weekend, most of the people at Queen of Apostles are not practising Catholics, but their parents desire a church wedding. One Italian couple show their displeasure by openly criticizing the course and refusing to enter the chapel until the last hour.

Back in the centre of the city, in the basement of a million-dollar Rosedale home, an "underground mass" is taking place. The congregation is comprised of middle-aged, middle-class women who are disillusioned with what they see as the misogyny of the Roman Catholic Church. Their Catholicism is spiced with feminist theology, chants about the female godhead, sessions where the sisters "share their journey" of faith and pain, and lectures about the positive aspects of wicca.

To the east, inside St. Mary of the People Church in Oshawa, the pews are occupied by mostly white, working-class people dressing in lightweight jackets, Blue Jays and Maple Leafs shirts. The majority appear to be bored and one middle-aged father of three daughters is asleep. The plump young cleric delivering the homily leaves his notes to talk about the evolving sexual abuse scandal. He is annoyed — not at the priests as much as at the press coverage. "Don't they know," he says, "that Protestants do it as well?"

The Roman Catholic Church in Canada and in Toronto is in a mess. Its schools turn out young people with little knowledge of their faith and less inclination to know more. There are so few priests that, in some areas, Catholics no longer receive Holy Communion. Priests who should be retiring are obliged to remain in parishes. Others, European imports whose English is basic, hear confession from penitents who know their words will not be understood. Catholic women are either angry or sad. Hardly anybody becomes a nun anymore and convents have become old-people's homes. A sister of St. Joseph who has known Ambrozic for years says, "My feelings are of disbelief. How can these men not understand how we feel? They organized a day to celebrate the religious of the city, priests and nuns and so on. The entire committee was men. When the service came, all I could see around the altar was a row of old male faces. It hurts. God believe me, it hurts."

The person appointed to remedy this heady mingling of discontent, apathy and fear was the direct choice of John Paul II, as part of his worldwide conservative campaign to "save the Church" from falling standards. One element of the Vatican's plan was to install a "Pope's man" whenever a liberal archbishop retired. Enter Ambrozic. The Vatican had been watching his progress for some time. Most Canadians had not, which was why his selection came as a shock. He had no real following within the Church in Canada and no profile whatsoever outside it. And many of those who did know him didn't appreciate his aggressive personal style, described by one priest as "the iron fist in the iron glove. No sweet talking, just a lecture." His profile was so low that, when the Canadian Conference of Catholic Bishops was preparing a shortlist of three people to replace Cardinal Carter as Toronto's archbishop, Ambrozic's name was reportedly nowhere to be seen.

According to traditional Catholic theology, the Church is a rock and the political and social shifts of the outside world are largely irrelevant. Democracy, modernism and equality are concepts of the present; the Church is an entity for all time. One reason Ambrozic is meeting with me is to get that message across, since he possesses — despite his façade of being a "frigging pessimist" — a certainty and a belief in the eternal and immutable truth of Catholic Christianity. He believes in the divine mission and infallibility of the Roman Catholic Church and will hear, or at least listen to, no other voice. He tells me about a nun who "asked what she could call me, what name she should use when she spoke to me. It was clear she wanted to call me Al. No, she will call me Your Grace and I will call her Sister. I'm not comfortable with immediate informality; I resent it sometimes." The anecdote is revealing: the archbishop believes it demonstrates his strength; his opponents would say it shows his weakness.

He is similarly sharp with his views on contemporary issues. On abortion: "No, never." On birth control: "Artificial contraception isn't the answer. It's too easy, too quick. It dehumanizes people." On the shortage of priests: "Look at parts of the developing world. They have no problems with attendance and vocations. And I believe that things will change here very soon. We're over the worst." On married priests: "It does us good to question celibacy. By questioning it, we're reminded of its importance. All these problems are good, they're challenges, they make us look again at what we believe." He might have added, to paraphrase St. Julian, all will be well, all manner of things will be well.

But Ambrozic and his followers increasingly resemble an island in a combative sea, its boundaries withering and diminishing as salty water erodes the soil. A Catholic academic who knew Ambrozic earlier in his career explained that "he could no more work as a priest in an inner-city parish, with all of its problems, than fly to the moon. He's not a bad man; he simply doesn't understand what is going on out there."

Ambrozic isn't so isolated that he's unaware of these criticisms. "I'm not alone, not out of touch, no, no," he says. "I have a number of priest friends, and, of course, my fellow bishops. Archbishop Marcel Gervais of Ottawa is a very close friend, has been for a heck of a long time. We bishops get together, we talk, we chew the fat . . .," and he laughs. He reflects for a moment and then adopts an almost confessional posture. "I've yet to ever love my neighbour as myself, never," he says, frowning, his voice trailing off.

Like the Pope, Ambrozic is at core an Eastern European who is distinctly uncomfortable with North American society and its presumed decadence, heterogeneity and lack of orthodox spirituality. He has a longing for what he perceives as older values, for the old European values. "Look at Europe, God bless us," he has said about immigration. "What's happening in Europe is that the white race is becoming extinct. North Africa is bursting at the seams with a demographic explosion, and I'm afraid that Europe is going to be overwhelmed again, not by military conquest, but by immigration from the Arab countries." He refers to the "disease of liberal" ideas and laments that people are "infected" by them; he derides the proclivities of our "sex-crazed society." It is all a problem of modernism. "God is God; we can't pick and choose, can't apply ideas like equality to divine revelation."

A sex-crazed society was certainly not the problem in his native Slovenia. There was little open homosexuality or, for that matter, black and brown immigration, particularly by 1948, the year in which Ambrozic's parents, shepherding their seven children, came to Canada by boat after leaving Europe and a series of Austrian refugee camps. The archbishop completed his high school education in these camps. "Ideas to be fought, ideas to be defeated," he remembers. "Communism was alive then, and it appealed to a lot of people." Ambrozic resisted and eventually entered St. Augustine's Seminary in Scarborough to study philosophy and theology. Ordained in 1955, he was attracted to the priesthood by its symbolism, and by "my very good family life, a Christian example." I pray therefore I am.

After briefly working in a Port Colborne parish, Ambrozic settled into a cocooned, privileged life as a student and a teacher: in Rome, in Germany at the University of Würzburg, at St. Augustine's, at the Toronto School of Theology. One pupil remembers him as "an inspiring teacher if you agreed with him. He was a genuine intellectual and really had the ability to make you want to pursue knowledge. But if you took a different approach politically, there was a coldness. Not nastiness, coldness."

It was a world in which he was seldom challenged and rarely opposed. That has all changed. Age sixty-three at the time of this interview, Ambrozic is in his third year of facing the full maelstrom of church politics, and a central irony of archdiocesan life — that forgiveness and love do not rank very high when it comes to internecine squabbling.

Cardinal Carter worked hard to hold together the fragile alliance that is the Catholic Church in Toronto. He courted the powerful, diplomatically manoeuvring with the grace of a renaissance cleric. He was comfortable with small talk and publicity, bursting with Quebec Irish wit and panache. He was a friend of Conrad Black and became an accepted face in powerful secular gatherings. According to his biographer, Michael Higgins, the cardinal "knew exactly how to get what he wanted and how to oil the wheels of influence." Where Carter was seen as perhaps too much the BMW driver, his successor was feared as a man on top of a panzer, someone who would roll back the advances made in the Church by new ideas.

Ambrozic is aware that he's viewed as an outsider. Accordingly, he resists the public glare because he is unsettled by its intensity. He stammers, sweats and digresses in the pulpit. During a function, even gatherings of the faithful, he is to be found in the corner of a room. "I'm not comfortable with all of that. I remember leaving a dinner organized by Carter, standing outside and not really participating in the chat of the guests. Someone came up to me and asked why I was there, suggested that I was a bit ill at ease. I said I was. 'Look,' he said, 'there was a time when Catholics were second-class citizens in this city. Because of Carter, because of small talk and the like, we're part of the Establishment; we're accepted.' He was right."

Ambrozic submerges his anxieties in copious bursts of work, and is busy from his predawn breviary until his night prayers, usually at 10 p.m., but frequently much later. On his schedule are myriad meetings, conferences, seminarian interviews, convocations, hospital visits, special and ordinary masses, blessings, funerals, interviews, prayers, ordinations. He's also in charge of an organization that has, until recently, been running an operating deficit. For relief, there are long, solitary walks, usually along the ravines near his Moore Park home. "I get rid of my hostilities that way, or try to," he says of his strolls that can last as long as four hours. "My frustrations begin to disappear."

Yet for all his peripatetic reflection, he does have the habit of saying things that should not be said. "I'd like to know why the British, French and the UN have done nothing to protect the Croats," he has said. "It's because the British and French favour the Serbs. I don't know why, except that a strong Serbian force would be a counterbalance to the German influence."

The statement contradicts his own commands to priests that they not become involved in politics, particularly complicated situations, as is the case in the Balkans. Then there's his comment about the late dictator Francisco Franco, who "was a conservative Roman Catholic and not a bad fellow, he's got a particularly bad press, certainly not a fascist."

The generalissimo certainly knew how to keep the Spanish Church in line. Ambrozic's difficulty is that the most challenging dissent comes not from revolutionaries with bombs but from good Catholics with bibles. Olivia Rehmer is a thirty-three-year-old mother of four, a homemaker who left the church when she was young but has returned with a vengeance. She leads a liturgy group for children at Sunday mass at St. Vincent de Paul Church on Roncesvalles Avenue. She is far from being a radical; she simply believes that St. Germaine Greer is just as important as St. Peter.

"Of course it bothers me," she says, "that, while women maintain the Church and have kept it alive over centuries, the people with all the authority are still men. I'm disillusioned. A few years ago, Ambrozic was coming to visit the church. We had altar girls, and the priest, a really good guy, said we'd have to not use them. We didn't. That made me mad. He was due to visit again two years ago, and we said, no way, the girls stay. In the end he had to cancel. But I mean, who is this guy anyway? Nobody likes him a whole lot, nobody I've spoken to."

Rehmer's frustration is not only over the issue of ordination of women. She's angry about the entire structure and hierarchy of the Church. "And it's not about new generations either, because we've seen that the only younger men who get any power are those who toe the line. I left the Church, I returned, thought that maybe I could cut through some of the crap. I do little things, refer to God as 'She' for the children during the liturgy groups. A little bit of good."

Now consider the story of two devout Roman Catholics, a brother and a sister, Stephen and Janet Somerville. One attacks Ambrozic from the right, the other from the left. They come from a family soaked in Catholicism. Their father was editor of the *Catholic Register*, the largest circulation church newspaper in Canada. Stephen is a priest at Blessed

Edith Stein Church on Thorncliffe Park Drive. He is a slim, approachable man with a pleasing voice and an avuncular manner. He is also committed to liturgical tradition and critical of any moves towards modernization.

"Oh dear," he says, "they even want to abolish kneeling at mass. Terrible. I've written an attack on this position." Father Somerville believes Ambrozic is too loyal to his fellow bishops and too willing to ignore their errors, even if they transgress orthodox Catholic theology (some, for example, favour inclusive gender language in the liturgy). "I saw a priest coming out of the Chancery office almost in tears after a dressing down," he says. "The man had criticized a bishop in a Catholic newspaper, and he was being dealt with. It appears that, in this church, an attack upon a bishop is the worst crime. I myself was fired from the editorship of a small Catholic journal — well, in fact, the thing was closed down — because I believe we were saying things the archbishop didn't want to hear, about the dangers of change."

The statement is doubly surprising: first, priests seldom criticize or even comment on one another; second, Somerville's conservatism should make him an ally of the archbishop. He wipes his forehead as if to indicate that he has had a close call and advises me to talk to his sister, Janet, who works for the left-leaning *Catholic New Times*, a newspaper that possesses a palpable anticapitalist feel, concentrating on issues such as Central America and female ordination. "Janet is the voice of reason on the *Catholic New Times*," he says a little condescendingly.

I explain to Janet that her brother recommended the interview. "Oh you met Stephen, did you?" she says. "I don't know what's happened to him. So right wing now." She is a recognizable type within the modern Catholic world. A secular nun. Sensible shoes, sensible thin nylon sweater, sensible trousers. There are many Catholic women who have remained single, probably celibate, waiting for the day they are allowed to become priests. Janet stares at me throughout our meeting, looking up to the heavens for five- or ten-second bouts before answering each question.

Of Ambrozic, she says, "Of course he's the wrong man for the job at a time of extreme change and movement in the Church, in the world.

He's not in tune with the aspirations of ordinary people." She pauses, then gives another one of those looks to the gods, or to God.

"At this paper, we're passionately rooted in the scriptural belief in justice, against domination, power, control. On the side of the poor, those who lack influence. I suppose, well, that the archbishop is biased towards another direction. Having said that, those of us who were nervous, alarmed when he was named as archbishop have been fairly relieved. As Bishop Ambrozic, he had been very active around the schools, controlling, smothering, doing things that teenagers would not put up with; you know, against modern sex education, the discussion of AIDS, teenage sex, real life I suppose. As archbishop, well he could have been worse, and we're prepared to sit it out." She is referring to the fact that some on the left feared Ambrozic would intervene on an almost daily basis with the details as well as the overall running of education and faith within Toronto Catholicism. He hasn't; he couldn't; he is simply too busy and understands that the task would be impossible.

Ambrozic is caught between Peter's rock and a hard place. He is aware of the complaints, the disapproval. "This saddens me," he says. "It really saddens me . . . criticism from within. I know it, I know it." This is one of those moments when Ambrozic indicates a form of weakness, even impotence. The truth is that he is a man who cares more about his Church than anything else and would dearly love to ease its suffering and expunge its divisions. He tries extremely hard but he cannot, in the long run, achieve his ends. It is rather like a well-meaning but extremely conservative father attempting to talk his nose-pierced, drug-taking son out of antisocial behaviour. There is no meeting place, no link, no common ground. Love exists, but communication doesn't.

There is also the changing nature of an archbishop's role. Indeed, some question the very basis of the office following revelations that Archbishop Robert Sanchez of New Mexico was involved in sexual relationships with several women and that Atlanta's Archbishop Eugene Marino was forced out of office after being caught in an affair.

"Yeah, there have been moments when I've longed for academic life," he admits, "and it never really entered my head that I would be a bishop. I'm an immigrant. Immigrants don't become bishops. But it's as difficult to pray as a professor as it is as a bishop. When I was a student, there was a problem, a problem that kept coming, a real problem of faith" — a pause, and he quickly changes the subject. "As an archbishop I have protection, I have a secretary, I've got various people, and if I don't feel like going, don't want to go somewhere, I've got someone to represent me, to be a wall around me."

And then Aloysius M. Ambrozic's press secretary reminds him that he has an interview with another journalist. "Oh, I don't like that man, don't want to see him," he says, raising his voice, suddenly strident. His press secretary reddens, halts and then begins a sentence. She is interrupted. "No, no, I don't want to see him, I don't like him. That's your job, to make up an excuse for me."

And here, encapsulated, is the conundrum of the archbishop of Toronto: the ring, the position, the man. The first is his symbolic link with the Almighty and is still in place; the second is under the combined siege of doubt and division but is holding; the third is willing, eager, committed but, according to most who are qualified to judge, unable to take the former two into the final years of the twentieth century.

A View of Celibacy in the Catholic Church

After the Second Vatican Council and the new liberalism of the 1960s, many windows of the Roman Catholic Church were opened. And so were some doors. Ranks of priests who had harboured reservations or doubts about their vocation decided it was time to leave the clergy. Since then, the priesthood has undergone a crisis: seminaries are dangerously underpopulated, the laity question the role of priests and sordid revelations shake the very foundations of the church. Even more men have abandoned the dog-collar.

Dominic is one of these men. He is an American who spends half of each year in Ontario. Scion of a New York–Irish family, he became a priest in his twenties and remained one for a decade. It was the combination of doubt about his role and a blossoming relationship with a woman, whom he later married, that obliged him to make the decision to leave. He is still a Catholic, still observes the sacraments and is raising his children in the Church. He knows several priests, some of them as friends. He feels nothing but sorrow and pity for them.

"It was as difficult to leave as it was to enter. Both leaps were incredibly difficult. It was mainly about celibacy. I was spending too much of my time, my energy, my inner strength on coping with it. Celibacy was preventing me from being the priest I wanted to be, preventing me from being the Christian I wanted to be," he says, fingering his wedding ring. "Celibacy had become an end rather than a means. That's the case with any number of priests, believe me. This was pain for no reason. A relationship with God can be deepened by denial, by sacrifice, I know that, of course. But it can also be soured and dirtied."

There is, in fact, no convincing basis or argument for priestly celibacy in the Bible, and the Roman Catholic Church itself did not always require it. Protestantism has never insisted on it, and Eastern Orthodoxy includes married as well as celibate priests. Considering its relatively meagre theological significance, the issue has become far more important within Catholicism than it probably deserves to be.

"It's got in the way, of progress, of unity, of God," protests Dominic. "Let's be realistic. I'd say that more than a third of priests have had or are having some sort of sex, and probably as many have homosexual feelings, many of them consummated. There are some orders that have separate houses for straight and gay men. It's not the homosexuality that shocks me but the fact that they are so dishonest about this. Condemning homosexuality publicly but ignoring it privately. Hypocrisy. The reason there are so many gay men in the priesthood is in the nature of our society. Gay men can disguise their sexuality in a homophobic society by becoming priests, not having to get married."

He stops for breath, eager to tell all now. "It will change, because of need. There are areas where there just aren't priests. North American and European parishes are desperate. When it reaches breaking point, then the Vatican will decide that it might just be time to question celibacy. What a coincidence. If only it could be done now, by choice rather than by need."

This seems rather cynical. "Remember, I was a priest. I know how these things work," he says, determined to stress his point. "If you could get an honest answer from every priest in Canada about celibacy, I have no doubt at all that the majority would be against it. But the Church is not a democracy. It would be tragic if sex scandal, abuse cases and empty pulpits had more influence than the wishes of good, faithful priests."

I ask Dominic if he would re-enter the priesthood, if it changed its ways and its regulations. He answers me with a joke.

"God visits the pope, asks him some questions. 'My son,' says God, 'will there ever be women priests?' The pope replies, 'Not in my lifetime.' God then asks, 'Will there be married priests?' The pope says again, 'Not in my lifetime.' God asks one last question. 'Will there be any change in the Church?' And again the pope says, 'Not in my lifetime.' As God is about to leave, the Holy Father says, 'Before you go, Lord, tell me: Will there be another Polish pope?' God stares at him and says, 'Not in my lifetime.' "

A pause and a smile. "I won't become a priest again, not in anyone's lifetime."

The Sorry State of Catholic Writing

I am not a fan of revolutionary literature. Usually so trite and predictable. Karol Wojtyla's *Crossing the Threshold of Hope* is, however, better than most; more radical and erudite and certainly more threatening to the established order. It is, in fact, glacial in its simplicity in that it echoes G. K. Chesterton's phrase from *What's Wrong with the World*, that "the Christian ideal has not been tried and found wanting. It has been found difficult and left untried."

The book had an initial print run of more than 20 million. And how indicative of the dreadful state of Catholic writing that the most successful Catholic writer of the late twentieth century should not be a Graham Greene, an Evelyn Waugh or a Flannery O'Connor but a John Paul II.

I suppose much of it is now up to popes. It has to be. Because if Catholic literature and journalism is left only to the Roman Catholic laity there are dark, Calvinist stormclouds ahead. That noble, rosary-long tradition of the Catholic intellectual and writer, once as enviable as it was inevitable, is dangerously close to termination. The dumbing of Catholicism in this country is connected, in particular, with the faith's embrace of assimilation and consequent secularism, and with a fear of being perceived as being different, alien, un-Canadian. The headlong rush of Catholic schools and colleges to be just like their non-religious counterparts and to expunge Catholicity from the arts curriculum has been gruesome. Why study a Catholic writer, teachers appear to be saying, when there is a good, pragmatic humanist to read?

Part of this cause and effect of Catholic decline can be witnessed in the numerous regional and provincial Catholic newspapers and magazines. None has a particularly large circulation and few have any content of quality. The two publications that claim something of a national voice are *The Catholic Register* and *The Catholic New Times*. The former is mainstream and conservative, its flavour indicated by one of its regular columns being titled "The Little World of Father Raby." When perusing *The Catholic Register* I cannot help recalling British novelist Frederic Raphael's damning comment about the insularity of the English newspaper *The Jewish Chronicle*. "I'll give you a typical *Chronicle* headline," wrote Raphael. "London Marathon: Goldstein 35th!"

The Catholic New Times is to the left of the *Register*. In private some commentators would claim that the *New Times* was established to balance the "jock church" *Register*. But in its own way this more flimsy if self-consciously more political newspaper has become equally obeisant to, in this case, liberal leaders and ideas. The journalism is, unfortunately, callow and relentlessly mawkish.

"This sort of thing is usually written by Gucci nuns," says Father George William Rutler, the author of the highly praised *Beyond Modernity* and one of those people who personify what hope there is for Catholic letters in North America. Rutler is one of the stars of the Ignatius Press in San Francisco, a house dedicated to publishing the Catholic classics and new works by Catholic thinkers. By "Gucci nuns" Rutler means media-friendly religious women, and their male equivalents, who seem more at home at launch parties than in churches.

Rutler has a reputation for wit and for technological and political conservatism, and with the likes of James Schall, Peter Kreeft and Thomas Howard on the Ignatius list he is attempting to resurrect the Catholic intellectual. He is, like so many of his comrades in this contemporary *Kulturkampf*, a convert.

Father Richard John Neuhaus, founder and editor of *First Things*, subtitled "A Monthly Journal of Religion and Public Life," began as a Lutheran and was raised in the Ottawa Valley. *First Things* is an intensely intelligent and urbane magazine, is increasing circulation at an exponential rate and is now required reading not only for thinking Catholics but for Protestant and Jews, who also write for what some now see as the Catholic version of *Commentary*.

"It was not so much that Catholic intellectuals were lost, more that they were told to leave and close the door behind them," Neuhaus told me recently in his New York office. "It is almost as if Catholics were embarrassed by it all. To a very large extent it can never be recaptured." He pauses. "It is a situation where a supreme effort might just restore us to how we were forty years ago. Depressing. But that's where faith comes in, isn't it?" Apparently Father Neuhaus, like that other Catholic intellectual in Rome, has crossed the threshold of hope.

Toronto's Divine Bookshops

Lipstick on the mouth of a statue of the Virgin Mary is all very well, but would the real lady have worn a deep crimson, or opted for a more subtle and implicit shade of pink? If the answer is to be found anywhere at all, it will be found on the pristine, polished shelves in the bookshop of the Daughters of St. Paul on Dufferin Street. This, the largest and best stocked of the Catholic bookshops in Toronto, is where the Roman righteous read. It does, of course, have theological competition.

The United Church bookstore hides itself away in glorious isolation on St. Clair East. The literary spearhead of Canada's most radical church prides itself on ecumenism and tolerance. This was best represented by a poster that once decorated its front window, featuring two adorable beavers rubbing noses, and the poignant statement "Love Is about Sharing." Thomas Aquinas? I inquired of the obese and hirsute man behind the counter, uniformed in a Sandinista T-shirt. "Oh I don't know really." A pause for a sip of very creamy coffee. "Someone told me it was an idea from the manager's mother, I think."

Love is seldom mentioned at any of the three Evangelical bookstores on Yonge, Lawrence and Royal York. Disguised under the initials EP, these establishments are strong on damnation, three-piece suits and Christian ashtrays. "I was in prison once, you know," I was aggressively informed by one employee, eager to spread the Good News of incarceration and liberation. "And then I discovered Christ. I bet that surprises you." Strangely enough, it didn't.

Nobody who works or shops at the Anglican Book Centre on Jarvis Street has ever been to prison, and very few of them have discovered Christ. But they are capable of choking to death an entire neighbourhood with the frankincense they have in stock, and some of the cassocks on sale are, in at least one sense of the word, quite divine.

Toronto, then, is unusually well endowed with religious bookshops, each bathed in its own national, ethnic and religious origins. National origin shapes the content, the style, the flavour of each store. The Daughters of St. Paul's Centre, for example, has slowly shed its Irish voice and gradually adopted the accents of Southern Europe. Portuguese missals fly around the room like Iraqi missiles, ostentatious and risible Italian wall decorations — "Real tears from the Madonna" "Jesus's wounds are guaranteed to light up when the lights are switched off" — are enough to turn the gentlest of souls towards Mecca and Shi'ite Islam. There was once a crusade by a group of British Catholics to expunge the vulgarity from the religion's memorabilia and objects of devotion. It goes without saying that they failed, miserably.

"We have to order for our public, order what is going to be bought. I'm afraid the old days are long, long gone," explained a delightful sister in a bland habit. "Chinese language works are becoming extremely popular, you know." *The Catholic Register*, which is sold in large numbers by the Daughters of St. Paul, is equally a product of its readers. It appears that there are few people who read the *Register* who can survive this modern world, with its whirling uncertainties and maelstrom of fears and anxieties, or even get through a working day, without a perusal of that journal's most popular column, "The Little World of Father Raby." A recent edition featured a most interesting letter from a concerned communicant from Moose Jaw. "I committed a mortal sin years ago, but did not confess the specific kind of sex sin it was. I've been worried ever since if the sin was forgiven, or my communion sacrilegious."

If the papists are swayed from the South, the Anglicans look towards Albion. How could they not? Theirs is the best, most sophisticated shop of its kind, and wears its deliciously camp air not so much on its sleeve, but more like an armlet. Flaming church garments rub shoulders with delicate icons, the works of puritanical missionaries are juxtaposed with slim but muscular volumes with gay vicars and God-doubting prelates. One almost expects an octogenarian female to enter with a plate of cucumber sandwiches and last week's edition of *Punch*, to announce that there has been a murder at the vicarage. No tacky translations here, and, interestingly enough, the Anglicans sell literature on other denominations. Anne Roche Muggeridge's eviscerating work on the post-Vatican II Roman Church, *The Desolate City*, for example, is more readily available here than in a Catholic bookstore. Broadmindedness, or some Jesuitical plot to undermine the scarlet rivals from Babylon?

The Anglicans also have the best sales in town. A complete crèche set from Germany, with each of the shepherds wearing his own individual and unique expression of adoration, and a baby Jesus in exact and appropriate proportion to a gratuitously Aryan-looking Mary, may be bought for under half the retail price by the middle of February. How fickle are the faithful. The music that is sold — more CDs than anything else, for this is still the church of the upper-middle classes — is elegant and expensive, evoking Cornish cathedrals, the age of Handel and, just as poignantly, that dear old lady with the cucumber sandwiches.

There are very few echoes of the green and pleasant land in the low church; the Evangelicals are inspired and often subsidized from the United States. The Bible Belt has expanded in recent years, and its body and bodies have become distended. If the back of the Protestant waistline begins somewhere near southern Chile — half of Central America is embracing fundamentalism, and the San Salvador branch of EP Books is running dangerously low on *I Was a Pimp for Castro Until I Was Born Again* — its buckle stretches to north of Toronto. On my visit to the downtown EP store I was accosted outside on the street by a young woman with sensible shoes and painted nails who asked me if I was a Christian. "Yes, a Catholic," was my response. "Aha! Then confess to the Lord, and kneel with me now to embrace the faith of Christ Jesus. Rome is idolatry."

The Evangelicals may be intolerant, small-minded and repellent, but at least they hold a tangible and consistent set of beliefs. EP Books is keen on salvation stories: prostitute turned into lay preacher, homosexual turned into father of ten, alcoholic turned into lemonade manufacturer; it is less enthusiastic about theology. "Theology is there in huge proportions," I was told by a friendly customer. "It's all in one place. The Bible."

EP is also the leading venue for audiovisual proselytizing. Whereas the Catholics are still pushing shoestring budget versions of *The Fatima Story*, where Portuguese actors mouth words they do not understand — Father De Silva says, "She is the mother of Christ" as though he were asking for a can of tuna and a pickled herring — the Evangelicals spend a fortune on recording their heroes and their views. One video, *Shadowlands*, about the life of C. S. Lewis is, I was told, extremely popular. The British television play was superlative, unprosaically pregnant with wit and charm. The version on offer in EP Books, however, has been edited and altered. No longer is Lewis's wife abrasive and difficult, no longer does Lewis act and pray as an Anglo-Catholic. This is Lewis the Squeaky Clean. Lewis the Evangelical.

Such a thing could never happen at the United Church bookstore. C. S. Lewis may still be the meat and potatoes of United Church Sunday schools on the Prairies, but in progressive Toronto he is virtually persona non grata. The place of origin for this church is, of course, Canada. The United — it sounds like a British soccer team — is the country's only indigenous church, the church of unity, compromise and sheer flummery. Popularly known — after a remark of Disraeli's about the English Tories and the Anglicans — as the New Democratic Party at prayer, the United Church has abandoned its Christian identity with such alacrity that rumour has it that it is now considering the ordination of practising diabolists. "But only politically correct ones," my informant urged. The words "compassion," "community," "abuse" and "sharing" jump out of the bookshelves with alarming regularity.

In the seventeenth century it was fashionable among Protestants to burden their offspring with such names as PraiseGod Barebones, TheLordIsGreat Smith and Christ AllPowerful Johansen. Imagine a generation of Community Watson, DomesticViolence Jones and PreferentialOptionForThePoor Forbes-Strutterford.

I was told that the shop's most popular titles concern the female Godhead or the church and homosexuality. "What about sin?" I inquired. "There's not much demand for that around here," was the stoical answer.

The ecumenical aspects of the shop extend to Matthew Fox, the Vatican-silenced Catholic author of such works as *On Becoming a Musical, Mystical Bear*; *Whee, We, Wee All the Way Home*; and *A Spirituality Named Compassion & the Healing of the Global Village, Humpty-Dumpty, & Us.* If all this is too heady, there are some rather beautiful posters of bucolic scenes for sale, with useful thoughts for the day inscribed at the bottom.

Yet trade is slow these days. When I asked one customer, an attractive

West Indian woman in her forties, why she had chosen this particular shop, she explained that her daughter's best friend at school had a bar mitzvah approaching, and she hoped that here she could purchase a card "with a bit of religion and a bit of fun."

It was Shaw, and if it wasn't it should have been, who said that the true Christian ought never to read, because it might lead him into bad habits. I repeat this to the disarmingly pretty nun at the Daughters of St. Paul. She smiles — do I detect a twinkle in those blue, blue eyes? — and pulls at her black, black dress. "Oh dear, do you think he was referring to this sort of thing?"

I think not. Perhaps, in fact, he was referring to the Edwardian equivalent of those beavers rubbing noses.

MORALITY

Veracity is the heart of morality.

THOMAS HENRY HUXLEY
UNIVERSITIES, ACTUAL AND IDEAL

Morality, Ethics and Social Values Never Go Out of Fashion

G. K. Chesterton, the grand knight of literary common sense, died in 1936, wrote myriad columns and books, and understood above all else that the basic tenets of morality, ethics and social values never fundamentally change, in spite of fashions.

It is interesting to speculate what the man would have said about some of the activities shaping contemporary Canada. There was, for example, the announcement that the City of Toronto spent $2,000 on a video made by drug addicts for drug addicts, explaining how to "shoot up" properly. The interesting logic offered to justify this home movie for junkies was that as drug addiction will always exist we should simply ensure the fatal habit is conducted properly and cleanly.

Why not extend the argument? Pedophilia will always exist so we ought to make a video for pedophiles explaining how to undertake their perversion responsibly and with minimum fuss; or even one for burglars, because they too will always be with us, giving little tips about the best way to break and enter. There is a culture war being fought and some people have already waved a publicly funded white flag.

Then there is the government's refusal in the last budget to reduce or eliminate funding for the National Action Committee on the Status of Women, the extremist organization that claims more than two million members but whose vice-president admitted to me on live radio that her mailing list has under 20,000 names. Which means the taxpayer is funding NAC at a rate of around $250 per head. I think I'll join. NAC is consulted on most legislation concerning women and is assumed to speak for the women of Canada — meaning every woman is radically pro-abortion, radically pro-lesbian, radically pro-NDP. Perhaps I won't join after all.

The old sage Chesterton would certainly have written a column or two about the abolition of an entire military unit just because a handful of its members had behaved badly, and might even have applied similar criteria to the House of Commons. And he would have pounced upon the introduction of repugnant speech codes forbidding us to use traditional language, and at a group of Toronto teachers calling for phrases such as "kill two birds with one stone" and "sabre rattling" to be expunged because they are violent, militaristic and doubtless lead to, well, to the 50 per cent of Canadian women who, according to a ludicrous survey last year, have been assaulted.

The foundation for so much of this hysteria and hypocrisy can be traced to the 1960s and to those affluent liberals who were at the forefront of the permissive society and argued that promiscuity, pornography and narcotics were acceptable in a mature, open state. They created a moral vacuum and people, just like nature, abhor such a thing. The hole has been filled with political correctness, aggressive minority interests and a contempt for authentic democracy.

Today we see many of those old red guardians, still in positions of power, cringing as the new leftist puritanism prevents them from indulging in Bollinger Bolshevism. There is, I suppose, something bitterly satisfying about this. It is more comforting to bathe in the knowledge that their ideas, just like the lunacies emanating from the current crop of zealots, have no staying power, the reason being that the best notions are based on the permanent things, the first things, the intellectualizing of the instinctive. We seldom have to be told what is truly right, we know it viscerally or we were told it by our parents before we could even spell morality or justice, before we could even spell.

But there is still something terribly wrong with the world. Many of us know it. Gilbert Keith Chesterton certainly did.

Ethical Law Takes a Holiday from Canada's Social Dynamic

In April 1995, a John Young was sentenced to two years in prison for selling pornographic videos depicting children in graphic acts of sex.

Some of the young people used in the film were impoverished and desperate street-kids. Two years in a Canadian prison with all of the facilities which that implies seems a meagre punishment, but at least another monster is out of circulation for a short while. And we can all congratulate Canadian justice, Canadian morality and Canadian concern for the vulnerable. A bad man has been caught and all is well in the world of the young.

Someone called Gerald Hannon apparently disagrees. He thinks that children are not being treated properly. Reviewing a book about the sexual abuse of children in *Xtra*, the homosexual newspaper of Toronto, Hannon wrote of the author, "She has let pity and outrage run away with her senses, and has produced a book that takes as its premise the notion that sexual contacts between children and adults can never be ethical. I find that position intellectually unsatisfying."

He went on to explain that he could not understand "how children's hockey differed from an organized child-sex ring. Both involved strenuous physical activity (adult coaches taking the role of the adult lover). Both involved danger. Both involved pleasure. Yet we approve of children's hockey and deplore child-sex rings."

I mention Hannon because he is by no means a marginalized individual who is usually silenced. *Xtra* is not a fringe newspaper but is a major alternative voice and the largest homosexual journal in the country. More than this, *The Globe and Mail* also saw fit to publish a feature article by Gerald Hannon earlier this year on the subject of pedophilia in which he referred dismissively to "police-constructed moral panic" on this subject about which he evidently knows so much. He also reviews books about sex and pornography for the same journal. His views appear to be respected. But Hannon does not sell pornographic videos. Our children are safe.

Then we have the Internet, the brave new device that is apparently going to change the world for the better and is championed by those clever souls who genuinely understand the future. One of the growth areas on this computerized cacophony is in child sex. Pictures of prepubescent boys fill the screen and the joys of child sex are described in grotesque detail. But it's okay, don't worry. Nobody is selling pornographic videos on the Internet. Again, our children are safe.

And of course there is highly respected author and broadcaster Sue Johanson, whose new book, published by a leading international company, explains all there is to know about sex. The author laments that children of eleven or twelve will miss a good deal of the book because they haven't had enough "life experience to tap into it." But Johanson is confident that "they will remember what's appropriate for them." Sue Johanson would never even dream of being involved in pedophiliac videos. Thank goodness our children are still safe.

Lastly there are those advertisers and television-producers who absolutely adore children. So much so that they use them to sell every product known to humanity and insert them into jarringly adult situations in comedies and dramas. They also present acts of nauseating violence, sometimes of a sexual or crypto-sexual nature, in programs that air in the early evening. But they do not sell pornographic videos. Of course our children are safe with them.

One distributor of kiddie-porn is in prison. He broke the law. At least the criminal law. The ethical law seems to be taking a vacation from the political and social dynamic of contemporary Canada. Nod your head in satisfaction that a malodorous exploiter of Dickensian proportions is in prison for a while, gasp in incredulity at his crime and wash your hands with the soap of indifference and the warm, comforting water of apathy. A little less filth is being sold to a bunch of fetid perverts.

And our children are safe. As safe, in fact, as an old established British bank.

Euthanasia Is Simply Wrong, Wrong and Wrong Again

Dr. Sheila Harding has a little story to tell. The Saskatchewan-based woman has a severely handicapped son, a boy who is obliged to undergo frequent surgery. One such operation occurred shortly after the Latimer case came to light, in which a man gassed his disabled daughter to death so as to "end her suffering." Dr. Harding's little boy heard about the incident. He was terrified. "Don't worry, Mommy," he said in desperate tones before one painful operation. "Please don't worry, I know I can stand it. Please, Mommy, you don't have to kill me."

I have held off from writing about this for quite a while. I wanted the bulk of the particularities of the Latimer case and the raw emotions provoked by it to have subsided. But now it is time to speak out on one of the most profound issues facing contemporary Canada. Time for this columnist to explain why he believes that euthanasia is wrong, wrong and wrong again. And to state quite clearly that the vortex surrounding the culture of death is capable of swallowing up not only evil people but good ones who wrap their misplaced compassion in a cloak of naïveté.

The issue is enormous but it speaks volumes if we explore the fundamental logical and moral basis of the argument of those who support the legislation of euthanasia. It would, they say, be voluntary and be based on free will. Simply, I do not believe that such a state of affairs is possible, even if it were desirable.

First, many people in the final stages of an illness are in no position to request death and the decision would have to be made by their doctor or family. Fine, say supporters of euthanasia, because families know best. Yet the same people who fight for euthanasia rights seem to be the first to tell us that families are often abusive. If so, surely we should not trust them to decide on whether a relative lives or dies.

Second, even if patients are clear of mind they would still be liable to enormous pressure from a society that is increasingly impatient with the ill and the handicapped and aggressive about the costs of caring for the terminally ill. Many seriously ill people become deeply depressed and temporarily suicidal. There might also be influences from families that, although still caring, are exhausted and indicate that life would be a great deal easier without poor old grandpa.

Third, and most important, so-called voluntary euthanasia has already been accepted and attempted in the Netherlands for some time.

In a universally respected study known as The Remmelink Report it was discovered that the "voluntary" part of the equation disappears extremely quickly. The report focused on 1990 and found that out of a population of 15 million there were 2,300 cases of voluntary euthanasia, 400 cases of assisted suicide, where the means of death is provided to the patient for self-administration, and 1,040 examples of involuntary euthanasia.

The latter involved a doctor acting without the request of the patient. Fourteen per cent of these victims were completely competent when they were "mercy killed" and the majority of the rest had never given any indication that they wished to be "put out of their misery." Another 8,100 people died after doctors gave them sufficient morphine to shorten their lives. Many of these patients were not even consulted about the decision.

Thus we have a large number of doctors killing an even larger number of patients without their consent. Many doctors also admitted to lying on their medical reports and stating that their patients had died from natural causes. If cases of dishonesty are added to the figures, says the report, the real number of people killed by doctors in Holland in 1990 was 25,306, almost 20 per cent of the total deaths in the country. It is probable that the majority of these were not voluntary.

The Dutch example indicates that any societal acceptance of voluntary euthanasia leads to an acceptance, even an encouragement, of non-voluntary "mercy killing" and a subsequent neglect of palliative care and training. Death has become a viable option. But, of course, we are morally superior to the people of Holland and such a thing could never happen here.

I have seen the future and it stinks of the odour of the morgue.

Violence Around the Abortion Debate

In April 1995, an anti-abortion group called Human Life International held a convention in Montreal. The press, bused in to the city with even more enthusiasm and alacrity than the rent-a-mob protesters, told the world that security at local abortion clinics would be increased, referring to the terrible, if isolated, attack in Boston earlier that year.

But was such a reaction justified in Canada? A similar phenomenon occurred when an abortion-performing doctor in Vancouver was shot. Anti-abortion groups were accused even though there was no pertinent evidence and no perpetrator had been caught. Similarly with the bombing of the Morgentaler Clinic in Toronto. Here, however, a CSIS report even said that pro-abortion zealots were suspected, having bombed the clinic so the Ontario government would then suppress pro-life activity. Oddly enough the media have been somewhat slow in picking up this particular news item.

But there definitely is violence around the abortion issue in Canada, as fifty-one-year-old Paul Nielsen can testify. For many years this Vancouver pro-lifer had experienced what he describes as "the usual sort of trouble on demonstrations. Punching, kicking, spitting. Oh yes, and threatening phone calls late at night." Until 1988 that is, when a Molotov cocktail was thrown through his office window. The firebombing shook him and his family but at least nobody was in the building at the time.

Not so in October 1993. Nielsen was asleep at his home, as were his wife and children. Suddenly a window was smashed. Nothing new there, bricks had shattered the windows for some time now. But on this occasion a marine smoke-bomb had been thrown and the fumes from this sort of device are so thick and toxic that they suffocate and kill extremely quickly.

"We were terrified," says Nielsen. "We managed to get out by sheer luck. The fire marshal told us that two more minutes and we all would have been dead. These things are deadly. What is even more awful is that we usually have our tiny grandchildren to stay, just babies, and if they'd been with us that night, I don't see how we could have made it." The press were informed but did not cover the case.

After this the Nielsens took precautions, but evidently not enough. In November another bomb was thrown through a window from a passing car. Now it was time for evacuation and for boarding up windows. A state of siege developed. Nielsen hired a security firm and the police monitored the house. "The stress is unbelievable," he says. "Imagine what this does to a young child, imagine the nightmares. Eight people almost gone, just like that."

This bewilderingly sanguine man stresses that he is not the only victim of such incidents. "At the end of last year a guy drove his car into a prayer circle outside an abortion clinic. If the people hadn't moved so quickly they would have been hit. Hardly made the news at all. Then there's Jim Hughes in Toronto. He's been thrown down stairs, he's been followed by a pair of guys with tire irons until the police came along, he had the bolts on his car wheels loosened — that one almost killed him. Pro-lifers are blamed for so much of the violence but this is rubbish. Pro-life means pro all life, not just the unborn. Congreve said, 'He that first cries stop thief, is often he that has stolen the treasures.' That's rather interesting."

What Nielsen would ultimately like is balance and equity. He knows that some people will dislike him because of his views and he believes, just as his opponents, that abortion is a life and death issue. He also knows that the majority of pro-life supporters believe in civilized and non-violent debate, and understands that this also applies to the vast majority of his opponents.

In his heart of hearts, however, he believes that the victims of attempted murder, of beatings and of casual violence are more often opponents of abortion than advocates of it. He would like the media to give it some thought. Before it's too late.

We Need a Little Help Defining Racism in Canada

Two black lawyers, each at the top of their profession, accuse each other of racism during the trial of a third black person, O. J. Simpson, for murder. The reason is that a white witness had the audacity to describe a particular voice as sounding as if it came from a black man.

A professor in a Canadian university is accused of racism and forced to fight a long and costly legal battle to clear her name. This is because she told an Iranian student that it was regrettable so many people in his country had been condemned by the Islamic government. The student, who had been receiving poor marks from the professor, thought the remark to be profoundly racist and offensive.

It is suggested that lawyers, policemen and teachers attend "racism awareness" courses. The sessions are not to be compulsory but the names of those who do not attend will be known and noted.

Racism. Such a minefield of political and social sin that we all surely need help in defining the terms of debate, particularly in a Canadian context. Here we go:

1) *I don't like Indian food.* Obvious, this one.

2) *I do like Indian food.* Don't be misled. Clumsy attempt to disguise guilt. Also an indulgence in imperialist rape of ethnic cuisine.

3) *I think I might vote Reform next election.* You're a Nazi.

4) *I think I might vote PC next election.* You're a Nazi from central Canada.

5) *Why don't we have crime statistics based on race? After all, we have them based on age, gender and class and we pay for the gathering of statistics in the first place.* The very suggestion is only one step away from the death-camps. Most crime is committed by bankers and businessmen anyway and if you've ever watched *Street Legal* on the CBC you'd know there is no link between crime and race and there never has been.

6) *Then why don't we release the statistics?* You're a Nazi.

7) *I sell Black Muslim newspapers in Canadian cities and call Judaism a gutter religion and think that white people are devils.* A sophisticated and sensitive call for justice. Compensation. Level playing-fields. Dead white males, etc.

8) *Immigration is healthy in moderation but surely we have a right as a nation-state to maintain a certain cultural homogeneity.* Where's your arm-band, Heinrich?

9) *I get the impression that too high a percentage of swarming and mugging crimes involve young West Indians. My Jamaican friends are outraged by this and are angry at white liberals who won't face the problem.* See numbers three, four and six. This is all about colour perception and you are a racist. Different cultures demand different things. And haven't you heard of slavery?

10) *Yes, but it was a long time ago and my ancestors risked their lives smuggling slaves to Canada and freedom. Also, Canadian soldiers and sailors died fighting African war-lords who refused to abolish slavery.* You're a Nazi who's read a book.

11) *I don't think Employment Equity is a good thing but I do think that every employer has a duty to form a representative workforce.* You're a sexist as well as a racist. The real world doesn't work the way you think. Employers hate new Canadians because, well, because they're new . . . and Canadians.

12) *There are dozens of documentaries about neo-Nazis on the television, often paid with public money, but these extremist groups seem to be powerless. Could it be that the people involved are neurotic buffoons who will say anything to a reporter just to be noticed and that our television journalists are too timid and callow to investigate real threats like drug-gangs and organized crime?* How do you think Hitler began, you moron?

13) *I thought Hitler began because of grotesque postwar depression, national humiliation, the rapid spread of communism and pervasive anti-Semitism.* Yes, just like contemporary Canada, but without the threat of the left, of course.

14) *Sorry, but I think Canada is rather a good country. I really don't see very much racism about, but I do read numerous articles in the liberal press about it.* Typical. Why don't you go back to where you came from.

How a Racist Won in London

The dénouement of denunciation was as predictable as it was inadequate. The people of a particularly run-down area of the rotted if not rotten London Borough of Tower Hamlets elected as their local councillor a member of the British National Party, a grubby little organization consisting of committed Nazis, social outcasts and skinheads.

The electorate spoke and its voice was jarring to the ear. All the mainstream British political parties condemned the result, and grey, grey Prime Minister John Major did his best to evince the appropriate form of anger on a public platform.

But the point has been missed. The election result in troubled Millwall has nothing to do with fascism, little to do with racism but much to do with a sense of powerlessness.

The same kind of men and women who are now being demonized in the press were lionized sixty years ago as the comrades who, arm-in-arm with the Communist Party and the local Jewish community (my family among them), halted Oswald Mosley and his British Union of Fascists as they tried to march through London's East End.

These dockland denizens are the industrial working class, the backbone of the Labour Party, the bulwark of the trade-union movement. They are soaked in the mythology of socialism and the people's struggle. And they have voted for a Nazi.

That the politicians who previously sought the Millwall vote are now castigating the Millwall voters should come as no surprise. It is far easier to revile the messenger than to consider the message.

The Conservative Party never stood a chance of winning a seat in the area and hence doesn't really care about the result; the Labour Party likes its workers bowdlerized and scrubbed, and anyway assumes that it will take back the riding in the next election.

What none of them will ask is why 1,400 people would vote for a party that possesses such sickening policies.

There is a lack of understanding and a clash between the more established white community in the area and the newer, Asian residents, and there is a tiny hard core of violent fanatics who have a far-right political agenda. This is so in many parts of Britain. Yet it has never in the past resulted in such an electoral shock — the last time a racist party won a seat was in 1976, but that group was more circumspect in its politics.

The reason that shopkeepers, postal workers, labourers, the unemployed and all the rest voted this way was because they felt impotent. Their grievances were ignored. Nobody was listening to them, nobody seemed to care. It is not the lust for power but the fear of powerlessness that provokes people into acts of extremism.

Margaret Thatcher's great wind of change brought myriad successes to Britain. But for the voters of Millwall, the nation's economic improvement was seen only vicariously through glossy advertisements and television dramas. It was passing them by.

They knew, and know, that bad housing, a filthy environment, poor schooling and unemployment are at least as hard on their Bangladeshi neighbours as they are on them. But they don't rationalize the situation.

The swines, right-thinking commentators now seem to be saying. How dare they not reflect upon their problems, debate them over a glass of sherry and then vote for a caring, compassionate social democrat who sees the election as a stepping-stone to greater political advancement.

Economic disadvantage is not the only motivation for feelings of powerlessness, and emetic Nazi parties are not the only conduit for these feelings. Beyond the tragedy of Millwall, we have middle-class Scots voting for a Scottish separatist party, comfortable Welsh farmers embracing Celtic nationalism. Why? Again, a sense of powerlessness.

These other marginalized voters might enjoy a full bank account and never fear street crime or inner-city decay, but London and genuine influence seem to be a very long way off; and the human condition has always been much more about the need for fulfilment than about economic well-being.

Thousands of miles from a district beside the Thames, there are accountants in Quebec City, policemen in Montreal, lawyers in Saskatoon and bankers in Calgary voting for groups beyond the three-party system that emphasize regional power or even complete independence. The factors of geographical distance, linguistic distinction and ethnic identity have turned out to be as important in the Canadian equation as any economic crisis.

When it comes to politics, both the rich and the poor are indulging in emotional spasms. Contemporary disenfranchisement is not about losing the vote but about losing a sense of individual influence over issues that shape one's life.

Until that fact is understood, British cockneys will shout instead of talk and Canadian voters will wonder whether established political parties, established federal systems — and even established countries — can really satisfy their needs.

Society's Moral Fabric Is Unravelling

So many words written, so many columns poured out of unilingual word processors from Halifax to Victoria. And all about a trivial vote about a trivial matter. If they go, they go. If they stay, they stay. Either way no gargantuan void will suddenly develop east of the Ontario border. We will all, I am sure, find a way. More important, surely, is that the whole Quebec issue has been a vast digression from the issues that really matter. The foundation of our culture, of any culture, is not language or geopolitics but family, children and morality.

And the traditional family is under attack from malicious and threatened people who have powerful friends and influential media allies. They mock the values that created the very society that, ironically, gives them the freedom and security to be so condescending and wrong-headed. Whereas illegitimate birth was once rare and disapproved of, it is now common and almost encouraged. Even though every survey and investigation proves that children need both parents, we deride any political leader with the courage and the candour to announce this fact in public. Will the Quebec referendum have any effect on this?

Hundreds of thousands of pre-born children are ripped in agony and terror from the womb because we have managed to justify the ultimate form of selfishness and have even glorified its practitioners. Yet if those babies somehow manage to make it into the world we now, under United Nations guidelines, give them the right to sue their parents and make a moral, and soon to be legal, crime for their mothers and fathers to gently smack them for naughtiness.

Our caring liberal state bombards our children with televisual images of violence, sexual perversion and greed, encourages both of these children's parents to go out to work and lauds the ideas of communal daycare. It caricatures and abandons the millennia-old and honoured notion of parental nurture and then looks to technology to introduce a special chip to replace those parents when it comes to censoring what tiny eyes see, tiny minds assimilate. Will the Quebec referendum have any effect on this?

While the liberal media trivializes and marginalizes the authentic family, it can barely contain its joy at any weird experiment with new, ostensibly familial forms. With the aid of test-tubes, an obliging third party or other tricks of science or promiscuity, lesbians have children and our editorial writers and opinion-makers tell us that this is beautiful, new, brave and inevitable. Our visceral instinctive and intellectual perception of what is ugly and ridiculous is dismissed as sheer bigotry.

When some of our religious leaders argue that the best way to prevent the spread of AIDS amongst teenagers is for them to lead a more restrained life, and that a million condoms do not one moral decision make, they are told by the chattering classes to mind their own business and that they know nothing about the reality of the situation. Yet still people die and still people cry. And rubber instead of resolution will, we are told once again, solve our problems. Will the Quebec referendum have any effect on this?

Multinational advertising companies and clothing manufacturers use and exploit sexual images, sometimes involving pre-pubescent models, to sell their products. Occasionally they go too far and have to apologize. They spend millions of dollars on such enterprises yet such amount of money spent on medical research would lead to the discovery of cures for several of the diseases that kill or maim our children.

Fathers are increasingly denied their role as parents by the legal system from their rightful place as equals in the upbringing of their children. Men taking their children on an airflight are now routinely advised by travel agents to obtain a letter of permission from their wives in case they are stopped by the authorities and questioned. In one case an airport official completely ignored a father, knelt down in front of a bewildered nine-year-old and asked, "Does your mommy know you are here?" It was an interesting start to a long-awaited holiday for father and son. Will the Quebec referendum have any effect on this?

If only the question was not so rhetorical. The sad reality is that in a week's time nothing will have changed. We fiddle while home burns.

Personalities

A biography is considered complete if it merely accounts for six or seven selves, whereas a person may well have as many thousand.

Virginia Woolf
Orlando, ch. 6

Irish Ires

The year is 1994. Two Irish politicians, two Hibernian thinkers in Canada simultaneously. One is Gerry Adams, leader of Sinn Fein, the gossamer-thin front for the Irish Republican Army. The other is Conor Cruise O'Brien, author, diplomat and consummate man of peace. Adams appears to be everywhere, in his manifestation as the champion of the IRA cease-fire. The newspapers report his speeches and his actions; he is questioned by intellectual featherweights on the CBC. It is obvious that hardly anyone concerned with all of this could even name a county in Northern Ireland, let alone decipher the internecine and interminable squabbles or the ancestral voices and vices of Irish politics, but the line has been thrown and swallowed.

Conor Cruise O'Brien is in Toronto to deliver the Massey Lectures (published by House of Anansi Press under the title *On the Eve of the Millennium*) and, indirectly, to give publicity to an extremely fine biography of him (*Conor*, published by McGill-Queen's University Press) by the Canadian academic Donald Harman Akenson. The man described by *The Atlantic Monthly* as "the only contemporary writer who can be compared to George Orwell and André Malraux" is hardly surprised that Gerry Adams is so successful, but he is very angry. "It's not so much the dumbing of America as the dumbing of everywhere. And less the dumbing of ordinary people than the dumbing of our leaders, of opinion-formers and opinion-shapers. We have been defeated by the sound bite, our concentration spans have been destroyed," he says, repeatedly linking the thumb and middle finger of his right hand and patting down the white hairs on his head. "Extremism is about simplistic solutions. That is what Adams offers, and that is why I oppose him."

The very essence of O'Brien's belief system is that it is the duty of every intellectual to challenge the political fashions of the day and, above all, to mistrust all forms of political or social extremism. For O'Brien this includes his native Ireland, it includes the country he is visiting and it includes his beloved Israel and the Middle East. These are, unfortunately, rare qualities in contemporary thinkers. But then

O'Brien is inspired more by the eighteenth century than the twentieth. More Burke than Burke, some would argue.

If it is true that we can see the depths of ignorance only from the heights of knowledge, this seventy-six-year-old, ruddy-faced Irishman in tweed jacket and open-necked shirt is the best of observers. His has been an intellectual and political road well travelled. It began with journalism in Ireland and continued with the civil service. Then came diplomacy the world over, a meandering into academe, and politics in Dublin — "a city where you can see a sparrow fall to the ground, and God watching it," he has said. He has been editor of Britain's *Observer* newspaper, a member of the Irish cabinet, a special assistant to the United Nations' Dag Hammarskjöld, head of the University of Ghana and then Schweitzer Professor at New York University. He is a stupendous traveller. As Akenson says pithily in his book, "This man, who was born free, was everywhere in planes."

Most of all, he has written. Perhaps the best modern book on his troubled homeland, *States of Ireland*, an extraordinary biography of Edmund Burke, *The Great Melody*, and a compendious and magnificently empathetic and crisp history of Israel and Zionism, *The Siege*. And articles, essays, arguments. People often quote the British conservative historian Paul Johnson's remark about the Burke book, that it was "by the greatest living Irishman on the greatest Irishman who ever lived." But then Johnson and O'Brien do have things in common. Politics, intellect, a taste for alcohol.

The drinking probably did O'Brien some good but it also did him some bad. People noticed the fact that at various functions he had evidently been investing heavily in the Scottish economy. He has since cut down and is relishing sixty-five-hour work weeks. "It's interesting, isn't it, what some people choose to notice," he says, rubbing his eyes, letting his gently Gaelic voice drop to a near whisper. "They don't ask what the last book was like, how effective a man might be as a diplomat, but speculate on how much he might have drunk over lunch."

The subject of O'Brien's Toronto lecture is "Religion, Ethnicity and Nationalism," issues heavy with Irish significance but also directly relevant to contemporary Canada. I wonder if he might be reluctant to discuss Canada, in Canada, at such a tenuous time. Not when there is extremism and political fashion to combat.

"If I was a member of the Parti Québécois right now . . . I would be extremely worried, extremely anxious to word that referendum to guarantee victory. And even if they win they could find themselves in a much more isolated position, a much more hostile world. If the worst happens, okay, perhaps the western provinces could separate and manage, Ontario could be independent in a loose relationship with the United States, but nobody would be terribly anxious to have Quebec as part of it, or even as a particularly close trading partner, not as it stands. Certainly not." A pause.

"This particular combination of linguistic and tribal differences is unique. But it isn't the really lethal cocktail that you find elsewhere. What is really interesting is the sharp decline in influence of the Catholic church in Quebec combined with the stability and intensification of the linguistic difference. They were felt to go together in the past, to be part of the same culture. There are parallels with Ireland. In the middle of the last century any criticism of the Catholic church was impossible. Now it is anodyne if you criticize the church . . . Though attendance at Mass is still over 80 per cent, perhaps the highest anywhere . . . The Irish attend Mass, they respect the pope — they don't take a blind bit of notice of what the pope says on subjects like contraception and so on, but they respect him.

"The animosities here are not as lethal as in Ireland, where people speak the same language. The friction appears to be worse when people speak the same language. In Canada the two linguistic groups are living in somewhat separate worlds and that cushions the anger."

But safety, particularly when it is wrapped in the malodorous blanket of conventional wisdom, is something that O'Brien has always eschewed. In Ireland he refuses to take the current cease-fire very seriously, seeing it as an act of political desperation by the IRA. He has never completely accepted the nationalist position and has deep sympathies with the Loyalists in the north. Some journalists like to think that this has made him a pariah in Ireland. "I might be one to the IRA. But I have no more craving for their society than they do for mine. The fellow travellers of the Provos are irrelevant to me, I welcome their hatred. As for the bulk of nationalists, they might disagree with me, gently deplore me. Most peopie either congratulate me or have no concern for politics."

It is on a region far from home, though, that O'Brien claims to have received the most acrimony and spleen. He is dreadfully unfashionable on the Middle East, supporting the Israeli point of view and daring to advocate Zionism in the English-speaking media, which have turned visibly away from the pro-Israel line they adopted until the mid-1970s. O'Brien's fellow Irishman, the playwright Brendan Behan, said, "Other people have a nationality. The Irish and the Jews have a psychosis." O'Brien has long been suspicious of what he sees as the international danger of Arab extremism and Islamic fundamentalism.

"When I was at *The Observer* I received letters from people about the Middle East that were quite obviously virulently anti-Semitic. I was surprised. So much passion. Endless comparing of Israeli actions with those of the Nazis, when there was no comparison at all. I've never attracted more hostility. In academic circles, in journalism, it is a very difficult path to tread these days."

It all seems so clear. This wonderful intellectualizing of an instinctive knowledge. Akenson captures some of this sagacious common-man flavour in his biography: "The ideal way to tell his story would be aloud, in an old pub, as part of a good conversation. It should be done on a weekday afternoon, when the place is given over to a few rays of sunshine coming through the grimy windows, and to old men sitting in corners, conversing softly. After a couple of pints they lean forward conspiratorially. One old fellow taps another on the knee and starts to talk about 'your man,' whoever that might be. That's how one wants to talk about Conor, with the sense that he might be coming through the door any moment, and, by God, things around here will pick up when he does."

I mention the passage to "your man."

"Oh, I'm not going to comment on anything in the book. Say nothing good or bad about what is written about you, runs an Irish proverb," he says, hitting me with a beguiling grin. "As to things picking up, well I don't know. I was at the UN for some time and I'm not optimistic about anything picking up there. The UN can do sweet bugger all about most things. That's what it's meant to do, to fail. One of the main functions of the UN is to be seen to fail, and then everybody can sit round and lament.

"Canada, on the other hand, has the resource repertoire to succeed. Be a damned shame if old divisions, rather regrettable ones, made that impossible."

As if, I suggest, in Canada you can see a dream fall to the ground, and God watching it.

Friend of the Fairies

There were fairies at the bottom of Sir Arthur Conan Doyle's garden. At least that was what the inspired father of Sherlock Holmes, Dr. Watson, Professor Challenger and Brigadier Gerard — a man knighted for his services to the British Empire — sincerely believed. He went to his death defending the honesty of a Yorkshire schoolgirl who claimed she had taken photographs of a group of gossamer-winged, wand-waving pixies. The photos still exist, the story disintegrated many years ago.

Conan Doyle's life was dominated not by detective writing, not by writing in any genre, but by an almost monomaniacal conviction that the supernatural was real, and that through a belief in and understanding of spiritualism our lives could be made abundantly meaningful. There exists a profoundly symbolic cartoon of Conan Doyle, his legs manacled to a tiny Sherlock Holmes, the miasma of smoke from the diminutive detective's meerschaum pipe enveloping and imprisoning the Gulliver-like creator. "Stop writing letters to me about Sherlock Holmes!" he wrote in June 1922. "It is of limited interest. Ask me, please ask me, about Spiritualism, about what really matters."

Conan Doyle always maintained that he had two birthdays: May 22,

1859, when he was delivered from his mother's womb, and November 14, 1893, when he became a member of the British Society for Psychical Research. To a large extent his conversion was inevitable. Born and raised a Roman Catholic and educated with posh papists at Stoneyhurst by members of the Society of Jesus, he rejected his religion almost as soon as he left home and his mother. The Jesuits had not then adopted liberation theology and eternal compassion, preferring beatings. But this Scottish, Irish, part melancholy, part visionary was soaked in spiritual longing. Once he qualified as a doctor Conan Doyle served as a ship's medic, and it was aboard a moribund whaler that the somewhat credulous, intensely imaginative young man sat down to tales of the after-life from hardened and cynical old sailors. He was prime for the taking.

The atmosphere of late Victorian and early Edwardian Britain — and North America and Europe were far from dissimilar in this respect — was thick with seances, mediums and ghostly apparitions. This was the breeding ground for Aleister Crowley, for the occult eugenicists as well as the less pernicious Christian Spiritualists. In short, any and every form of vaguely theological alternative was considered.

A more sophisticated and cerebral New Age mentality abounded; there were plenty of Shirley MacLaines. Arthur Balfour may not have tripped the light fantastic in innumerable Hollywood musicals, but he did possess celebrity, influence and the ability to legitimize extreme ideas. This one-time prime minister and foreign secretary was a devoted Spiritualist and believer in the supernatural. His public acceptance and approval of these beliefs enabled an entire generation of the middle and upper classes to overcome the hurdle of peer disapproval.

Yet it was a prosaic young girl who mangled her vowel sounds and wiped her frequently running nose on her sleeve who brought Conan Doyle into the fold. Florrie Cookes was born in London in 1854, and from her early teens she was thought by the initiated to be a gifted, acute medium. She floated to the ceiling of the family's Hackney home on the most unlikely occasions, sometimes accompanied by her sister, but usually solo. More often she would be found insensible on the floor, exhausted after communicating with the dead: a tiny but perfect conduit for the thoughts and desires of the spirit world.

In 1870 the girl's father placed her in the charge of two more experienced mediums, Frank Herne and Charles Williams. Within a year Florrie was holding her own seances. She managed to produce a spirit, John King, and then his daughter, Katie. These were tactile presences, touching the men who were seated around the table, even fondling the women. Some pondered on the physical similarities between John King and Frank Herne, and the way little Katie's eyes and cheek bones so resembled those of Florrie Cookes.

By 1873 Cookes was the most famous medium in London. She invited the authoress Florence Marryat to a seance, where spirit Katie King stripped naked, crying out, "Now you see that I am a woman!" (Marryat later commented, "which indeed she was.")

In 1880 a skeptical sitter realized that one of Cooke's new spirits was wearing stays; he made a grab at her, and she ran away screaming insults and punching her fists into the air. Florrie Cookes's own clothes were found lying behind a nearby cabinet. Arthur Balfour, his political star ascending, poured parliamentarian scorn on the entire affair. Arthur Conan Doyle had less to lose. At around the same time he was invited by a patient of his, "a general whom I attended professionally," to monitor the results of a bout of "table turning." He thought those results beyond doubt. Soon he was writing letters to the local press, and signing them "Spiritualist."

He had been irrevocably seduced by a compendious, seminal volume written by a friend, F. W. H. Myers. *Human Personality and Its Survival of Bodily Death* was the most important Spiritualist book of its time. "A great root book from which a tree of knowledge will grow," Conan Doyle wrote to his mother. In 1,200 pages Myers propounded his view that human personality was not simply a combination of physical and mental elements, dependent on the material existence of the body and the brain. Myers believed that the personality was essentially supernatural, that the conscious self was simply the tip of an "inverted iceberg, the rest of the personality being separable from it and superior to it, and connecting it with the soul." He coined the term telepathy, saying it was "like islands in a stream; certain human beings are able to release themselves from the confines of the physical bases of subsidiary thought and can establish contact between the islands, and build up connections with personalities which had survived the physical destruction of the brain."

This was the science and the philosophy Conan Doyle needed to expunge any skepticism that had survived the Cookes affair. Heroic delusions were one thing, considered explanation quite another. He later wrote in one of his Spiritualist manuals, *The New Revelation*: "Myers was an enormous advance. If mind could act on mind at a distance, then there were some human powers which were quite different to matter as we had always understood it. The ground was cut from under the feet of the materialists, and my old position had been destroyed . . . If the mind, the spirit, the intelligence of man could operate at a distance from the body, then it was a thing to that extent separate from the body. Why should it not exist on its own when the body was destroyed?"

There exists a short film of Arthur Conan Doyle. It is shaky, the cameraman has no notion of framing and continuity, and it is quite often a little out of focus, but it manages to convey the delightful essence of the man. He grins a great deal, talks to his dog, flirts with the camera with a confidence rare for filmed subjects in the 1920s. Some of the ten minutes of the piece are concerned with Sherlock Holmes, but the bulk is spent on Spiritualism. Any questions as to why he embraced the movement, why he believed so much of its content when even some zealots were more selective are answered therein. A serenity comes to his face when he discusses Spiritualism. He is no longer an author inundated with letters from Sherlockian fanatics, but a man of faith in comfortable seclusion from the fools and knaves who surround him. He wears the look of all men of genuine belief, of monks, priests, the authentically holy. It is the mask of certainty.

Spiritualism became his vocation. The overwhelming and international success of Sherlock Holmes — it is argued that Holmes is the most famous literary creation in the history of language — made Conan Doyle a world figure. He was invited to address audiences in almost every major city, and whenever he spent an evening lecturing about Holmes he devoted his mornings and afternoons to talking about spiritualism. He came to Canada, for instance, on several occasions, and was fascinated by a poltergeist sighting in Montreal.

"The electric lights were switched off at untoward moments, and the pictures were stripped from the walls. Twice the husband was assaulted by pillows until his incredulity had been buffeted out of him. Prayer seemed of no avail."

Doyle was moved and shaken by the psychic immensity of Winnipeg.

"On our first night . . . we attended a circle for psychical research which has been conducted for two years by a group of scientific men who have obtained remarkable success. The medium is a small, pleasant-faced woman from the Western Highlands of Scotland. Her psychic gifts are both mental and physical. The circle, which contained ten persons, including my wife and myself, placed their hands, or one hand each, upon a small table, part of which was illuminated by phosphorous so as to give some light. It was violently agitated, and this process was described as 'charging in.' It was then pushed back into a small cabinet made of four hung curtains with an opening in front. Out of this table came clattering again and again entirely of its own, with no sitter touching it. I stood by the slit in the curtain in subdued red light and I watched the table within. One moment it was quiescent. A moment later it was like a restless dog in a kennel, springing, tossing, beating up against the supports, and finally bounding out with a velocity which caused me to get quickly out of the way. It ended by rising up in the air while our finger-tips were on it and remaining for an appreciable period."

Winnipeg had more than dancing tables to offer. Later during his stay Conan Doyle met a local medium named Mrs. Bolton. She led a group of Spiritualists in a round of "Lead, Kindly Light," then "sank into a trance, from which she emerged with an aspect of very great dignity and benevolence," and proceeded to lecture the good citizens on the conditions of heaven and the possibilities of transforming water into wine. Arthur Conan Doyle rather liked Canada.

He was not so enthusiastic about France. In September 1925 he was made acting president of the International Spiritualist Congress in Paris. Interest in contact with the deceased had never been greater; so many tens of thousands had been killed during the war, few had not lost a husband, son or lover. Four thousand people attended the congress and there were riots outside the building by those who had not managed to obtain official tickets. The police were called, their barriers were smashed, fights and beatings occurred. In an effort to inject some order into the proceedings and calm the mood of the delegates Conan Doyle began the day with a slide show. The projectionist was drunk, and if the slides were not shown upside down they bore little relation to the notes being read by the acting president in his broken and heavily accented French. Skeptics began to laugh. More fights. Somebody shouted out from the middle of the hall, "Look out, you're treading on my ecto-plasm." A believer broke a chair over the head of a heretic. Conan Doyle lost his temper and stormed off the stage.

The following year another mass meeting was organized, this time in London's Royal Albert Hall, to commemorate Armistice Day. This jamboree was far more of a success, with less Gallic playfulness but more Anglo-Saxon organization. Conan Doyle rose from his seat in the front row of the impressive auditorium, he was wearing his medals from the Boer War, his walrus moustache was neatly combed and his slightly distended stomach slowed his ascent to the front of the stage. He took a breath, then another, and looked around the audience in a careful, deliberate pause.

"I ask all who are sure they are in touch with their dead to rise and testify," he bellowed without the aid of a microphone. Another pause. Some members of the audience began to stand, then more. Finally, over three thousand men and women stood up laughing, some crying. There were tears in Conan Doyle's eyes as well. He said in a softer but still audible voice, "Thank God there are so many. I prophesy that within five years to such an appeal every man and woman in this great hall shall arise." He took a moment to hold up his hands towards the roof as if bearing an invisible trophy, and surreptitiously brushed a tear from his cheek. "We are not testifying to faith, but to fact."

Across the Atlantic there existed another man of genius who refused to believe that physical death was the conclusion of life. This son of a Brooklyn rabbi had not attended medical college or one of the better British public schools. He was a magician. Better still, he was Harry Houdini.

The escapologist was passionately interested in the supernatural, but was also committed to exposing fake Spiritualists; and the frauds, he believed, composed the majority. The image of Conan Doyle and Harry Houdini strolling along the streets of Manhattan together, arm-in-arm, sharing a music hall joke, is quite delicious. There was an affection between the men that bordered on platonic love. In 1920 Conan Doyle wrote to Houdini: "I see that you know a great deal about the negative side of spiritualism — I hope more on the positive side will come your way. But it wants to be approached not in the spirit of a detective approaching a suspect, but in that of a humble, religious soul, yearning for help and comfort."

The friendship deepened. The two families became close, staying with each other and sharing holidays. Conan Doyle made some headway with his friend, introducing him to more plausible seances, finally drawing out a "we had some success" from Houdini after one particular meeting. But Houdini was cognizant of too many of the tricks of the trade to become a convert; when he was unable to prove fraud he became splenetic and resentful. The two men began to argue. Houdini delivered diatribes against Spiritualism at the end of his magic shows, sometimes referring to his Scottish friend and mocking his attitudes. Such was the strength of Conan Doyle's beliefs that he was prepared to abandon friendship rather than tolerate jibes at Spiritualism. The two did not speak again.

Houdini eventually died of peritonitis in Montreal, caused by a punch in the stomach from a college student eager to prove his strength.

Some years before his death Houdini had devised a code of signals and knocks, which he revealed only to his wife and to Conan Doyle. If after I die I want to communicate with you, he declared, I will use the code. It will be proof of an after-life.

A medium named Arthur Ford contacted Conan Doyle shortly after Houdini's death and swore that Houdini's spirit had woken him one night and given him the details of a special code. He was questioned, and his answers were accurate. Conan Doyle was euphoric. He was then informed that Houdini's parsimonious widow had sold the code to the *Brooklyn Eagle* — it had been published and was hence common knowledge throughout New York City.

Conan Doyle's involvement with Spiritualism was, in fact, characterized by a succession of disappointments. In August 1925 he opened a Psychic Bookshop and Museum near to Westminster Abbey. He invested most of his savings and spare time into the project. He lost a small fortune. A direct hit from a German bomb during the Second World War destroyed the majority of the books, papers and artefacts.

In 1930 he fell out with the Society for Psychical Research. Their journal had published an eviscerating review of a book of psychic mysteries by a friend of Conan Doyle, Marquis Scott. The review implied that the book was a hoax, perpetrated by its author. Conan Doyle demanded contrition, and when none was forthcoming resigned from the society he had joined thirty-seven years earlier. The review, of course, was merely the latest of many petty internecine squabbles and personality battles inside organized Spiritualism.

If disappointment did not weigh him down the critical judgment of others most certainly left its impression. Simply, enemies never bothered him, but doubting friends did. He defended the homosexual Sir Roger Casement, for example, who had spied for the Germans during the First World War so as to aid the Irish Nationalists; calls for Casement's blood were general, but Conan Doyle believed that the wretched man was clinically insane and should not be executed. He never wavered in his defence of the unfortunate aristocrat. He laughingly dismissed frantic, bloody letters accusing him of treachery, but took to his room for hours when an old friend called on him and expressed disapproval of his support for Casement. Unfortunately it was friends who tended to poke fun at his spiritualism, sometimes inevitably. How could they take seriously Conan Doyle's suggestion that his second wife, Jean Leckie, had definite psychic powers when she herself thought the idea was absurd?

And then there was the case of Lily Loder-Symonds. She had been a bridesmaid at Conan Doyle's second wedding and was an old and trusted family nanny, but a chronic lung complaint drove her to her bed. Concerned about her future at the Conan Doyle home she suddenly developed the power of "automatic writing." Her position became only slightly more secure. Then she began to write down messages from her brothers, all of whom had been killed at Ypres in 1915. Conan Doyle was subsequently in awe of her, and invited her to become a permanent guest in his house.

Battles were also lost. Conan Doyle's anti-Catholicism occasionally bordered on the hysterical. Some of his historical romances display a lamentable bigotry towards the Roman Church. Once a Catholic, often an anti-Catholic. In 1929 he engaged the Jesuit Father Herbert Thurston in a public debate. Thurston had recently published a critical work entitled *Modern Spiritualism*, and Conan Doyle replied with *The Roman Catholic Church — A Rejoinder.* The two men had been at Stoneyhurst together, and Thurston had been the more astute intellect even then. Neutrals had no doubt as to who had triumphed. A less courageous individual would not have thrown down the gauntlet against Thurston in the first place.

Although he was a hussar for his cause, the noblest of partisans, he left his flanks unguarded and vulnerable to ridicule. Rather than embrace certain aspects of the supernatural and reject others, Conan Doyle believed that each of the phenomena was related and mutually dependent. He eschewed those Spiritualists who were contemptuous of other, less formulated psychic ideas. On fairies, for example, he wrote this in *The Edge of the Unknown*: "All these evidences as to fairies sink into insignificance compared with the actual photographs which I have published in my *Coming of the Fairies.* These, in the enlarged edition, cover cases from Yorkshire, Devonshire, Canada and Germany, and show varying sizes as already described. Since its publication I have had an excellent one from Sweden."

In the summer of 1929 two Californian friends of the Conan Doyles, Doctor and Mrs. Wickland, came to Britain for a visit. While the four were out together, Mrs. Wickland "physically identified herself with the spirit of a murdered ostler." Why is it, Conan Doyle asked a cousin, that they laugh at me?

He wrote over twenty books on Spiritualism, including *The Wanderings of a Spiritualist, The Case for Spirit Photography,* two volumes of *The History of Spiritualism* and *An Open Letter to Those of My Generation.* Some were published by the small Psychic Press, but others by more reputable and secular houses such as G. P. Putnam's or Hodder and Stoughton. He dedicated the first, and possibly the best of these volumes, "to all the brave men and women, humble or learned, who have had the moral courage during seventy years to face ridicule or worldly disadvantage in order to testify to an all-important truth."

Yet he knew as the end of his life approached, that the battle, if not the war, had been lost. His legacy was, of course, Sherlock Holmes, that most pristine example of the materialist, and opponent of all things beyond nature. Conan Doyle used him as a safety valve, to siphon the cynicism and irony of which he was capable. He was sometimes naïve, but seldom entirely foolish. In a revised work he wrote these telling words, exotic with ambivalence and doubt:

"We who believe in the psychic revelation, and who appreciate that a perception of these things is one of the utmost importance, certainly have hurled ourselves against the obstinacy of our time. Possibly we have allowed some of our lives to be gnawed away in what for the moment seemed a vain and thankless quest. Only the future can show whether the sacrifice was worth it. Personally, I think it was."

Poor Sir Arthur.

Revisiting Amis the Elder

Novelist Martin Amis tells the story of when he was a young boy and his father Kingsley took him to a wrestling match. One fellow was doing particularly badly and, with his head in an arm lock, suddenly saw the famous author of *Lucky Jim* in the front row. He fixed the author with a stare and shouted, "Help me Lord Jim, help me. What should I do?" Lord Jim knew exactly what to do. He got up and left.

Knowing what to do appears to have been a constant in Kingsley Amis's life, according to biographer Eric Jacobs. The London-born, Oxford-educated author knew when to adopt the persona of the angry young man, when to abandon it for a more orthodox and conservative status, when to thrash the establishment and when to join it. He also knew how to write. From his teaching days at the University of Swansea in the early 1950s and then at Cambridge, Amis's poetry and stories were accomplished and astute. But the watershed — the dividing and defining point in this man's life — was the publication of *Lucky Jim* in 1954.

With well-placed research and an insight into his subject, Eric Jacobs confirms what anyone who has read *Lucky Jim* has speculated about for some time, that the hero, Jim Dixon, is largely an extension of Amis himself. Dixon is a university teacher with liberal and anti-establishment views, a naïve if determined young man who sees through the pomposity of his peers and has no tolerance for the bubble reputation when he thinks it deserves to be burst.

The book is as funny today as it was half a century ago and, as Jacobs emphasizes, the satire on university life of the 1950s has a rippling effectiveness today as we grimace through the campus correctness of the 1990s.

In the five years following this phenomenal success, Amis wrote *That Uncertain Feeling*, *Take a Girl Like You* and *I Like It Here.* These were still satire and there was still anger on display but a new ideology was now apparent, the old hostility towards the establishment transformed into a resentment of radicalism and leftism of the 1960s. His work became increasingly xenophobic, tinged with misogyny. The author was increasingly tired of what he saw as vacuous attempts at progress.

"The delusion that there are thousands of young people about who are capable of benefiting from university training, but have somehow failed to find their way there, is a necessary component of the expansionist case," he wrote. "More will mean worse."

The born-again satirist captured an entirely new audience with his new incarnation and his major novels of the 1970s, *Ending Up* and the highly accomplished and successful *Jake's Thing*. Both reflected the novelist at his most wicked. He was, without doubt, a genuinely witty man: "Outside every fat man there was an even fatter man trying to close in" and "He was of the faith in that the church he currently did not attend was Catholic."

He also tried his hand at espionage fiction, a beloved reading genre of Amis's, with *The Anti-Death League* in 1966, and the supernatural with *The Green Man* in 1969.

By the 1980s, however, Amis began to resemble a dramatic character who has somehow strayed into a play from the wrong period. He had the lines and he knew the plot but the context and the ambience were all wrong.

More than this, Jacobs shows us the contemporary man as a stew of feelings and emotions, with his work tasting of just such a recipe — spicy and pleasant but leaving one just a little unsatisfied. There are anachronisms, such as his penchant for soft pornography, smutty jokes, a yearning for certainty and a suspicion of everything that began after his own maturity. They are charming at times, pathetic at others. The inescapable conclusion is that the best of Amis was long behind him. But the best was supremely good. The rest was merely packaging. Eric Jacobs wraps the gift rather nicely.

Call Me Madam . . . DAMN IT!

We're in Richmond Hill on a grey, bland Tuesday morning. There's a small block of apartments, as bland as the day, made of colourless brick and large, unexciting windows. It dribbles rain: a *donk, donk, donk* sound on the roofs of the parked cars. At the front of the building an esurient dog chews through last night's garbage bags; the hound is not disturbed. There is nobody around: this is consummate commuter land.

An expensive Toyota pulls up outside the small block of apartments. The driver is furtive, excited. He is wearing a faded grey overcoat, too large rubber overshoes and a Chinese fur hat with long ear pieces. He smokes furiously, then stops, throws the half-completed cigarette to the ground and rubs it innocuously with his shoe. He pauses, looks at the building before him and steps forward. A dozen paces. Two more. The last one. He rings the buzzer of an apartment on the third floor, and, as obsequiously as he can, responds to a peremptory demand from the other end of the intercom. "Please may I have permission to visit and serve my mistress?"

There is no response. But the buzzer sounds, and the automatic door lock is opened. He walks to the silvery-grey elevator; the doors are open. It is surprisingly quiet. He pushes button three, feels his lower stomach grind with a mixture of fear and desire. His mouth is dry, his legs rather unsteady. The elevator bumps to its stop. Doors open. He walks along old mauve carpet to a brown door. Knocks. The door opens immediately. The Toyota driver sidles in, pulling an envelope from his coat pocket. His hand trembles. His mistress, a defiant blonde in thigh-high leather boots, leather miniskirt and taut leather jacket, watches as he respectfully deposits it on a small hall table, next to a domestic Rolodex. She doesn't deign to count to see if the requisite $175 is there. She knows it will be.

"Take off your clothes carefully, fold them neatly, and place them on the chair," she commands.

The Toyota driver strips naked, shivering a little though the room is far from cold. He walks past his mistress, eyes ahead, past the out-of-tune piano, the lavishly framed photograph of Mistress Jacqueline Première's daughter, past the well-thumbed copy of *Recipes Only* lying next to the even more well-thumbed copy of Simone de Beauvoir's volume on the Marquis de Sade, into what he has imagined for so long: a suburban torture chamber.

He waits to be whipped. He wants to be whipped, to be beaten and humiliated. It is why he is here.

The first time he came to "serve" he had brought with him, as Mistress Première had demanded, a two-page essay, which he had presented to her, naked on the floor on his hands and knees, as an offering of his good faith. The paper listed his secret erotic imaginings; she had read it slowly, while he waited, thrilling to the idea of humiliation. Later, she showed him to the bedroom, where there is a large bed bought from a department store. In harmless-looking drawers under the bed are the tools of his pain: the chains, restraints and poles, the spreader bars (designed to keep the legs apart to heighten the humiliation, to open to the disdainful inspection and use of the mistress every bodily orifice). His breath is short as he walks into that bedroom, down the hallway to heaven. He waits there submissively for his darkest dreams to be penetrated by this woman, his mistress, his dominatrix . . .

Mistress Jacqueline Première (which is her professional nom de guerre; her real one is almost as extraordinary) is a dominatrix by trade, a woman who physically and emotionally whips, beats and humiliates men for money. There is no sexual contact, at least of the conventional kind; there is certainly no penetration, and not always an orgasm. This is primarily an eroticism of the mind. The lady — for that is what she is, and to forget it is to provoke an immediate and painful response — is, and will remain, in perfect control throughout. It is what the treatment demands.

It *is* treatment. It is therapy. It is fantasy. Ten months in a British drama school taught her how to act, how to make the fantasies believable, the fantasies of troubled men, carefully typed (not by their secretaries). She demands these typewritten fantasies whenever a new client presents himself; these offerings list fetishes, fantasies, experiences with previous mistresses. While the "slave" reads the rules of the house, Mistress Première studies the essay, discovering from its revelations what he desires, what he needs.

The house rules are extensive, elaborate and essential. Nobody under twenty-one years of age is allowed to visit, anyone under the influence of alcohol or drugs is ejected from the apartment. Limits are vital. The rules explain that if the word "red" is shouted, the mistress immediately stops whatever she is doing. If "orange" is used, it signifies a wish to stop temporarily, and discuss what is happening, perhaps alter the degree of abuse. "Green" is the signal for events to continue. There are peremptory suggestions and caveats. Slaves will shower from head to toe and wash their hair. On no account must they touch their mistress, unless she specifically requests some form of service or worship. "I will not tolerate" is ubiquitous, the aura of authority powerful and all-embracing.

The Toyota-driving slave reads what is on offer. Cross-dressing is self-explanatory. He may wear a wig, put on high-heeled shoes and female underwear, be forced to make tea and perform menial chores, dust the apartment. Bondage and discipline (B&D) is listed. This implies chains, restraints and poles, spreader bars, whips, riding crops and nipple clamps. He reads of foot and leather fetishes. If he opts for this he will have to kiss Madam's boots, give an enforced foot massage. If he opts for more punishment, he will be "shown the instruments."

The whips on display would have done justice to HMS *Bounty*. Some are cosmetic, designed to titillate but not injure. Others are for real. Wounding, bleeding, cutting, scarring instruments of pain. They nestle alongside a riding outfit: hat, tight white jodhpurs, black topcoat and, of course, leather riding boots — the pair bought for an ungrateful mistress by an adoring and specifically lascivious slave. A pair of thigh-high boots — plastic, cheap looking — higher than could be worn in the street, are on offer as well, as are a heavily laced bodice, an evening gown for the more discerning customer, and an assortment of straps and chains. "I should have a separate torture dungeon. Really should. Some of the girls downtown do," she explains. Difficult, in a one-bedroom apartment.

This client's scenario holds no surprises for Jacqueline. "I took advantage of a girl in the office, Madam, I had sex with her in the washroom. You're my boss, what will you do?" Bad acting, but genuine desire. "I know I shouldn't have done it. Now you're going to punish me, aren't you?"

She insults him, verbally abuses him, makes him feel small, pathetic, absurd. He crawls around the room, unprotesting and contrite. He is then bound and chained, tied to the wall and unable to move. His mistress whips him, beats him with a riding crop and a paddle, producing a flat, wet sound that delights the victim. There are satisfied sounds and groans, followed by silence or heavy breathing. There is no verbal communication for a moment, and then a sharp threat or warning. The punishment is relatively gentle this time; the slave is a polio victim. After an hour he is released, and ordered to masturbate while Mistress Première turns her back in contempt and apathy. He dresses, expresses his gratitude and gets back into his sensible car. He will return. They always do.

There are dominatrices in every country, every city in the world. Toronto boasts some of the wittiest and wickedest. Some of them give golden showers, others don't; some indulge in anal penetration, others don't; some allow physical contact, others don't. Some are young, some late-middle-aged. Some attractive, some distinctly plain. They occupy the twilight world between sex and psychology, using the weapons of gesture and innuendo as much as they use violence and physical pain.

There are, and always have been, men who obtain sexual fulfilment by receiving abuse from women. They may need it for an hour a month, or on a daily basis, but without it their sexuality will always be incomplete and unquenched. They are also on the increase: the threat of catching AIDS has ensured that — intercourse never takes place in a domination session. The range of domination is enormous. Death has almost certainly ensued in one or two cases, and broken flesh is common. Jacqueline Première is more subtle, more in control of her profession. She is proud of what she does.

The Wife's Tale. Jacqueline Première has been married three times, all to highly dominant and successful men. The last husband was a jockey. He was good. Very good. Good enough to ride a winner of the Kentucky Derby. Jacqueline was submissive, and subsequently abused. No physical punishment took place, but emotional and psychological pressure and exploitation were a perennial aspect. The choice of such men seems to be inevitable; a congenital and subconscious desire on the part of the pliable to pick an inimical partner.

"Only someone who has been genuinely submissive and has experienced domination by another can really understand what it's all about," she explains articulately, fingering the hem of her tiny leather skirt. "It can be awful, painful, depressing and disgusting. It can also be fun." A pause. "It can give you a buzz, make you feel alive, turned on, sexy. I administer domination and humiliation so well because I received it . . . so well."

The Divorcée's Tale. She was broke. Broken. Living in the United States, she found herself the next-door neighbour of a professional dominatrix. They became friendly, chatted, had coffee, while clients moaned and groaned in their voluntary confinement. Jacqueline sat in on a session — many of the men who attend a dominatrix fantasize about two women being present at a scene but very few can afford to pay for such a luxury — and stored the information away at the back of her mind. Back in Canada she began a strip-o-gram agency, but "became tired of the girls not bothering to turn up for work." A laugh. Other enterprises were attempted, all failing in their turn with nauseating regularity. Desperate, and daring, she recalled the acquaintance in Los Angeles. She made further inquiries, gave it some practical and ethical consideration, and set up shop as Richmond Hill's finest.

The Dominatrix's Tale. "I am not a prostitute. I am not, do you understand, a prostitute." Insistent, a little intimidating, those eyes seldom breaking their stare. "What I do here is about stress management and psychology, as much as about sex." A sip of coffee, a straightening of her skirt. She throws her head back. Increasingly comfortable. "Men ring me up and ask me if I'm beautiful. I always give the same reply. Does a real estate agent need to be particularly beautiful to do what she does? This is not about sex — not about sex. There is no sexual contact, not even any physical contact from slave to mistress unless they touch my feet, paint my nails or something. I'm controlling them," she explains, with emphasis and passion, "and there can never be any humiliation for me. If I expose my boobs, show them my genitalia, let them touch me, I am letting them get the upper hand. That's why I won't give golden showers — it's degrading, for me!"

The entire experience is about mind control, mind games, mind exploitation. From the initial telephone call to arrange an appointment, through to the return call from her to them to confirm authenticity, to the sound of the downstairs buzzer, and the slave's arrival at her front door, Jacqueline Première is in control. Her tones are clipped, harsh, nasty. It takes time for that façade to slip during the interview. She welcomes me with a teacherly "sit there," and a face set in superiority.

The style is contrived, but necessary. The temptation to laugh at an obese accountant dressed as a housemaid, tottering about the apartment in high heels, is huge. And a mistress has to avoid repugnance. There are men who want their anuses bombarded with every instrument known to perversion, who want to be defecated upon, to be burned, to be choked until they vomit. The question begs: Why?

"Very few of the men I see are homosexual, even fewer effeminate in any way," she says. "Many are married, many have kids, I think a lot of them are very happy."

The phenomenon is not confined to our age, and says nothing about the latter half of the twentieth century that it doesn't about the eighteenth or nineteenth. The lust for humiliation is disturbing. The attachment of humiliation to role reversal, and inherent warped perception of female identity is perhaps more unpleasant. To become a woman is to become dominated is to become a slave. The equation provokes obscene and terrifying conclusions. The expatiations of psychiatrists, however, are universally rejected by mistress and slave alike. They have a symbiotic relationship, and agree that only those who experience the living or receiving of domination can fully comprehend it.

"My clients are powerful, successful, secure, clever, wealthy. Wimps don't come to see me, they're dominated every day of their lives. It's as though there's something inside us that needs a balance. I see men who give orders, don't take them. Women telephone me, but none have shown up yet. Role reversal means more than men pretending to be women, not all of them want that."

A long pause, and a glance around the apartment. "It means winners becoming losers; it means husbands becoming wives; it means aggressive becoming passive. They masturbate, they have orgasms, but that is never, never the most important part of a session. It's almost incidental."

The complete truth is almost impossible to find. It isn't that either half of the act is telling lies, simply that they don't, can't, know. If would-be slaves knew exactly why they needed to be humiliated, they wouldn't need to be humiliated.

Nick, average and ordinary, would not be out of place in a family restaurant or a law firm. However, he suffers, therefore he is. "My desires," he writes in his essay to Mistress Première, "stem from a basic fear of women combined with a strong sex drive and a vivid imagination. I long to spend time with an attractive woman but I lack the confidence to take the lead. Therefore, I dream of meeting a woman who will accept my submission and take charge."

He dwells on two fantasies. In the first he meets a woman in a bar. She is wearing a short leather miniskirt. After inviting Nick home she informs him of her requirements. "She tells me she is only interested in men who are willing to submit to her and that if I am not willing to serve as her slave, I should disappear now! When I agree, she orders me into the backseat, hands me a black leather hood and tells me to pull it over my head. Next she handcuffs my hands behind my back and makes me lie on the floor, covering me with a blanket. We drive for maybe half an hour, then enter a garage and I hear an overhead door close after the engine stops.

"She helps me out of the car, but leaves the hood and cuffs in place and buckles a collar around my neck. Then she pulls me by the leash into the house and down a set of stairs into the basement. My hands are refastened over my head and a spreader bar is placed between my ankles, then the hood is removed. The room I am in is dimly lit, with stone walls and a concrete floor. My hands are chained over my head to a stout iron ring in one of the heavy wooden beams. The woman I had met in the bar stands to one side, hands on her hips and a leather whip hanging from her wrist. Another woman is beside her, dressed in black leather from head to toe.

"She gags me with a ball gag and then strips my clothes off, cutting them with a knife to pull them free. She explains that if I survive the night, I will be freed, but that from this moment on I will remain their slave. She tells me that I must come to them whenever they call and do whatever they ask.

"By use of punishment and reward they teach me to serve and to obey. By morning I am indeed their slave forever."

A second fantasy follows similar lines, this time involving a professional mistress. Amateur dominatrices do exist (in the United States there are cases of slaves being swapped around and entire personalities being smashed) but for the most part are exactly what they usually begin as: fantasies. Jacqueline Première is a health fanatic, loves her mother (and does not tell her what she does for a living) and has no desire to lead a grown man around like a dog. Mind games.

Nick's written requests are as enlightening as his obsessions. After asking that no marks be left on his body, he writes: "I am happily married with two children. My wife is aware of my unusual desires, but has no interest in dominating me; however, I want our meetings to remain confidential . . ." He reports of other mistresses he has visited; one a success, the other an appalling failure. A cattle prod was employed, electric shocks given. "I was terrified and didn't enjoy the session. I felt this session was more abuse than domination."

Robert's essay dwells on why he is as he is. Its candour is staggering. "My attraction to all this goes back to childhood. I am a preacher's son and, as a child, was aroused to self-flagellation and masturbation by stories of the floggings and abuse of Christian martyrs. My most intensely erotic sensations are achieved through B&D and S&M sessions. The 'dark side' ritualism fascinates me — the celebration of total submission to a superior power. My Puritan legacy is manifested in a sense of essential unworthiness, in the need to first endure pain and humiliation before earning the right to experience ecstasy.

"Professionally, I act in a judgmental capacity and I suspect my exploration of bondage, discipline and masochism is a case of the judge seeking his own judgement. It is a kind of stress management with freedom achieved through bondage and submission." Robert's fetishes concern feet and footwear. His limits are extensive, he suffers from "a hernia problem." He understands, however, that he is a slave, "only useful as a vessel for Madam's pleasure and correction."

Steven is from Etobicoke. He works for the Ontario government and attended a university in the United States. He has never written an essay, frightened that it may be used for blackmail or other financial or moral pressure. He is not a regular client of Jacqueline Première, but instead varies the dominatrices he visits; he tries to see a different mistress each month for perhaps a six-month period. He claims to have never been unfaithful to his wife.

"Of course I felt guilty in the beginning, but not now. I don't see this as disloyalty to my wife. No, I wasn't beaten at school or anything; I just developed an obsession for leather and dominant women, sometime after my first marriage broke up. I've asked my wife to do this type of thing, she obliges. But it's done with love. I don't want love. I trust the women I see now."

A draw on a cigarette, a moment to collect his thoughts. "I depend on them . . . With the AIDS scare I'm damned glad to see these women, and not ordinary hookers. Once you're trapped, that's it: prostitutes, domination, all the same depth of need. Thank God I don't risk catching anything. And I can look my wife in the eye and tell her I've never had intercourse with another woman while we've been married. Sounds deceitful, ridiculous. Really? I've learned to live with something I can't understand. I've been lucky, I've built up relationships with women who understand me. But they can't last. You see, when familiarity develops, the mystery and the fear evaporate. If you could quantify and package the answers to lust, there'd be some very rich people around."

The paradox at the core of sexual domination is a beguiling one for client and mistress. A regular, long-term slave is an oxymoron. The more empathetic and willing the mistress, the more pleasure for the client in the short term, but only in the short term. Jacqueline Première knows that one of her weaknesses is her tendency to dialogue, to discuss, to listen after the business aspects of the meeting have terminated.

"I can't quite bring myself to kick them, physically or otherwise, out of the door. Some mistresses do. I know it. I've seen it. I can't. This is a very lonely profession indeed."

She yearns for a friendly cup of tea and a chat; they want a wicked push and a contemptuous frown as they leave the apartment. Only one in three of the men who make appointments over the telephone actually arrives in Richmond Hill. She tries to compensate for the isolation — can't talk about your work over the checkout counter at the local mall — by humour and variation.

"I was about to tell one of my slaves to clean my silver spoons last week. Found out I was out of silver polish, so I whipped him instead." A mixture of laughter, embarrassment and regret. "Sometimes I'll ask for presents, for flowers or perfume or soap, or possibly a new instrument to use in the sessions. I'm not greedy. Some girls are, they'll order everything they can, exploit a slave's needs. Not me, I just need to feel pampered, need to be made to feel special; I have feelings too," she says, with a flavour of sadness in that otherwise stern demeanour.

"If someone was able to set me up in a real dungeon, then there would be less loneliness, more clients. A bedroom isn't the best place, especially in my home." She refers to the elaborately realistic venues some mistresses work from; with mediaeval-style torture racks, imitation slugs and slime, and sufficient devices of pain to keep the Marquis de Sade as happy as a madman can be. Such a scenario is possible, if unlikely. Jacqueline Première's fate is to be the suburban queen of domination; to sit by the telephone and wait for Jack and Barry and Bernard to ring, and to arrive with their silk nightdresses — for their use, not hers — and bulging lists of lusts.

"Will you wrestle with me, Madam, will you wrestle with me and win please, Madam?" inquires one optimistic telephone caller.

"No, I won't," replies the opponent of his dreams. "I'm not a wrestler, I'm a mistress."

And the phone is slammed down, and the tenacious canine nibbles at last weekend's take-away, and Richmond Hill, safe and secluded, doesn't know the half of it.

The Indiscreet Charm of Robertson Davies

(Note: This column was published in 1994. Robertson Davies died in late 1995.) Robertson Davies has never owned and never worn a cape. No doubt of this. He is sure of it. His wife is sure of it. His friends are sure of it. Yet there exists the belief in literary circles that he habitually dons such a garment. A senior arts producer at the CBC even told me that he once saw Davies "rushing across Queen's Park with his cape whirling around him. Quite a sight." Indeed.

So how, why, the canard? As though he had stepped out of one of his own novels, Robertson Davies has a screen about him, composed of many colours and shades and images. He knows it, better than anyone. Probably because he created it.

It's indicative that a deeply researched biography of him by Judith Skelton Grant is titled *Robertson Davies: Man of Myth*, and equally indicative that the book does not fully explain him. It explores and analyses the facts of his life, which is the wrong approach. Reality lies elsewhere, beyond and beneath tangibles.

"There is something funny about me," he whispers, "I create myths." And then he turns in semi-profile, and as his head sweeps round I swear that there is a twinkle in his eye. And he knows I can see it. He's done this before. Robertson Davies has conjured up a magic, puckish effect and instantly reversed the balance between interviewer and interviewee.

Apart from the fact that this man is a trained actor and has mastered the alchemy of managing an audience, we are also on Davies territory. This is his country seat, the Caledon East home where he and his wife spend most of their time. The 150-acre view is soaked in verdancy, an hour away from the metropolis's urbane blight and in comfortable seclusion from the fools and knaves of literary society. Upstairs, like some sort of engine room, is the office. A large framed photograph of Davies's great hero Carl Jung, postcard pictures of W. B. Yeats, Richard Wagner, Bernard Shaw. The Davies coat of arms. The lilting regularity of a ticking timepiece. Studied serenity. This is the retreat, the hiding place from a Toronto that is not, truth be told, the city that Davies knew nor the city of Davies's writing. Davies is like a conduit, along which is passed the Canada of memory, the Canada that might have been, and the Canada that, on a particularly good day, still is.

There is no resemblance whatever between Davies and the bulk of younger or more CanLitesque writers. There is something about contemporary literature, and about contemporary Canadian literature in particular, that defines itself not by its breadth and width but by its smallness, not by what we are allowed and encouraged to say but by what we are not.

"Yes, and people like that hate me. I remember some years ago a friend of mine was a member of a three-person committee making a decision about the Governor General's Award. I had a novel in that year. Its name came up. A lady said, 'Oh, we won't even consider that. I wouldn't give that man anything under any circumstances.' " He sits comfortably back in his chair. "They think I'm antifeminist. The feminists are a very special group. They're not very numerous, fortunately. Otherwise I should be in the poorhouse.' "

He is eighty-one years old. His recent birthday marked an *annus mirabilis* for Davies, but not one that he particularly welcomed. The long-promised biography by Skelton Grant is at last published, by Viking/Penguin. It is not that it is a bad book but that it takes itself so terribly seriously.

"She's written to women I took out once or twice to a movie, years ago. A sort of questionnaire. Did he take you to see *The Bride of Frankenstein*? Did he put his arm round you? Was there any romance?" He laughs, throwing his head back. "I mean, it isn't important. The book is a bit like that. She hasn't got me. Or so I've heard. Haven't read it, you know; my secretary has, though." Gently dismissive, dismissively gentle.

What Skelton Grant does achieve is a complete if distended chronological account of Davies's progress from his childhood in Thamesville, Ontario, through his time at Upper Canada College, Queen's University, and then Oxford, to his work as an actor at London's Old Vic, and then his return to Canada, journalism both at *Saturday Night* and the Peterborough *Examiner*, and, eventually, Massey College. And then through to writing novels. As the biography says, it happened relatively late (he was thirty-eight) in Davies's life. But it is also the meaning of his life and far too few of the more than 800 pages of the biography are devoted to this so-important theme.

The best response Davies could possibly deliver would be another novel. And *The Cunning Man*, published in 1994 by McClelland & Stewart, is particularly important, not merely because he has reservations about the biography but because *Murther & Walking Spirits*, in 1991, was less well received than most of his previous books. He admits to this without any prompting. *The Cunning Man* is a return to former glories.

"Toronto is the hero really," says Davies. The book traces three student friends through their separate vocations — priest, doctor, teacher — and tells how they and the city change and develop. There are rows at the York Club, mysteries at the altar in St. Aidan's church, artistic salons, miraculous cures, and delicious digressions about typically eclectic and eccentric Daviesian subjects, such as tsarist bordellos and the German bombing of London.

Suddenly, almost without my noticing, Davies is away from the plot of his book and back to the new literature, of the Canadian kind. "I wonder if Canada does want great writers?" Davies asks. "We want to project a certain national image. If something bad happens we run immediately with food and bandages and we're astonished when roughnecks shoot at us. It's a silly, Sunday-school approach to life that doesn't work. A more bland, YMCA-secretary creature than the popular idea of a Canadian you couldn't conceive. And that is not a concept that includes any kind of writer of determined opinions."

A pause. "Nowadays everybody has a kind of carbuncle that you can't touch or they scream. It's hard to make jokes about anyone, about the Scots, the Jews. Even Irishmen." Dodgy ground here, yet he laughs and laughs. "I doubt if the people who are imposing all this on us actually believe any of it. One of my principles all of my life is that if you want to know about somebody look at what the world sees and then look at the exact opposite." And he looks over his glasses at me.

What has pushed Robertson Davies outside favoured-author status in this country, but made him an international literary doyen, is that he evinces a contempt for fashion and convention. And what is more, Canada's greatest man of letters doesn't care. "Oh, yes, they call me an elitist. But what is elitism? Preferring the better to the less good." A longer pause this time. "You can't win, so bugger them all."

An ethnic literary allusion comes to mind. Davies's fellow Welshman Dylan Thomas set *Under Milk Wood* in the fictitious town of Llareggub — think about it, backwards. The link is vital. To understand Davies one has to understand his Welshness. There is a Celtic quintessence about him, a shadow of Merlin, a powder of wizardry. The Welsh. Never as fashionable as the Irish, not as successful as the Scots. Few in number, dark of feature and of temperament. There is depression just around the next unpronounceable corner. It's in Davies's books. The sombre and sober anguish of Canadian village life, composed of a heady and spicy stew of unhappy ministers, wretched spinsters, uproarious humour and mysterious mythology.

There are living examples of this jarring juxtaposition in Davies himself. Just after discussing old age and death, where he makes a running-away gesture when he talks of the soul, he offers me a sherry, and asks if I would like some gin in it? Gin? In sherry? "My tutor at university started me on it.

"Part of being old is realizing that we have to be optimistic. I am optimistic," he says. "I have some sort of belief in an afterlife, not the stupid idea of eternity of the body, but something, certainly. I used to have friends in the university who said, 'You know, the tragic outlook on life is the only viable way of thinking.' What they were doing was glorifying their own gloom. Usually they were men with horrible wives." That laugh once again, Davies aware that he has made a politically incorrect comment. "Well, much of life does fall down to a joke in a way. When you hear people talking grandly and philosophically and splendidly you're sometimes aware that they're icing the cake of their own insufficiencies."

Yet another anecdote. "I was at Oxford with Teddy Heath, you know." The Red Tory leader of Britain during the early 1970s. "He was an exact contemporary of mine at Balliol. My heart sank when he became prime minister. Not one idea to rub up against another. Sad. He knew no god but he. But you know, one of the reasons I felt so sad when he became prime minister was that I used to sing in the Balliol College choir, which he conducted, and he was a lousy conductor. And a man who couldn't lead a choir of thirty people could not lead a nation of several million."

So, let's talk some more about politics. "Oh no, I'm not very political," he says, contradicted by the meat of what we have been discussing for the past two hours. "Anyway, time for lunch, and I'm sure you'd like to inspect the plumbing." I am being given a hint.

And Robertson Davies has never worn a cape. But we still search for it. We shall never find it, and that is for the best. The enigma is much of the pleasure.

Memories of Scarborough

Suddenly everybody in Beverly Hills is a hockey fan. At Duke's Coffee Shop on Sunset Boulevard, nudged in among heavy metal tattoo parlours and esoteric compact disc stores, there's a Los Angeles Kings poster on the wall. Most of the denizens of this hip watering hole look as if they wouldn't know the difference between a blue line and a coke line. This isn't hockey country. It's only the transitory glamour of Wayne Gretzky that has provoked the fashion. One cannot help thinking that if Los Angeles made it to the finals on an international curling competition, Rodeo Drive would immediately witness an explosion of "Go Curling" caps, and Rolex-laden men would materialize from dark, expensive corners to explain that "curling is where it's at — Burt Reynolds has curled for years."

And then, through the door walks a compact figure, quite slight, with voluminous red hair, wearing a grey and black hooped jersey and jeans. He looks wary, even nervous. On his head is a blue baseball cap emblazoned with the words "Toronto Maple Leafs." He would not raise an eyebrow at the Rivoli or the Squeeze Club — a somewhat anonymous and unassuming individual, shooting out "excuse me," "sorry" and "thank you" to those he passes. He must be Canadian.

Mike Myers sits down, apologizes for being a little late and asks me if I have any news of the NHL draft in Quebec. As we begin to converse, a man strides up and asks him what he thought of the Stanley Cup playoffs (this is some months after the event). As the man leaves, Myers edges close to me and whispers in a conspiratorial way, "That guy wrote the screenplay for *The Mighty Ducks*," and smiles broadly. He presumably shares the real fans' disgust with the trivializing of Canada's national sport in a laughable American movie. This is a man who really knows the game; it's part of his love for Canada. He would, he admits, "come back to live in Toronto in the space of a heartbeat."

The history of American show business bursts with anecdotes of self-exiled emigrants unable, if not unwilling, to return home. Groups of white-shirted, white-trousered English stars playing cricket in the Hollywood hills, Scandinavian actresses appalled by the blandness of the New World. For a comic like Myers, the difficulty is even more profound. Los Angeles, after all, is a city where irony does not run very deep. An official street sign proudly proclaims, ADOPT A CANYON: THIS AREA SPONSORED BY BETTE MIDLER, and nobody so much as breaks into a smirk.

Well, almost nobody. Myers knows what Hollywood is all about and has chosen only to rent a house in the city while filming the sequel to *Wayne's World*, the hit movie based on the character he made famous on *Saturday Night Live*. New York is where he lives, though he does not call it home. But tonight, in L.A., "we're going to Milton Berle's eighty-fifth birthday party. We're just basically going to sit there and look at famous people. Famous people that don't make it up to Toronto. Neat, cool. I'm still overwhelmed, but I'm also homesick. I am so homesick."

Home was Scarborough and the border area between Scarborough and North York. First an apartment on Eccleston Drive, near the intersection of the Don Valley Parkway and Eglinton East; then another apartment on Don Mills, north of Fairview Mall, around the area known as "The Peanut." So Myers and his two elder brothers, Paul and Peter, grew up surrounded by the comforting immutables and appealing eccentricities of suburbia. His parents had emigrated from Liverpool in the 1950s, and his father worked as an insurance and encyclopedia salesman in Toronto. He died in 1991, and the scar is far from healed.

"This was his, you know." Myers points to a crested gold ring that he uses as a wedding band. "It's the badge of Edinburgh University. He didn't go there, but he sold the *Encylopaedia Britannica*, and when he was made salesman of the year he was given this as an award." Myers is evidently moved. "He'd drink ten cups of tea a day, always standing up, never sitting down. He'd tap his ring finger against the side of the cup over and over again like this," — he imitates the action — "saying, 'D'you wanna cuppa tea, lad, wanna cuppa tea?' "

He pauses. "If I think of *Saturday Night Live*, *Wayne's World*, all of it, all the praise and the money, I still believe that I'm most proud of the fact that we carried out my dad's wishes; he wanted to be taken home to Liverpool and have his ashes sprinkled on the Mersey. We did it, all of us. The family from Canada and cousins from Liverpool went there and did it. My brother sang Beatles songs. It was lovely. You know, the Mersey flowing into the ocean that finally comes to Canada. I'm so proud of that." We are a long way from comedy, but a little nearer Mike Myers.

Life in Toronto informs Myers's conversation and permeates his work. His character, Wayne Campbell, is Mike Myers growing up in Scarborough; Garth Algar, Wayne's best friend, is named after his brother Paul's girlfriend, Toronto book publicist, Liza Algar; Aurora, Illinois, Wayne Campbell's hometown, is Scarborough. Scarborough is to Mike Myers's Aurora what Orillia was to Stephen Leacock's Mariposa.

Myers admits that the more time he spends away from the city the more he misses it. He cried when the Leafs lost to the Kings in the Stanley Cup semifinals. His most treasured possession is the hockey uniform given to him by the Leafs' Glenn Anderson, "sweater, helmet, socks, pants, everything. I did a video for the team. What a nice man

Glenn Anderson is." He subscribes to *The Hockey News* and longs for ketchup-flavoured potato chips. "You can't get them here. I was in Toronto and had to have some, just had to. I went out, bought a packet, and there was a *Wayne's World* special offer on the side. God, that was special. Very cool. Very, very cool."

He says that he would like to buy a house somewhere off Queen West and commute to New York for *Saturday Night Live.* But is this practical for someone who is as hot a property in New York and Los Angeles as it's possible for a comic actor to be? Myers is the victim of a paradox: his success confines him to a place he would rather not be. It was ironic that during the Stanley Cup games in L.A., Wayne Gretzky helped arrange tickets for him so that he could cheer for the Leafs.

Myers always knew he wanted to do something in movies. He appeared in television commercials for K Mart (and other companies) as a child, shot Super 8 films as a youth, rehearsed comedy routines with his companions as a teenager.

"Crazy stuff," recalls his best friend, Toronto actor David Mackenzie. "I had this habit of singing Al Jolson songs to the traffic, a sort of weird expression of something. So Mike wrote a little film called *Kill the Singer*, where the community gets together to stop this annoying person singing Al Jolson numbers. They hire a killer to get rid of him. Absurd. Very funny. To me, his success has always been inevitable. It was like he had a huge key in his back; you just wound him up and off he went, entertaining people, making them laugh. When streaking was fashionable, he ran through a field next to the school completely naked, wearing only a football helmet. Now he was just eleven years old then. The image is pretty strong for me. I think it was an Argos helmet."

Myers developed a comedy act at home, worked on it with friends and, when he was seventeen, began to take workshops with Second City Comedy Troupe. While at school — at Lescon Road Public, Dallington and J. B. Tyrrell — he soaked himself in comedy techniques, in film theory and in the study of performers such as Peter Sellers. He applied to York University to study film, with an entrance essay entitled "Joseph Campbell's Monomyth Cycle and *The Spy Who Loved Me*." On the day he was accepted at York, he was offered — and took — a full-time job with Second City.

He was a member of the troupe for almost two years, learning all the time, improving his technique. Yet the pull of British comedy was strong, coming from his parents and from the enormous influence of Monty Python. In 1984, he left Second City, cashed in his savings and went to work in London. He lived in Shepherd's Bush, teamed up with Cambridge University Footlights graduate Neil Mullarkey, and played at the Edinburgh Festival and on the London cabaret circuit. "I lived with a guy whose stage act was to melt a block of ice in sixty-nine different ways. His name was Melted 69. I loved it, but I missed Canada, my family, hockey, Letterman and Doritos."

He also missed the opportunities that only North America offered. A year and a half after he left, Second City contacted him and wondered if he might just consider coming home. Might just consider? He was on the plane as quickly as he could make the arrangements. It was impossible to develop Wayne Campbell in Britain where the cultural references of North American teenagers were unknown. Back in Canada, he played Wayne and other characters anywhere he could. For the next four years, he worked with Second City in Toronto and in Chicago. There was an innocence and a hilarity about him that won critics and convinced producers like Pam Thomas (then married to comedian Dave Thomas). In early 1989, she set up a meeting for Myers with *Saturday Night Live*; with no audition, Myers got the job.

"He was obviously incredibly gifted and had an enormous vitality and energy," recalls Lorne Michaels, creator and executive producer of *Saturday Night Live.* "He was also, and still is, very committed to his characters; he won't betray his creation for a cheap laugh, the way some comics do. I met him five years ago, and it was obvious straight away that here was something special."

As simple as that? I ask. From high school to *Saturday Night Live* in seven years?

"Well," says Myers, "in some ways, yes, as simple as that. I've been helped a great deal by people, and things have happened fast, no doubt. And sure, a lot of it has to do with Wayne Campbell."

So who is Wayne Campbell, and what is his world? In essence, he is the apotheosis of the ordinary. Living in suburbia, battling puberty, playing rock music in the basement family room, the host of a cable TV talk show. Wayne and his friend Garth, ever gauche and clumsy, discuss the events of the day from the perspective of head-banging, teenage suburbanites.

"I'd been working on this guy since I was thirteen years old," says Myers. "It's heightened reality, not naturalism. It's based on small, previously unarticulated truths. For me, the greatest thing I got to do in a movie was to enjoy 'Bohemian Rhapsody' in a car. I'd never seen anybody do that in a movie, listen to rock music in their car like that. But we used to do it in real life. We went round in a friend's car, a brown Dodge with a vomit stain on the side. We'd go hunting for art-tarts at the Ontario College of Art. You know, the Don Valley Parkway has got yellow lights; it was always our yellow brick road from Scarborough to downtown. Am I being pretentious? Slap me if I'm being pretentious.

"When my brother Peter got his first car, a Toyota Celica, for $1,000, we'd go out to McDonald's on Warden and Sheppard, or Wendy's if we wanted the exotic. Or Tim Horton at Sheppard and Don Valley Parkway. We'd play Queen music in the car. Some of that doesn't transfer down here, of course, but that almost pleases me. I like to think of it as letters to home, the enemy within being a good guest in a foreign country."

American critics have called Myers the most original and talented product of *Saturday Night Live* in years, recalling the triumphs of John Belushi, Dan Aykroyd and Chevy Chase. Since those early days of movie spin-offs and international success, *Saturday Night Live* had lost some of its required viewing cachet. *Wayne's World* injected "Excellent!" "Not!" and "No way! . . . Way" into the language and helped to re-establish *SNL*'s slipping crown. Tristar was so impressed with Myers's box office attraction that it decided to back his $20 million film, *So I Married an Axe Murderer*. Such is the studio's enthusiasm for the man that it flew him and his family to London on Concorde for the *Wayne's World* press junket. Unless catastrophe strikes, Mike Myers can point his career, in the short term at least, in any direction he wants.

In Hollywood, people are pigeonholed as they arrive at the airport, and Myers insists on stepping beyond categorization. He is anxious to do more, to prove to a notoriously fickle industry that he can be someone other than Wayne Campbell. He emphasizes his other characters, and then before I can stop him, even if I had wanted to do so, breaks into Linda Richman, the host of *Coffee Talk*, pronounced *cawfee tawk*. The accent drips Manhattan Jewish matriarch — glutinous, rich and extremely difficult to imitate without sliding into caricature and offence.

"So people ask us why we suffer so much. Well, I'll tell you. The Talmud says . . ." I laugh, the woman at the other end of our table reading a biography of Sir Richard Burton laughs. The waiter laughs. The star of *Coffee Talk* is complaining about the heat and the economy. "Talk amongst yourselves. Here. I'll give you a topic. Progressive rock is neither progressive nor rock. Discuss."

Linda Richman is Myers's favourite character right now. She is based on his mother-in-law. When Linda Richman discusses her broken heart on *Saturday Night Live*, complaining that her daughter Robin is marrying a goy, she is borrowing from life: Robin is Myers's wife, actress Robin Ruzan, and the goy is Myers himself.

"No, she doesn't mind, she loves it," he says of Robin's mother. "She's great. She says, 'Sure, you can do me on television, but who will watch? Who in the world would find me exotic?'" And then he is at it again, pretending that he's got copious amounts of jewellery jangling from his gesticulating arms, rattling off Yiddish expressions in onomatopoeic splendour. He does the character for his in-laws at their Passover meal, and they love him for it.

He met Ruzan in Chicago more than six years ago, after a game between the Leafs and the Blackhawks. "I saw her in a bar opposite the Second City Theatre. Now we're married. I've always said there are various rites of passage: birth, first day of school, last day of school, loss of virginity, driver's licence, college, marriage, death. I'm nearer to death now. Hey, I'm nearer to death now. No, wait a minute, I've just got my driving licence here, so forget all that. I might live longer, but I sweat a lot — I haven't mastered reverse yet, so I have to drive around the block a lot to find parking places and get into them from the front." He's off into character again — first as Wayne, then as Linda Richman.

Such is the success of *Coffee Talk* that Barbra Streisand — "a voice like butter, like butter" — has appeared on it, as have Madonna and Roseanne Arnold. "It's like *Field of Dreams*: if you write it, they will come," and he delivers a haunting, over-the-top voice that is supposed to sound like the ghostly suggestions Kevin Costner hears in the movie.

Madonna was so taken with Myers that she suggested he interview her for *Interview* magazine. The pair spar and flirt for a page until Madonna finally says, "Would you ask me some questions that have a resonance to my life? This interview is mostly about what you're interested in: toys and hockey." Myers responds by asking if she believes in psychics and wondering if she has ever contacted the spirit world. He revels in armed combat with preconceived ideas and will invariably lunge at them with fists and feet.

This aspect of his personality is embodied in Deiter, the character he created to host *Sprockets*, an avant-garde arts show on *Saturday Night Live*. Based on a German waiter Myers met on Queen Street, this pouting neurotic-obsessive dresses in black, crosses his legs to an impossible degree, brings a pet monkey onto the set and orders his crew to dance in a mechanical, robotic way whenever the whim takes him. Perhaps the funniest moment in *Saturday Night Live*'s recent past occurred when Myers had *Wayne's World* costar Dana Carvey impersonate James Stewart on *Sprockets*, reading some of Stewart's ridiculously banal poetry. When asked why he had written about his pet dog, Carvey/Stewart told a story about a prostitute in Mexico and a fight with a broken bottle. Surreal, satirical and extremely un-American — this was humour with a European cutting edge.

"Taking chances is what comedy is about," he says, rubbing his face with his hands. "You cannot be safe and be funny. It's very Canadian to be safe, and that's good, but sometimes we can afford to push a bit harder. These little history lessons on television about our past, for example, they're great, sure. We should know about our past, should know that Mary Pickford was Canadian. But knowing that we invented various strains of rust-resistant wheat? I don't know about that."

We are interrupted by a fan who asks what Myers is up to at the moment. A brief, somewhat embarrassed hiatus. "That never happens to me usually, I swear to God," he says. But it probably does, and it certainly will. The life that Myers remembers and longs for is most likely impossible now, even in his idealized Canada.

"Gun control, peace prizes, multiculturalism, two languages, universal health care," he explains enthusiastically between bites of whole wheat toast. "Nobody hassles you, no street crime. That's what I like about Toronto, about Canada." Yet when he got married in Toronto, he was obliged to book hotel rooms under a false name for fear of the media discovering the event. He is famous. He will be more famous. What secures him to humility and stability is a heady mingling of nostalgia, family ties and a leaping humour.

We are discussing the CBC, Canada and hockey again. Myers digresses to when he was a boy travelling in the car with his father to pick up his mother from work. "I remember that *As It Happens* would come on the radio just about the time we got into the car, as we went out, and they would introduce the presenters. My dad would say, 'I wish my name was Alan Maitland, what a great name.' Then he'd go into this whole thing, 'Hi, let me get that, I'm Alan Maitland.' 'Hello, mate, I'm Alan Maitland.' No reason for it really." Unattached, Python-like.

He then discusses his mother. "You know those Battle of Britain movies and the women with the baccarat sticks in the bunkers with their headphones saying 'Jerries over Norfolk, scramble thirteen, scramble.' That was my mom." The accent is perfect — his parents are British, after all — but pushed just over the limit, making it instantly hilarious, emphasizing the rigidness of the vowels, the constipation of the consonants. "My cousins from Liverpool always had one ambition: they wanted to be able to say 'asshole' like North Americans. They can't do it, can't do it. The British can't say 'asshole.'" And then he is into Simon, the little English boy in the bathtub on *Saturday Night Live*: "Mummy, would you like to see some of my drawings?"

"He's always been funny, and nobody is particularly surprised by his success, really," explains his brother Paul at a side table at the Squeeze Club in Toronto, a Myers family hangout. Paul Myers is a rock musician who bears an uncanny resemblance to his younger brother. "There's always been a certain vulnerability about him, too, something that comes across in his humour. I remember when we lived in an apartment as kids. I took his clothes away one day and pushed him into the hall of the apartment block as a joke and locked the door. He stood there naked, banging on the door, but I wouldn't let him in. In the end, he asked the neighbours for help. They were East Indians, and they put him in a sari for the day until my mom came home from work. I suppose he learned to be funny."

"I don't know about that," says Myers. "My brothers were the funny ones. I remember my mom saying, 'Your brothers are funny, but you're not. Don't try. You see, you try and you get frustrated, that's the problem. Just sit and laugh, laugh with the rest of us.' When I could make my brothers laugh, that was the ultimate. Their judgment has never become a devalued currency. They're still my harshest critics and my biggest supporters. It helps me keep my expectations in control, which isn't always the case in Los Angeles. There were no expectations with *Wayne's World*, but the universe has been very kind. Lorne Michaels has been very kind. I was the first person from *Saturday Night Live* he took to Paramount. Imagine, the man in charge of *Saturday Night Live* taking me to a big studio. A guy from Forest Hill taking a kid from Scarborough into the movies."

We are back in Beverly Hills. The man from Myers's publicity office, who had introduced us earlier and then diplomatically sat at the other end of the restaurant, is hovering now and checking his watch — it is clear the interview is over. As we finish our conversation, a local in a Who T-shirt walks past and says loudly, "Hey, Wayne, yeah, like, yeah." Myers is a professional actor again, seen as Wayne, the Midwestern kid, not as Mike, the Toronto success story. He pouts, falls into Wayne and jokes about the problems of being recognized. He is trying to make me laugh, and I oblige — I can't help it. I am still laughing as I leave the restaurant, so much so that I forget the bill. Myers says nothing. He's a Canadian. The man from his publicity office is an American, and he asks me if my magazine is picking up the meal. I am embarrassed; I apologize and ask if the place will take Canadian dollars. Therein lies a tale.